D1072689

THE
INTERNATIONAL
DESIGN
YEARBOOK

THE INTERNATIONAL DESIGN YEARBOOK

1985/86

EDITOR
ROBERT A.M. STERN

GENERAL EDITOR
STUART DURANT

ASSISTANT EDITOR
PENNY McGUIRE

ABBEVILLE PRESS · PUBLISHERS · NEW YORK

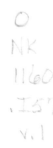

O
NK
1160
.I57
v.1

The Publisher and editors would like to thank the
designers and manufacturers for submitting work for
inclusion in this book. They would also like to thank
Susan St Clair for compiling the bibliography.

Designer: Peter Bridgewater

Library of Congress Catalog number 0883—7155
ISBN 0—89659—573—0

Copyright © John Calmann and King Ltd and
Cross River Press Ltd

All rights reserved under international and Pan-American
copyright conventions. No part of this book may be
reproduced or utilized in any form or by any means,
electronic or mechanical, including photocopying,
recording, or by information storage and retrieval
system, without permission in writing from the publisher.
Inquiries should be addressed to Abbeville Press, Inc,
505 Park Avenue, New York 10022.

Typeset by Composing Operations Ltd, Tunbridge Wells
Printed and bound in Hong Kong

First Edition

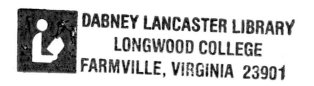

DABNEY LANCASTER LIBRARY
LONGWOOD COLLEGE
FARMVILLE, VIRGINIA 23901

C O N T E N T S

PREFACE

This is the first volume of an international, annual review of domestic design. It shows the best, most characteristic and most innovative recent designs of furniture, lighting, textiles, ceramics, glass and product design. The *International Design Yearbook* will not only chart the progress of contemporary design, but also reflect the view of a leading figure in the design world. Each year the selection will be made by a different guest editor.

Robert Stern, one of the leading exponents of Post-Modern architecture, both as a practitioner and a theorist, has chosen the works to be included in this volume. He has selected examples in all styles – for their aesthetic excellence and as examples of current movements in design.

Post-Modernism predominates, but alongside pieces by Memphis or Alchimia are works which show that Modernism is not merely surviving but flourishing. Robert Stern has also chosen to represent the vogue for reviving classic designs of the last hundred years by including a chapter on reproductions of works by such masters as Mackintosh, Hoffmann, Le Corbusier and Eileen Gray. Current preoccupation with the past is not only shown in the work of contemporary designers, but also in the popularity of these revivals.

Within each chapter, the pieces have been grouped according to style. The commentary relates each of these groupings to present trends and developments. The Appendix contains biographies of each designer, and the addresses of manufacturers and major retailers who supply the designs illustrated. The bibliography lists current writing on the area.

Design, like architecture, is now in ferment. The *International Design Yearbook* enables us to stand aside and take yearly stock of this exciting diversity.

INTRODUCTION

This is the first volume of an annual review of decorative art, comprehensive and international in scope. The project is, I think, well timed, coming at a moment when Post-Modernism has achieved its most important goal, replacing the belligerently present-oriented focus of Modernism with an attitude toward design that is far more open to influences from the past, from the physical context, and from culture in general than had been the case for the past sixty years. Post-Modernism has dominated architecture for the past dozen or so years, so it is hardly surprising that the work of its allied disciplines, the decorative arts of furniture, textiles and accessories, should reflect a new formal freedom and philosophical depth as well.

Post-Modernism originated as a somewhat self-conscious, iconoclastic reaction against the late, enervated Modernism of the 1950s and 1960s. But the time of jokey, awkward early youth is now behind it and Post-Modernism has matured into the significant creative trend of our time. While its detractors and, perhaps, too many of its early polemicists, have presented it as a kind of trivial pursuit of aesthetic titillation – sleepwalking through the streets of history, as one critic likes to say over and over again – it has in fact had a much more profound impact on design by reopening the dialogue between the present and the past, a dialogue that had been the fundamental fact of architecture from the Renaissance until the First World War.

By its very fixity, the past offers the designer the best opportunity to comment on the madshow fluctuations of the present. The forms of the past, explored in interaction with present-day techniques and programmes, have opened up what had become, by the 1960s, the dead end of 'good design'. The Post-Modern condition in design has its parallels in other fields – in the interest museums, academicians and auction houses show in reviving 'minor' artists, and in the expansion of the concert hall repertoire to an encyclopaedic conception of the past, reviving entire periods of history – the Baroque, say – and fleshing out more recent tales with the contributions of peripheral individuals. In all the arts, then, the Post-Modernist sensibility moves us towards an appropriately complex conception of history that is not linear, and not progressive, more a mosaic than a coherent composition. Modern architecture is once again seen as a continuous evolution stretching back to the Renaissance, when the idea of history returned to Western civilization, and we see the anti-historicizing Modernism of this century as just one of its phases, most like the Mannerism of the sixteenth century.

Hence the breadth of this book, the diversity of its contents, the rampant pluralism it documents, embracing even the 'good-design' good taste of Late Modernism, with its emphasis on technologically inspired functionalism. It is important to stress that given Post-Modernism's anti-revolutionary premise, the door has not been slammed shut on the aesthetic achievements of the previous generation. Post-Modernism has opened up a wider, richer and ultimately more honest view of the past and its relationship to the present, yet the Modernist impulse still remains a central fact in current production, particularly in the field of mass-produced design objects. Its morality of the present continues to obsess both designers and the media, who all too frequently value stylistic innovation above qualitative issues of functional fit, craft or – to speak the word that dares not be spoken – beauty.

What then, does this have to do with the design of objects – consumer goods, if you will? Although the selection contains works that are pugnaciously Modernist in their form and philosophical meaning, I would argue that Modernism is dead as a vital fact of contemporary design; dead not just of consumerist boredom but because it reflected the values of an outmoded stage of industrial production. Its approach was typological, exemplified by the belief, for example, that there was an ideal chair, scientifically determined by the constituent facts of mass-production and suitable for every place and occasion where one might sit down. Reacting to the collapse of a rigidly stratified society, it vaunted an opposing ideal not so much of equality as of sameness, which it achieved in the aesthetic vacuity of the machine aesthetic of the 1960s, epitomized by the work of Charles Eames or George Nelson, a mode appropriate to a manufacturing process that demanded that designs be produced in thousands upon thousands of copies.

Unsympathetic observers will seize on the Post-Modernist explosion in the decorative arts as evidence that the market needs innovation simply to stimulate sales. Kenneth Frampton, who nostalgically awaits a return to the austerity of the *Neue Sachlichkeit*, regards the entire movement as 'consolatory consumerist kitsch'. Yet the fact of consumer capitalism is not so much to be overlooked or lamented as to be understood as a constituent fact of our time and served by the designer, just as he serves the standards of craft and aesthetics. After all, people who buy designer furniture generally already own something to sit on, and their Le Corbusier chairs are probably not falling apart. That some will throw away their chairs when the market tells them they are out of fashion may seem unfortunate, but it is what capitalism and industrialization are all about – choice.

Surprisingly, modern industrial production poses greater problems for decorative design than it does for architecture. Modern building, despite some architects who insist otherwise, remains an issue of craft: each building is essentially a one-time effort, and even its seemingly mass-produced industrial components are typically adapted to the architect's own specifications. No self-respecting architect with artistic pretensions, for example, will use an off-the-shelf curtain wall when designing a skyscraper. Architecture has thus remained comparatively free of industrialization – even Mies van der Rohe, the supreme artist of the engineer's aesthetic, detailed his steel and glass curtain walls in such a way that they had to be assembled in an essentially handicraft manner. In the decorative arts, however, the marketplace enforces a more complex interaction between the project designer and the engineer-technician. If it is to reach a wide market, even the most basic object of daily use must take advantage of machine production, but at the same time it must achieve a certain complexity to avoid being 'knocked off' by every two-bit cabinet-, metal- or wood-working shop. Mies's buildings remain unique because he used expensive materials expensively put together, while his classic steel-tube chairs – one personification of a high-tech aesthetic – are ripped off every day because they in fact require very little in the way of present-day technology. Perhaps the current situation is epitomized by Robert Venturi's wittily historicist chairs for Knoll, which merge three different modes. Their decoration refers to traditional works of exquisite handicraft; they are fabricated in an ordinary, vernacular material – plywood – but this is so elaborately contoured, in part to prevent design piracy, that the chairs are raised to the level of high technology. A Post-Modern aesthetic realized in Modernist terms?

There is of course a lot of top-quality work being done that still reflects the Modernism of the mid-century. The best of this sees the aesthetic for what it is – a style that refers to a moment that is by now irrevocably part of the past, but which can still shed aesthetic and philosophic light on the present. This can be seen in the architecture of Richard Meier, whose romantic recapitulations of the early International Style infuse their fifty-year-old themes with a new sense of materiality and sensuality. The insufferable and once seemingly insuperable moralism of Modernism is left far behind. In his Hoffmannesque furniture for Knoll, Meier has expanded the horizons of his aesthetic nostalgia to *fin de siècle* Vienna. His approach is unlike Venturi's:

Meier gives us not a hint of irony, nor are his designs subjected to the same sort of production constraints. What they lack in aesthetic tension, they make up for in visual grace.

There are three dominant trends in the Late Modern work. There is, first, a new sense of lyricism, of artists lavishing aesthetic refinements on an established industrial vernacular. Christina and Lars Andersson's *Maximus* seating, which marries the Bauhaus to the standard park bench, or Minale Tattersfield's folding chair, *Skeleton*, among many examples, are attempts to soften clichéd, industry-based designs. There is, among the Modernist-inspired work even a note of whimsy or wit — although one is never quite sure whether it is intended. Thus a second, and, as it turns out, more portentous trend, leads designers to conceive of ordinary objects and furniture as miniature buildings. This is a time-honoured point of view — one thinks of Biedermeier's terrible fronts. But in the current work, problems of scale and character intrude, and the most ordinary elements begin to swallow up space and even the user's best intentions. Engineering — and not architecture — is explored for self-conscious poetic effect. Marili Brandão's *Tiete* looks like a model of a suspension bridge; Ivana Bortolotti's *Tenso* chair, like a bay of SOM's tented airport in Riyadh; and Els Staal's bench series, like fragments of a space frame.

A third trend seeks to revivify Modernism by injecting it with a conception of form-making that is no longer machine-based, but biomorphic and, at least to look at, sympathetic to user needs. Ferdinand Alexander Porsche's reclining seat *Antropovarius*, with its arching back of steel vertebrae, is a spectacular example of the philosophy that makes medicine taste bad so that you know it is doing you good.

The aesthetic speculation of Post-Modernism has increased the curiosity about the recent Modernist past, revealing a number of promising aesthetic directions that were abandoned in the push toward stylistic uniformity but which now provide designers who prefer an abstract mode with an avenue of escape from the tired moralism of orthodoxy. Constructivism and De Stijl, for instance, are no longer pictured as mere false steps taken on the road of Modernism, but as bold flowerings of aestheticism cut short by the hard white winter of the International Style. For many designers today seeking to link up with the good old Modernist values, Rietveld in particular seems to be an emblem of a golden age of experimentation free of dreary moralization — for example Denis Balland's and Gijs Bakker's folding chairs, Danilo Silvestrin's table, *Hommage à Rietveld*, or even so simple a design as Stefano Casciani's *Albertina* chair, where the compact cube of a Le Corbusier armchair is pulled slightly apart, freed of its tubular-steel bondage, and rendered in garish De Stijl primary colours.

Although Modernism still plays an important role, both as a continuing theme and as a style to be revived, the dominant trend of this volume lies elsewhere, in a kind of aesthetic free-for-all so emblematic of the new sensibility that the popular press tends to see it as *the*, rather than *a*, Post-Modernist style. This spirit of aesthetic mayhem is best exemplified by Memphis, which chips away at the Archilles heel of Modernist orthodoxy with infectious glee. Memphis is inspired not by the heroic Modernism of the 1920s, with its dream of a technocrat's world, but by the low-brow commercial vernacular of the 1950s. Memphis revives a time when Modernism still seemed to glow with the promise of utopia, and when the vocabulary of Surrealism had passed into the everyday decorative alphabet as a talisman of a new, democratic, post-war age. The boomerang curve and gold-thread counter tops of 1950s luncheonettes are the fodder of Memphis's imagination — most explicitly in Michele de Lucchi's small table, *Cadetto*, aptly displayed with a soda fountain, shaker and straw.

Memphis is, in its own way, a fulfilment of Robert Venturi's argument of twenty years ago, a demonstration that a designer can take a popular vernacular, accept its vocabulary of signs and symbols, and transform it into art. Memphis succeeds at being decorative and witty; the quirky contrasts, playful scale, and totemic abstraction of its furniture capture the exuberance and optimism that the style once possessed — and as revived, it is both sophisticated and touchingly naive.

One can see Memphis's influence throughout this book — in the work of Studio Alchimia, for instance, which applies a subtler wit to more high-brow sources, or Swedfun's somewhat sophomoric efforts. It shines through as well in Hans Hollein's absurdly seductive couch, *Marilyn*.

The greatest contribution of the new Milanese school is not the revival of a particular style but simply its spontaneity, its riotous ribaldry and madcap mayhem. Something of the same sensibility can be found in a number of the American entries, where the source material is rooted both in consumer kitsch and a countervailing tradition of provincial Classicism — a confusion that reflects the chaos of America's built landscape. For Frank Gehry's *Fish* lamps the sources lie both in the found object of the 1960s and the sort of endearing decor one might find in a Las Vegas wedding palace. In the work of Stanley Tigerman the spirit is sometimes more fay, as in his cartoon baroque *Cherub* plates; occasionally more ambiguous, as in his double love-seat, whose sinuous ripples of plastic laminate hover somewhere between ergonomics and Classical-moulding profiles.

One sees a more scholarly approach to Classical traditions coming out of the English craft schools, in Lucie McCann's Serlian bench and Martin Grierson's desk, *Partners*. One can also find it in the voluptuous Belle-Époque styling of Charles Jencks's tea service for Alessi, in Paul Chiasson's restudying of a *Classical Cabinet* for Formica, or in my own firm's candlesticks.

This scholarly approach brings up the fundamental issue of Classicism — the idea that certain things achieve a canonical status, that they are worthy of continuous veneration, that they become 'classics'. For furniture, the sure sign of such canonization is when someone sets out to re-create a period piece faithfully. Reproduction furniture has been a commonplace of the market since the nineteenth century, and helped fuel the indignation of early-modern moralists such as William Morris. One notices today the attention given to reviving Hoffmann and Mackintosh, representatives of a time when tradition and modernity were last held in balance. Their availability is a boon not only because it places beautiful objects on the market, but because it stimulates current design. The best achievements of another era also provide a standard against which to judge our own efforts. So it is that Hoffmann chairs now adorn the interiors of the hitherto ascetically anti-historicist Charles Gwathmey, that his firm's recent furniture evokes the craft traditions of the Wiener Werkstätte, and that, at least in some commissions, this sense of connection with the past is filtering into its architecture.

But the scope of reproduction furniture goes further. Now, ironically, we revive even the classical statements of the Modern Antichrist itself. While the present-day production of furniture by Mies and Le Corbusier — designs now more than fifty years old — can be seen as an example of continuity, they were not in fact in production until Knoll revived Mies in the 1950s and Cassina did the same for Le Corbusier in the 1960s. We now have a spate of revivals of craft-oriented, early-modern masters, whether Saarinen's tasty or Rietveld's aggressively picturesque chairs, both subjected to the same preposterously accurate scholarship as repro Sheraton. Modern is not modern anymore; Modern is not moral anymore. There is room enough, demand enough, and talent enough for us to have the best of the past and the present.

For the future, the important issues raised by this book are not the differences between Modernism and Post-Modernism, though they are fundamental to setting the stage. The critical point is that the design of an object is only so convincing as it relates not to the task (there have been chairs almost as long as there have been backsides), but to an aesthetic need. The decorative arts must fulfil their function in relation to the demands of a particular aesthetic. The irony is that one might think that objects would allow designers to explore ideas in miniature before doing big buildings, but the reverse is in fact the case. Most compelling objects reflect established trends in architecture. This was true in the past because craftsmen were responsible for furniture, and their conception of design was less thoughtful and less scholarly than that of architects; theirs was a craft, not an art. Today it is true because technology is so complex – and therefore so expensive – that one cannot afford to invest in a production line until one is sure that an architectural trend is firmly established; it must have built many buildings to legitimize an aesthetic direction. The very best decoration, from Adam to Aalto and beyond, has been part of an overall architectural schema. The rest runs the risk of being just so much stuff.

Robert A.M. Stern

FURNITURE

Architects have always enjoyed designing furniture. Their handwriting invariably shows and their furniture echoes their buildings. Schinkel's was nobly Neo-Classical, William Burges' playfully Gothic, Josef Hoffmann's was discreetly avant-garde, while Gerrit Rietveld's furniture was obsessively Euclidean. Le Corbusier's furniture, however, was commonsensical and inventive at the same time. It is hardly surprising that several of his pieces are still 'in print'.

Robert Venturi's furniture is unashamedly eclectic – like his architecture – borrowing, as it does, from succulent, comestible Queen Anne, Biedermeier, or even Art Déco. It would be interesting to see what would happen if a furniture manufacturer – like Alessi with their coffee services or the Formica Corporation with their promotion of Colorcore – were to commission a series of suites of furniture from a selection of major contemporary architects.

Furniture design mirrors the architectural manners of the day. But it has its own traditions and, probably because of its dependence for its effects upon the intelligent deployment of creative craftsmanship, it is a largely autonomous field. Great designer-craftsmen – like Louis Majorelle in the 1900s, or Émile-Jacques Ruhlmann in the 1920s – were the inheritors of a tradition which had its roots in the eighteenth century.

Not so the present generation of craftsmen, whose allegiance is more likely to be – though it is often a superficial one – to the Arts and Crafts Movement which flourished before the First World War. But there is, as yet, no real consensus of ideals or practice among the craftsmen and craftswomen who represent the contemporary Crafts Revival. Craftsmen now, like Romantic artists, seek to assert their individuality in all they do.

All the main current approaches to the design of furniture are represented in this section of the *Yearbook*. Undoubtedly, the most conspicuous of these is that of the Post-Modernists. The Post-Modernist approach is extrovert, jestingly historicist and, of course, eclectic. A group of chairs by a young British designer working in Milan has a distinctly 1950s air about it – pert and spikey. Post-Modernism encourages such expeditions into the recent past. Post-Modernism also encourages the expression of sensuality, and has made it respectable even. Post-Modernist drawing-room furniture can be as sensual as the chaise-longue in the boudoir of a nineteenth-century concubine.

Modernism – a kind of absolute style, a style without style – still has its adherents, as this chapter of the *Yearbook* demonstrates. Dieter Rams' credo, 'quiet is better than loud, unobtrusive is better than exciting', could have been uttered by any of the original Moderns – Mies van der Rohe, or Marcel Breuer, or Walter Gropius. But unobtrusiveness and lack of excitement, after all, can lead to a certain ennui.

Post-Modernism has revived the conception of design as an artistic, as opposed to a soberly scientific, activity. For all its wilful brashness it has brought new energy and delight to the activity of designing. This is nowhere more evident than in the design of furniture.

1 ACHILLE CASTIGLIONI AND GIANCARLO POZZI
Folding bench, *Camilla*
Frame of drawn and forged steel, fire-
lacquered green. Seat and back of
stratified laminate, pink. Also available in
white with plum-coloured seat and back.
H 97 cm (38 in). W 62 cm (24 in). L 101 cm
(39 in)
Manufacturer: Zanotta, Italy

2 LESLIE JOHN WRIGHT
Deck chair
Laminated Huron pine. The chairs are
stackable and handpainted in various
enamel colours before being rubbed back.
Prototype.
H 70 cm (27 in). W 75 cm (29 in). L 190 cm
(74 in)
Manufacturer: Leslie John Wright, Australia

3 JEAN CLAUDE DUBOYS
Folding chair, *Programme Attitude*
Wood.
H 82 cm (32 in). L 65 cm (25 in). W 80 cm
(31 in)
Manufacturer: Attitude, France

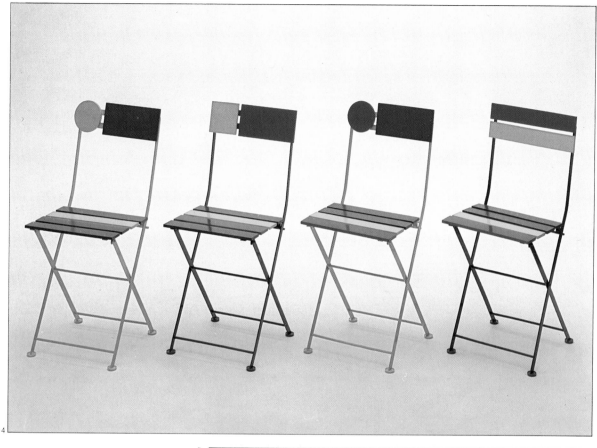

4 DENIS BALLAND
Folding chairs, *Ligne Kis*
Lacquered steel frames with plastic rollers,
seat and back of lacquered timber battens.
H 84 cm (33 in)
Manufacturer: Fermob, France

5 VICO MAGISTRETTI
Armchair, *R 513p*
Rattan and round rattancore, leather
bindings. Available in different colours:
natural, aniline, walnut, rosewood, red
mahogany, green, grey, opal, or lacquered
white, ivory, blue, red, pink, black.
H 71 cm (28 in). W 103 cm (40 in). L 80 cm
(31 in)
Accompanying sofa *R 513 d*
H 71 cm (28 in). W 165 cm (65 in). L 80 cm
(31 in)
Manufacturer: G. Gervasoni, Italy

6

■ The trestle table has a long history; one thinks of the planks of wood on triangular trestle legs that have been used for working surfaces, harvest dinners and the like, since Breughel's day. The modern versions, here all Italian, vary from the refined folding tables by Lucci and Orlandini, de Martini's Italianate version of the Scandinavian, and Castiglioni's deliberate evocation of *artiginato;* to Citterio and Nava's exquisite glass and steel trestle.

De Martini's trestle has accompanying chairs. He says of his creations: 'I set out to experiment with wood in very thin section, seeking to express a play of stays and struts, of extreme lightness and extra-ordinary solidity. . . . I am reminded of the first flying machines, then of musical instruments.'

7

8

6 ANTONIO CITTERIO AND PAOLO NAVA
Table, *Quadrante*
Part of a range of furniture that includes various cabinets with sliding doors, shelves and drawers. Table structure of metal with transparent or coloured glass top.
L 210 cm (82 in). H 72 cm (28 in)
Manufacturer: Xilitalia, Italy

7,9 ROBERTO LUCCI AND PAOLO ORLANDINI
Folding tables, *Caramella*
Wood and laminated plastic.
H 73 cm (28 in). W 80 cm and 70 cm (31 in and 27 in). L 80 cm and 100 cm (31 in and 39 in)
Manufacturer: Ciatti, Italy

8 ROBERTO LUCCI AND PAOLO ORLANDINI
Folding table, *Fast*
Steel, with top in wood or laminated plastic.
H 73 cm (28 in). W 80 cm (31 in). L 158 cm (62 in)
Manufacturer: Lamm, Italy

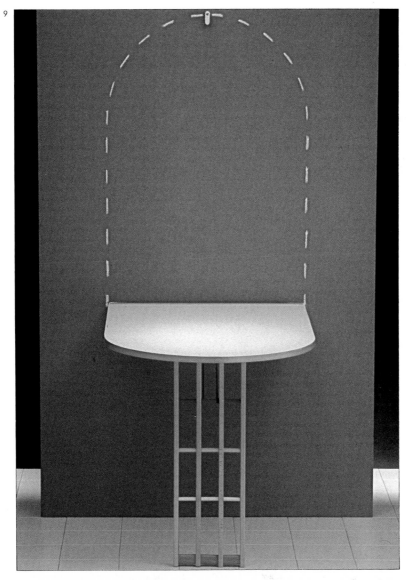

10 PIERO DE MARTINI
Table, *Ariante*
Ash frame with natural and black-ebony stained finish. Can be square, round or rectangular. The latter can be extended by the addition of two semicircular hinged leaves.
Square model H 74.5 cm (29 in). 125 cm × 125 cm (49 in × 49 in). Round model H 74.5 cm (29 in). D 135 cm (54 in). Rectangular model H 74.5 cm (29 in). 175 cm × 90 cm (68 in × 35 in), closed; 260 cm × 90 cm (102 in × 35 in), open
Manufacturer: Cassina, Italy

11 PIERO DE MARTINI
Chair and armchair, *Alcina*
In black lacquered ash. Removable seat cushion with polyurethane foam padding and removable fabric or leather upholstery.
H 78.5 cm or 71.5 cm (31 in or 28 in). Seat H 47 cm (18 in). W and L 51 cm (20 in)
Manufacturer: Cassina, Italy

■ The steel-frame folding or stacking chair (illustrations 11 to 18, also in materials other than steel), whose natural habitat was — and is — the European café, continues to be a popular subject for designers. Achille Castiglioni, for example, did a series of such chairs for Zanotta, including the *Rosacamuna* and *Irma* chairs. Marco Zanuso designed another, the *Celestina*, for the same firm. And here is a new series.

12 GASTONE RINALDI
Chair, *Desy*
Chair with tubular steel structure, stove-enamelled with epoxy powders in various colours or chromed. Seat in flexible foamed polyurethane on elastic webbing. Backrest of solid rubber. Upholstery can be covered with fabric or leather.
H 75 cm (29 in). W 43 cm (16 in). L 50 cm (19 in)
Manufacturer: Thema, Italy

14 JOUKO JARVISALO
Folding chair, *Flap*
Metal parts chromed or epoxy-coated steel tube, wooden parts, painted birch plywood.
H 82 cm (71 in). W 45 cm (17 in). L 49 cm (19 in)
Manufacturer: Inno-tuote, Finland

13 GASTONE RINALDI
Chair, *Lisa*
Folding chair with a tubular steel structure, stove-enamelled with epoxy powders in various colours or chromed. The seat of beech plywood is covered with granulated rubberized fabric in black, grey or yellow. Backrest in beech covered with the same fabric.
H 73 cm (28 in). W 50 cm (19 in). L 62 cm (24 in)
Manufacturer: Thema, Italy

15 MINALE, TATTERSFIELD & PARTNERS
Chair range, *Skeleton*
Epoxy-coated tubular steel, various upholstery finishes. The range includes a stacking chair, five-star base-swivel chair with gas lift, beam seat, fast-food seating system. All chairs are available with or without arms and a range of accessories: linking system, writing tablet, briefcase rest. Available in bright colours.
H 84 cm (33 in). W 51 cm (20 in)
Manufacturer: Cubic Metre Furniture, UK

12

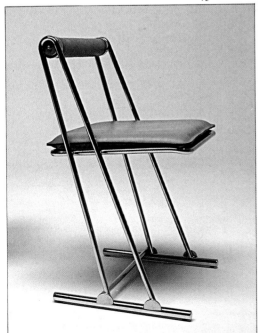

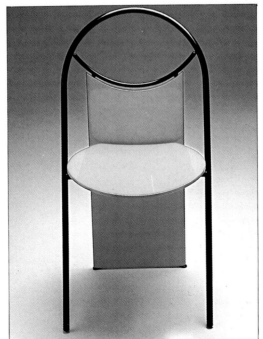

13

14

15

16 AD.SA (PIERRE PAULIN)
Stackable chair, *Fauteuil 800*
Moulded polypropylene.
H 72 cm (28 in) overall, seat H 45 cm
(17 in). W 54 cm (21 in)
Manufacturer: Stamp, France

16

'The ultimate proof of the primacy of personal design in public esteem is the reputation of Michael Thonet. This Rhineland cabinet-maker went to Vienna to decorate palaces and finished by inventing the bentwood chair on which café society has sat, and largely still sits, all over the world. He made it dirt cheap; he made it by the million. . . . And now he is remembered as the designer of the most sought-after rocking chair (more sought after than the Kennedy rocker) in the world, the favoured bentwood throne of the leaders of modern design.' Peter Reyner Banham, 'The Chair as Art' (1967).

The problem with inventing a type is that it is a hard act to follow; but the idea of 'progress' is hard to resist. Thonet's styling-up of the basic chair has not always been successful; but Gerd Lange's chair shown here, and using materials other than wood, is one of its most satisfactory — and more stylish — products.

The graceful chair by AD.SA (Pierre Paulin) is a new variation on a now familiar theme: the stackable, moulded polypropylene chair; but the shape is pure Thonet.

17, 18 GERD LANGE
Stacking chair, *Thonet-cut*
Wood, metal, plastic frame. Upholstered. Metal-tube reinforcing is anodized or lacquered in different colours.
H 82 cm (32 in). W 43 cm (17 in). D 48 cm (19 in)
Manufacturer: Gebr. Thonet, Austria

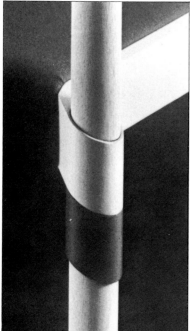

17 18

19 PIERRE MAZAIRAC, KAREL BOONZAAIJER
Dining chair, *MB*
Metal frame, leather back and seat.
H 78 cm (30 in). W 48 cm (18 in). L 55 cm (21 in)
Manufacturer: Metaform, Netherlands

■ The chair by Jonas Bohlin is made of two planes of concrete held by a metal frame with an appropriately rusty finish. 'No,' said the young man on the Källemo stand when it was first exhibited at the Copenhagen Furniture Fair, 'it is not a joke.' The company had made one hundred of them, and had sold fifty.

The chair (*above left*) by Mazairac and Boonzaaijer is a descendant of the tubular structures of the 1920s; Breuer, Stam/Thonet and Corbusier come to mind. Visually satisfying for its lightness and elegance; and for the way the apparently continuous metal tubing describes the outlines of invisible planes.

20 JONAS BOHLIN
Chair, *Concrete*
Steel frame, concrete panels. One of a hundred signed pieces. The chair is also produced in steel and birch; and coloured blue, red, green, grey/brown, white or natural birch.
H 90 cm (33 in). W 57 cm (22 in). L 50 cm (19 in)
Manufacturer: Collection Källemo, Sweden

22 GIJS BAKKER
Folding chair
Coloured metal tubing and plywood. This chair, summoning up the ghost of Rietveld, appears with thin counterposing planes, two-dimensional, and seemingly designed for the tall and angular; or for those addicted to the elbow-on-a-level-with-the-ear position.
H 85 cm (33 in). W 65 cm (25 in)
Manufacturer: Designum, Netherlands

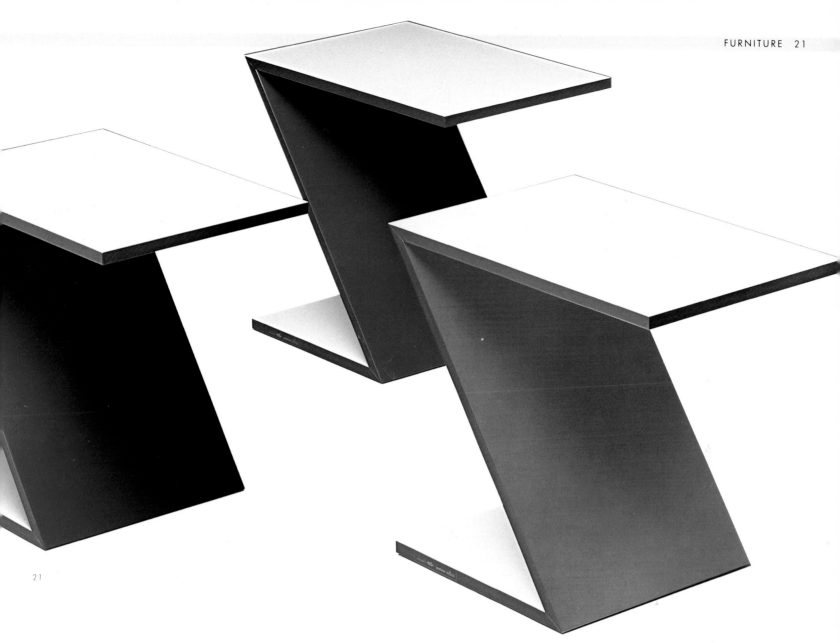

21

21 DANILO SILVESTRIN
Table, *Hommage à Rietveld*
Lacquered wood. The formal reduction to three surfaces is
emphasized by colour.
H 60 cm (23 in). W 46 cm (18 in). L 69 cm (27 in)
Manufacturer: Rosenthal Einrichtung, West Germany

23 DANILO SILVESTRIN
Desk, *Hommage à Mondrian*
Lacquered wood.
H 83 cm (32 in). W 90 cm (35 in). L 190 cm (74 in)
Manufacturer: Rosenthal Einrichtung, West Germany

22

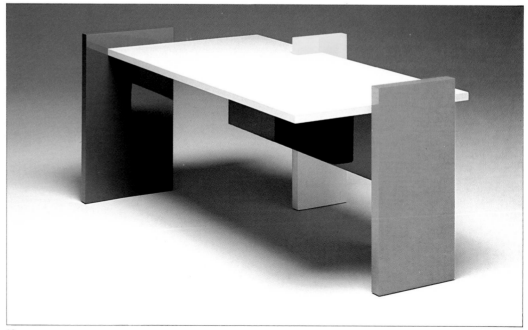

23

24

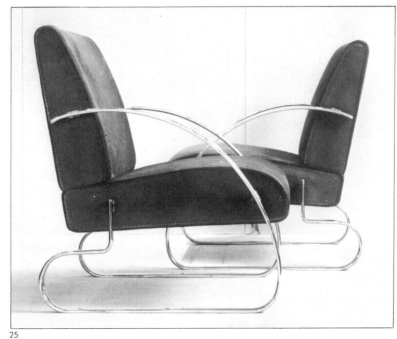

25

■ Rodney Kinsman is one of the most interesting of today's British designers, generally treading a cautious Modernist path. Most recently he has produced spare, anti-tactile furniture for Bieffeplast. Despite the title, *Vienna*, the elegant aesthetic can be traced back to the British 1930s. Whether deliberately induced or not, the reference that springs to mind at the sight of Jorgen Kastholm's curious armchair, with that unsettling combination of thin and athletic metal frame and bulky body, is 1930s, Practical Equipment.

24 RODNEY KINSMAN
Vienna Series
Small table made of painted steel with two glass shelves (1 cm [½ in] thick). Grey. H 69 cm (27 in). D 26 cm (10 in)
Table, painted steel with glass top (1.5 cm [1 in] thick). Grey. H 72 cm (28 in). D 75 cm (29 in). L 140 cm (55 in)
Armchair of grey-painted steel tube. Seat and backrest upholstered and covered with fire-proof grey velvet in virgin wool or cotton fabric. H 68 cm (26 in). D 52 cm (20 in). L 54 cm (19 in)
Sofa constructed out of grey-painted steel tube. Seat and backrest upholstered and covered with fire-proof grey velvet in virgin wool or cotton fabric. H 68 cm (26 in). D 52 cm (20 in). L 98 cm (38 in)
Manufacturer: Bieffeplast, Italy

25 JORGEN KASTHOLM
Armchair, *Geo-Line*
Timber frame with steel tubing. Fabric upholstery. Longer units can be built up into a sofa unit.
H 72 cm (40 in). W 68 cm (30 in)
Manufacturer: Franz Wittmann, Austria

■ Guido Gerli's chair is designed for a youthful market and there is a standard lamp to go with it: 1920s steel-frame tube-cum-Bertoia-cum-modern supermarket trolley.

26

26 GUIDO ALESSANDRO GERLI
Chair, *Basic*
Armonic steel. Can be dismantled into four pieces.
H 79 cm (31 in). W 49 cm (19 in). L 52 cm (20 in)
Manufacturer: Robots, Italy

■ 'The very essence of furniturization – or a better word, still, *fauteuillage* – is the precedence of appearance over performance, form over function. Le Corbusier's celebrated *fauteuil grand-confort*... looks marvellously comfortable with its huge cushions of soft down. But when you sit in it, it slowly slides you forward onto the floor with your knees up, and breaks your spine by reverse flexure in the process. Architects buy these chairs purely out of reverence for the name of the designer, admire them, but avoid sitting in them': Banham in 'The Chair as Art'. One is reminded of these observations on inspecting the chairs and sofas shown here; not that they are necessarily uncomfortable, but that although they are supposed to serve a similar function – easy domesticity – one is left with the Object as Art. Even Venturi's and Miles Carter's pumped-up, sumptuous sofas, one imagines, would be acquired first for what they represent.

27

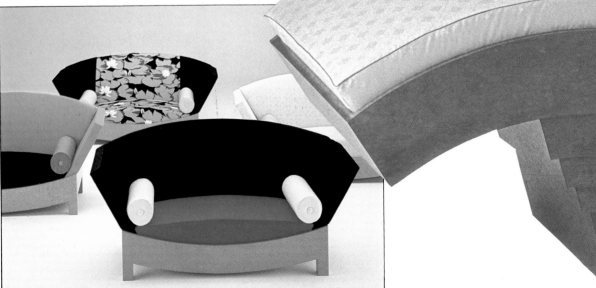

28

27 ROBERT VENTURI
Sofa, *Venturi Collection*
Traditionally inspired comfortable sofa. Can be upholstered, as here, in Venturi tapestry.
H 84 cm (33 in). D 110 cm (43 in). L 221 cm (87 in)
Manufacturer: Knoll International, USA

28 PAOLO PIVA
Sofa, *Arca*
Structural steel body embedded in cold-expanded polyurethane; upholstery of Du Pont Dacron II covered with fabric or hide. The back of the sofa is adjustable, and the small glass tables under the arms can be rotated. Colours can be ecru-white, yellow, maroon and brown.
H 72 cm (28 in). W 98 cm (38 in). L 205 cm or 245 cm (80 in or 100 in)
Manufacturer: B&B Italia, Italy

29 HANS HOLLEIN
Sofa, *Mitzi*
Wood frame, plywood back and side. Padding in polyurethane of different hardnesses, covered in fabric.
H 97 cm (38 in). D 87 cm (34 in). L 210 cm (82 in)
Manufacturer: Poltronova, Italy

30 MATTEO THUN
Chaise longue, *Rainer*
Wood frame, upholstered fabric and tapestry. Part of the Anthologie Quartett collection.
H 94 cm (37 in). D 85 cm (33 in). L 203 cm (79 in)
Manufacturer: Anthologie Quartett, West Germany

31 STEFANO CASCIANI
Armchair, *Albertina*
Frame of steel. Different upholstery of fire-resistant polyurethane foam. Available without roller on back.
H 90 cm (35 in). W 68 cm (26 in). D 65 cm (25 in)
Manufacturer: Zanotta, Italy

32 HANS HOLLEIN
Sofa, *Marilyn*
Wood frame, padding in polyurethane of different hardnesses.
H 93 cm (36 in). D 75 cm (29 in). L 238 cm (93 in)
Manufacturer: Poltronova, Italy

29

30

31

32

33

33 RONALD CARTER
Sofa, *Hardwick*
Designed to make use of Bute Fabric's
handwoven tapestry. Natural-wool fabric
cover over solid-wood frame, foam and
metal springing. Two pieces of handwoven wool tapestry placed and held in
position over the back and the seat.
H 68 cm (26 in). seat H 32 cm (12 in). W
210 cm (82 in). D 104 cm (41 in)
Manufacturer: Peter Miles Furniture, UK

34 PAOLO PIVA
Armchair, *Aura*
Metal frame covered with fabric or leather
upholstery. Marking a return to softer
rounder shapes, *Aura* is also available as
a two- and three-seater sofa.
H 75 cm (29 in). W 80 cm (31 in). D 72 cm
(28 in)
Manufacturer: Franz Wittmann, Austria

36 RUD THYGESEN AND JOHNNY SØRENSEN
Chair, *Bistro*
This chair is part of a furniture system
comprising several different types of
chairs and tables. The furniture is designed
to be stacked. Each piece is extremely
light – the chair weighs less than 3.5 kg
(7½ lb) and the tables can be stacked by
one person. The designers and
manufacturers have invented a method of
construction using an advanced lamination
technique, which does not involve either
screws or dowels. Though light, the
furniture is extremely strong and is suitable
for public or private use.
H 70 cm (27 in)
Manufacturer: Magnus Olesen A/S,
Denmark

34

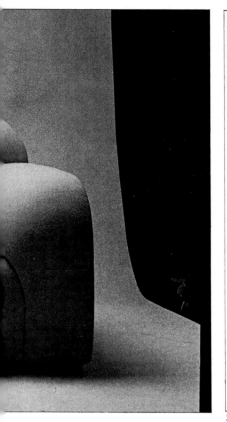

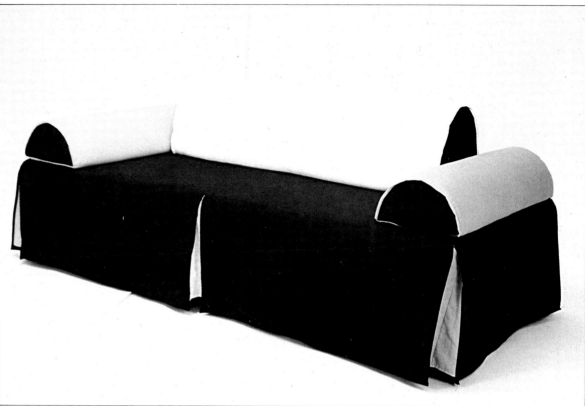

35

36

35 JOHAN HULDT
Sofa, *Flag*
Epoxy-enamelled steel-tube frame, pure-cotton covering. The cover can be removed for cleaning; and the sofa can be used as a bed.
H 76 cm (29 in). W 193 cm (76 in). L 88 cm (34 in)
Manufacturer: Form Program, Sweden

■ Since its flowering in the early days of the postwar period, Danish design has been associated with the 'acceptable face' of Modernism; concerned with the pure and elegant, rather than the Brutalist form, and with respect for the human body.

One of the most successful partnerships has been that of the architects Rud Thygesen and Johnny Sørensen. Together they have designed some of the best modern Danish furniture (mainly in wood), for three furniture factories – Magnus Olesen, Botium and Erik Boisen's Mobelfabrik – who co-ordinate the production of their work. The main influence is evidently Aalto. In general there is nothing superfluous in their work and the detailing is superb. Despite the austerity conveyed by their economy of line, the refinement, craftsmanship and silkiness of the wood make the furniture wholly sensual.

■ The aptly named *Mantis* chair by Pep Bonet (illustrations 42 and 43) recalls Ernest Race; but more particularly Dennis Young's *Shell Chair* of 1947–8.

The Skipper series evokes 1950s stretch fabric and large moulded forms: Festival of Britain mixed with Dali's Surrealist Mae West Lips, designed in 1936.

Festival of Britain appears to have affected Lynne Wilson's design of seating for Mobilia Italia; while Zanotta – a firm with a reputation for eccentric quality – has endorsed the British High Street aesthetic of the same period (Cintique comes to mind) and has thereby raised it from – to British eyes – the mundane to the chic.

37–38

39

40

41

42

43

37–38 LYNNE WILSON
Seating, *Lotto*
Steel frame and legs. Seat and headrest in polyurethane foam with fabric or leather covering. Comfortable and particularly suitable for contract furnishing.
H 99 cm (39 in). W 82 cm (32 in). L 83 cm (32 in)
Manufacturer: Mobilia Italia, Italy

39, 40 CLAUDIO SALOCCHI
Armchair, two- and three-seater sofa, *Feeling*
Steel frame, upholstery in fabric or leather.
Armchair H 85 cm (33 in). D 90 cm (35 in). L 85 cm (33 in)
Sofa with two seats H 85 cm (33 in). D 90 cm (35 in). L 140 cm (55 in)
Sofa with three seats H 85 cm (33 in). D 90 cm (35 in). L 198 cm (78 in)
Manufacturer: Skipper, Italy

41 DE PAS, D'URBINO, LOMAZZI
Sofa, *Valmara*
Steel frame. Different upholstery of fire-resistant polyurethane foam. Back is of down in sections. Seat cushions of down/polyurethane. Double covering; the first one of nylon cannot be removed; the second, available in various fabrics, can be taken off for dry cleaning, though the leather covering cannot be removed.
H 82 cm (32 in). Seat H 42 cm (16 in). D 82 cm (32 in). L from 88 cm (34 in) to 200 cm (78 in)
Manufacturer: Zanotta, Italy

42 DE PAS, D'URBINO, LOMAZZI
Sofa, *Bastina*
Steel frame. Different upholstery of fire-resistant polyurethane foam. Back is of down in sections. Seat cushions of down/polyurethane. Double covering; the first of nylon cannot be removed; the second of various fabrics can be taken off for dry cleaning, though the leather covering is fixed.
H 75 cm (29 in). Seat H 42 cm (16 in). D 78 cm (30 in). L 88 cm (34 in) to 200 cm (78 in)
Manufacturer: Zanotta, Italy

43 PEP BONET
Armchair, *Mantis*
Wood, steel, with fabric or leather upholstery.
Manufacturer: Levesta, Spain

■ As a homage to the 1950s, Richard Sapper's folding chair is slender, beautifully detailed, and refined. In particular, it recalls the style of the British designer, Robin Day, who produced during the early 1950s a series of similarly sparely designed chairs for the British furniture firm, Hille.

44

44 RICHARD SAPPER
Small folding armchair, *Nena*
Structure of PRFV (plastic-reinforced fibreglass). Knuckle joints and crosspieces of powder-varnished die-cast aluminium. Seat and back in weather-proofed plywood. Upholstery can be either fabric or leather. Once folded the chair can be easily stored in confined spaces or hooked against the wall.
H 83 cm (32 in). W 76 cm (29 in). L 55 cm (21 in)
Manufacturer: B&B Italia, Italy

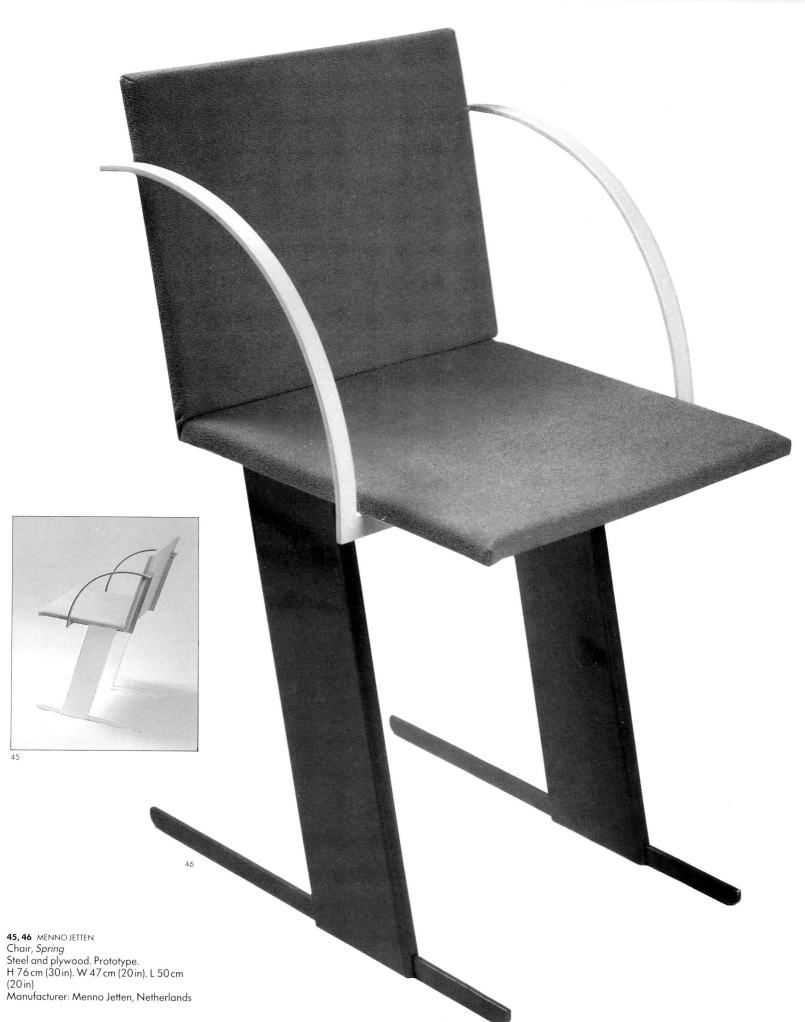

45

46

45, 46 MENNO JETTEN
Chair, *Spring*
Steel and plywood. Prototype.
H 76 cm (30 in). W 47 cm (20 in). L 50 cm
(20 in)
Manufacturer: Menno Jetten, Netherlands

47 TAKASHI SUDO
Stool, *Zip*
Steel and leather.
H 101.5 cm (40 in). W 43 cm (17 in).
L 38 cm (15 in)
Manufacturer: Zoeftig and Co, UK

47

48 BURKHARD VOGTHERR
Chair, *T-Line*
Metal, polyurethane moulded foam,
integrated fabric in various colours.
H 100 cm (39 in). W 75/76 cm (29½ in).
D 68/75 cm (26/29 in)
Manufacturer: Arflex, Italy

48

49

50

49,50 FRANCO RAGGI
Armchair, sofa, stool, *Elba, Elbalunga, Elbapouff*
Armchair and sofa backs in natural or grey stained wood,
seat in lacquered wood. Upholstery as required. Elba and
Elbalunga are designed for formal and informal use.
Chair *EL/1* H 82 cm (32 in). W 77 cm (30 in). L 92 cm (36 in)
Sofa *EL/2* H 82 cm (32 in). W 77 cm (30 in). L 120 cm (47 in)
Stool *EL/3* H 38 cm (15 in). W 62 cm (24 in). L 50 cm (19 in)
Manufacturer: Cappellini, Italy

51

52

53

51 UGO LA PIETRA
Sofa, *Agevole*
Frame and base of shock-resistant grey-painted steel-section. Seat sprung with crossed elastic belts, feet of black injection-moulded PVC. Agevole is the name of the range which also includes an armchair, three-seater sofa and coffee table.
H 78 cm (30 in). W 75 cm (29 in). L 150 cm (59 in)
Manufacturer: Busnelli Edizioni, Italy

52 UGO LA PIETRA
Armchair and sofa, *Pretenziosa*
Frame of polished chestnut, slides of copper-plated and polished aluminium-section. The cushions can be removed and the covering zipped off.
Armchair H 78 cm (30 in). W 102 cm (43 in). D 80 cm (31 in)
Sofa H 78 cm (30 in). Seat H 39 cm (15 in). L 154 cm (60 in)
Manufacturer: Busnelli Edizioni, Italy

53 UGO LA PIETRA
Armchair, sofa and table, *Flessuosa*
The coffee table is made of glossy polyester-lacquered wood, coloured lilac and pink. Armchair and sofa have solid-wood frames and are sprung with crossed elastic belts. Upholstery is of variable-density polyurethane covered with cotton fabric. The armchair is also available with a high back.
Armchair H 88 cm (34 in) or 130 cm (51 in).
Sofa H 88 cm (34 in). W 125 cm (49 in).
Table H 60 cm (23 in). D 55 cm (21 in)
Manufacturer: Busnelli Edizioni, Italy

54 UGO LA PIETRA
Armchair and sofa, *Pratica*
Frame of shock-resistant, grey-painted steel-section and solid wood. Seat sprung with crossed elastic belts. The ample arms and plump shapes make *Pratica* extremely comfortable. Armchair H 94 cm (37 in).
L 99 cm (39 in)
Sofa H 94 cm (37 in). Seat H 44 cm (17 in).
Manufacturer: Busnelli Edizioni, Italy

54

55 PAOLO DEGANELLO
Armchair, *Torso*
Steel frame and elastic webbing, padded with polyurethane foam and polyester. Feet with black ABS points. Fabric or leather upholstery; the seat and back can be of different materials. A sofa and a bed are available in the same style.
H 82 cm (32 in). D 88 cm (34 in)
Manufacturer: Cassina, Italy

■ Belotti's *Man Ray* chair for Alias looks unwieldy; 1950s foam with a punkish aspect; the metal frame punches through the soft fleshy-looking body like an ear-ring through an ear lobe.

56

56 STUDIO GIANDOMENICO BELOTTI
Armchair, *Man Ray*
Steel frame painted in black epoxidic powder, or chromium plated. Seat in high-quality polyurethane covered in cotton or velvet.
H 82 cm (32 in). W 70 cm (27 in). L 60 cm (23 in)
Manufacturer: Alias, Italy

■ Public furniture in Scandinavia is generally well made, pleasing to look at and designed to be durable. Andersson's serpentine bench with its slatted back and seat has a traditional appearance. The curving steel frame recalls Artifort furniture of the 1960s. The Pelikan café furniture, compactly designed, also has a 1960s look; though the chairs have a curious slit seat.

57, 58 PELIKAN DESIGN (NIELS GAMMELGAARD AND LARS MATHIESEN)
Chair and round table
Galvanized or painted steel tubing, grey-rubber seat and back bracket. This café system also includes a bar chair, a small table and a rectangular table.
Chair H 71 cm (28½ in)
Round table H 70 cm (28 in). D 55 cm (21½ in) or 90 cm (35 in)
Manufacturer: Fritz Hansens, Denmark

57

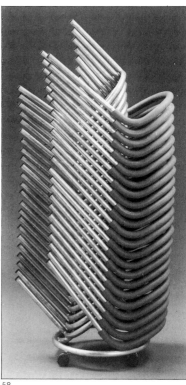

58

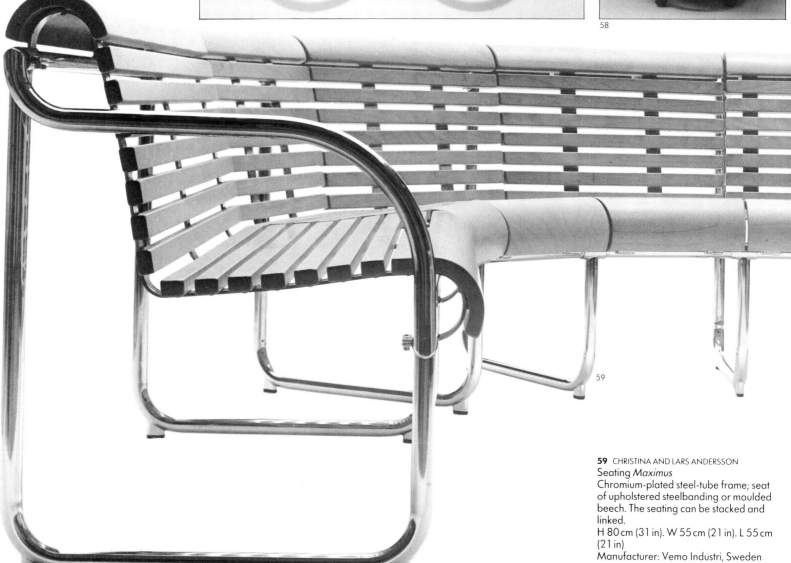

59

59 CHRISTINA AND LARS ANDERSSON
Seating *Maximus*
Chromium-plated steel-tube frame; seat of upholstered steelbanding or moulded beech. The seating can be stacked and linked.
H 80 cm (31 in). W 55 cm (21 in). L 55 cm (21 in)
Manufacturer: Vemo Industri, Sweden

■ These two pieces – *Antropovarius* by Ferdinand Porsche and *Veranda 3* by Vico Magistretti – are truly sophisticated structures: high technology as opposed to the semblance of it. Porsche's chair looks as though it were designed for a car or a plane. When fully extended, its curving backbone and ribs give it an unmistakably anthropomorphic appearance.

The ancestry of *Veranda 3*, with its unfurling mechanism concealed by upholstery, can be traced back to the hugely successful *Maralunga* sofa designed years ago, and more immediately to the splendid *Veranda* chair on which Magistretti said you could 'eat, sleep or make love'.

With *Veranda 3*, 'I intended to create space by using the furniture itself, so that instead of adapting the geometry of the walls, the occupants could follow their own tastes. They can sit as they like, facing each other or grouped as if in front of a fireplace – or in a large circle resembling an Indian encampment, as in the IBM hall in Madison.'

60

60 VICO MAGISTRETTI
Three-seater sofa, *Veranda 3*
Black or white lacquered wooden base. Glossy dark-green or matt-black enamelled steel feet. Steel seat frame, polyurethane foam and polyester padding, fabric or leather upholstery. The three sitting units, with folding backs, are linked but independent. The central unit is fixed; the two side ones are movable, rotating around a pivot fixed to the base. This can be used as a table top when the side units form a semicircle.
Fully extended head rest H 110 cm (43 in). Seat H 41 cm (16 in). W 85 cm (33 in). L 260 cm (104 in)
Manufacturer: Cassina, Italy

61–62 FERDINAND ALEXANDER PORSCHE
Reclining seat, *Antropovarius*
Steel structure with leather upholstery. The chair can be adjusted to a number of positions, from upright to lounging. Designed according to the most advanced ergonomic principles, the structure is made of adjustable triangular elements and can be controlled by a simple handlever. Base, structure and arms are black: upholstery available in a range of colours. The leather covering of the cushioned back is pierced to allow air to pass through it.
H adjustable 75 cm to 122 cm (29 in to 48 in). W adjustable 96 cm to 165 cm (38 in to 65 in). L 72 cm (28 in)
Manufacturer: Poltrona Frau, Italy

61

62

64

■ Since Charles Eames produced his now classic swivelling, tilting chairs in the late 1950s for Herman Miller International, there have been endless and more or less opulent variations on the same theme. Some recent and spidery versions by Oscar Tusquets are shown here. The alertness of their design, and of the accompanying stacking chair, is pleasing. Visually there are similarities between it and the *Airmail* chair by King and Miranda for the Italian firm, Marcatre.

63

63, 64, 65 OSCAR TUSQUETS
Chairs, *Varius* range
Steel with seat of polyester and polyurethane. Upholstered with cloth or leather.
Secretarial chair H 76 cm to 84 cm (29 in to 33 in)
Operational stool H 84 cm to 95 cm (33 in to 37 in)
Desk chair H 84 cm to 92 cm (33 in to 36 in)
Management chair H 87 cm to 95 cm (34 in to 37 in)
Four-legged chair H 83 cm (32 in)
Manufacturer: Casas, Spain

65

■ Kartell was the first firm to mould nylon products; the first to introduce injection-moulded ABS lamps and the first to manufacture chairs entirely in plastic. Throughout thirty-five years of corporate history, Kartell's image has been reflected by the quality of its products; which from the 1960s onwards have included furniture. The famous children's chair by Marco Zanuso and Richard Sapper was designed in 1964, and that was followed shortly afterwards by the now classic Joe Colombo chair. In any case the list of names associated with Kartell design — Anna Castelli Ferrieri, Franco Albini, Sergio Asti, Gae Aulenti, Joe Colombo, Isao Hose, Gerd Lange, Vico Magistretti and Ettore Sottsass — is an impressive compendium of distinguished designers.

Kartell continues to produce pure sculptural objects whose design gives form and function equal billing, and makes excellent use of colour. The newest Kartell trolley shown here is, as usual, a beautiful piece of taut design in the Modernist tradition: 'large enough for a Christmas turkey and with a rim high enough to prevent it falling, and equipped with a removable bottle tray'. The same goes for the elegant table; though a hint of Post-Modernist caprice appears in the Studio Alchimia-style arrowheads around the base.

66 ANNA CASTELLI FERRIERI
Table with centre leg, *4310*
The top is made of expanded ABS finished with antiscratch paint, the leg of ABS, and the feet of nylon technopolymer glass fibre. Colours: white, yellow, black, red or green. Injection moulded with no screws or metal parts, the table is sturdy and virtually indestructible. Suitable for domestic and commercial use, indoors or out. The tables are particularly suitable for restaurants because their central support permits unobstructed leg room when they are pushed together.
H 72 cm (28 in). W 8 cm × 80 cm (31 in × 31 in)
Manufacturer: Kartell, Italy

66

67 CENTROKAPPA
Trolley, *4564*
Top and handle in ABS. Upright and castor support in polypropylene. Colours: trolley body in white and black; handles in white, black, red, yellow or green. Bottle holder in ABS, coloured black and white.
Trolley H 70 cm (27 in). W 45 cm (17 in). L 75 cm (29 in)
Bottle holder H 10 cm (3 in). W 18 cm (6 in). L 20 cm (7 in)
Manufacturer: Kartell, Italy

67

The furniture in this section has been loosely classified as Light Engineering. Protière's delicately webbed chair (illustration 75) for Pallucco was one of the most appealing at the 1984 Milan Furniture Fair; though it must be said that as another variant of 'The Chair as Art' it is for those for whom comfort is not the first consideration.

Ivana Bortolotti's tensile structure and Marili Brandão's adjustable divan (illustrations 68, 69 and 76) are visually intriguing and practically ingenious. Bortolotti's chair folds up compactly; while Brandão's hammock-like divan can be turned into a bed, and the back-rest adjusted by means of the nylon cords. These two pieces formed part of the 'Seven Living Ideas Project', sponsored by B&B Italia, and presented in Milan in 1984. The project was a laudable attempt by B&B to give young designers a chance. The company commissioned designs of settees and chairs from seven fourth-year Industrial Design students at the Istituto Europeo di Disegno, and working under Roberto Lucci and Paolo Orlandini. The aim was to produce furniture for a young public; and all the models were collapsible or could be folded up.

The British company, One-Off, has recently been attracting a good deal of attention internationally. Its furniture, like the rocking chair and extending light shown in illustration 74, is, one feels, punk translated into hi-tech. The chair's aggressive angles and the tangled wires of the light, whose arm reaches out by remote control like the arm in the classic nightmare, all constitute a mocking comment.

68, 69 IVANA BORTOLOTTI
Chair, *Tenso*
Tensile structure in 20 mm aluminium tubing and steel-wire rope. The netting seat is threaded with nylon. Extremely compact when dismantled, this prototype was produced for 'Seven Living Ideas Project,' sponsored by B&B Italia's Research Centre and the Istituto Europeo di Disegno, Italy.
H 100 cm (39 in). D 85 cm (33 in).
L 100 cm (39 in)
Prototype

70 ELS STAAL
Bench series
Laminated wood panels and steel tubing.
The bench can be demounted. The range
is particularly suitable, the designer says,
for institutional use. The bench can be
upholstered.
Heptagonal bench H 73 cm (28 in).
D 216 cm (85 in). L 92 cm (36 in)
Two-seater bench H 70 cm (27 in).
D 160 cm (63 in). L 72 cm (28 in)
Wall-mounted bench H 70 cm (27 in).
D 180 cm (70 in). L 65 cm (25 in)
Prototype

70

71 ALBERTO SALVATI AND AMBROGIO TRESOLDI
Easychair, *Miamina*
Structure of eight chromed or lacquered
tubes fixed on a central moulded joint
which allows the chair to be folded up.
Covered in Missoni fabric. The chairs are
sold in a bag containing the folded
structure, upholstery and headrest.
H 97 cm (38 in). D 90 cm (36 in). L 97 cm
(38 in)
Manufacturer: Saporiti, Italy

71

72 NIELS GAMMELGAARD
Folding chair, *Jarpen*
Steel tubing and net, painted red, white or
black.
H 38 cm (14 in). W 65 cm (25 in). L 66 cm
(26 in)
Manufacturer: Ikea, Sweden

72

73 ISAO HOSOE, WITH ANN MARINELLI
Articulated free-standing wall, *Snake*
Extruded PVC tubing, ABS connectors. A self-supporting
room divider and screen. Can be made to assume various
serpentine forms.
H 85 cm (33 in) to 181 cm (71 in)
Manufacturer: Sacea, Italy

73

74 RON ARAD
Rocking chair
Structure of tubular, PVC coated steel springs. Chrome
finish. Aerial light. Die-cast aluminium base, steel body and
halogen lamp. 12 v, 50 w. Finished in textured epoxy-
coated chrome. The arm of the light can be extended and
moved up and down, as well as round and round, by
remote control. The dimming mechanism is also part of the
remote-control unit.
H adjustable from 60 cm to 72 cm (23 in to 27 in). W 79 cm
(31 in). D adjustable from 66 cm to 78 cm (26 in to 30 in)
Manufacturer: One-Off, UK

75 RÉGIS PROTIÈRE
Chair, *Lizie*
Tubular steel frame and drawn-steel rods. Seat in natural
beech or aluminium; polyurethane powder finish.
H 71 cm (28 in). W 51 cm (20 in). L 50 cm (19 in)
Manufacturer: Pallucco, Italy

74

75

76

76 MARILI BRANDÃO
Adjustable divan, *Tiete*
Also converts into a bed. Frame in steel tubing and
sections. The angle of the backrest can be altered by
nylon cords. Prototype by a fourth-year industrial-design
student designed for the 'Seven Living Ideas Project,'
sponsored by B&B Italia's Research Centre and the Istituto
Europeo di Disegno, Italy.
H 70 cm (27 in). L 200 cm (78 in). D 83 cm (32 in)
Prototype

■ As a designer, David Wolton inclines towards engineering and the performance-per-pound principle – an approach that eschews self-conscious ornament or display of the craftsman's art: Buckminster Fuller rather than John Makepeace. A hop merchant and publisher, he belongs to the tradition of the inspired English amateur; for the past twenty years he has designed and made a series of original softwood chairs and stools. They are intriguing for their combination of slender elegance and a deliberately orange-box quality. Their apparent fragility belies remarkable strength. The chair has a box frame with legs diagonally braced, and the seat tilts slightly forward, accepting the position naturally adopted by anyone working at a desk. The stool, one of a series, is similarly constructed. Our subliminal recognition is prompted by the fact that it closely resembles the stools used by Ancient Egyptians, familiar from tomb reliefs and paintings.

77 DAVID WOLTON
Chair, *C8*
Wooden box-frame and bent wood, vertical-rail back.
H 96 cm (38 in). Seat H 45.7 cm (18 in). W 42 cm (16½ in).
D 35.5 cm (14 in)
Manufacturer: David Wolton, UK

78

77

78 DAVID WOLTON
Stool, *S7*
Wood, morticed struts.
H 33 cm (13 in). W 30.5 cm (13 in) × 30.5 cm (13 in)
Manufacturer: David Wolton, UK

■ The table, by its nature, lends itself to architectural forms. Here Kurokawa's table, described by flat planes, is an essay in restraint. The wood of the post-and-lintel base appears the dominant fabric, so that the thin translucent top floats in a surreal fashion like a sheet of water.

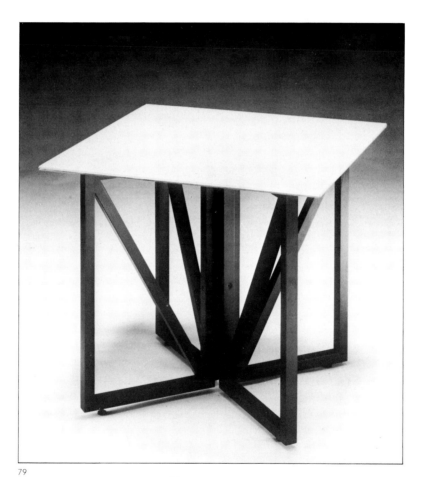

79

79 KISHO KUROKAWA
Coffee table, *Edo*
Wood structure, table top of two layers of glass; legs finished with black matt polyurethane paint.
H 33 cm (13 in). W 90 cm (35 in). L 90 cm (35 in)
Manufacturer: Kosuga & Co, Japan

80

80 LELLA AND MASSIMO VIGNELLI (VIGNELLI ASSOCIATES)
Table, *Ambiguità*
Top of green or red granite, base of slate, column of white Carrara marble. The table top can be rotated and arrested by means of a mechanism. The borders of the two long sides, and of one end, are sanded smooth, while the remaining end is left unfinished.
H 72 cm (33 in). D 90 cm (41 in). L 235 to 250 cm (107 in to 113 in)
Manufacturer: Casigliani, Italy

81 GWATHMEY SIEGEL AND ASSOCIATES
Table, *De Menil*
Wood: mahogany, cherry, ash and ebony. The base, the bull-nosed edge and penetrations are one solid piece of wood; the top is a veneer of another. The table comes in three shapes, square, circular or rectangular.
H 46 cm (18 in). D 106 cm (43½ in). L 106 cm (43½ in)
Manufacturer: ICF, USA

81

82 GIULIO LAZZOTTI
Table, *Siena*
Low table with top of marble, stone and terracotta, base of black or white wood.
H 30 cm (11 in). D 105 cm (41 in). L 123 cm (48 in)
Manufacturer: G.B. Bernini, Italy

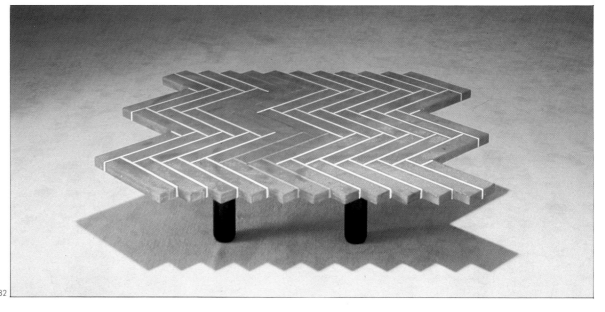

82

83 ALBERTO SALVATI
Table, *Lisitski*
Metal structure on a chiselled cement base. The base can be doubled in size to support a bigger superstructure. The metal part supporting the glass top is made up of a series of various coloured elements, reminiscent of abstract art.
Rectangular tops H 72 cm (28 in).
D 100 cm (39 in). L 200 cm, 220 cm or 240 cm (78 in, 86 in or 94 in)
Square tops H72 cm (28 in). D 130 cm or 140 cm (51 in or 55 in). L 130 cm or 140 cm (51 in or 55 in)
Round tops H 72 cm (28 in). D 130 cm or 140 cm (51 in or 55 in)
Manufacturer: Saporiti, Italy

84 AFRA AND TOBIA SCARPA
Oval table, *Polygonon*
The top is produced in marble, transparent or blue-cobalt glass. Octagonal base is of steel plate coloured by adherent and scratch-resistant film.
H 72 cm (28 in). D 169 cm (66 in). L 130 cm (51 in)
Manufacturer: B&B Italia, Italy

85 ALBERTO SALVATI
Series of tables in different heights, *Nuvole*
Top and base-blade made of wood, lacquered with metal legs in various colours.
H 72 cm (28 in), 35 cm (13 in) or 29 cm (11 in)
Manufacturer: Saporiti, Italy

86 TOSHYUKI KITA
Table, *Tavolo Altobasso*
Top lined with plastic laminate, available in black or white. Pedestal lined with striped rubber. Height adjustable by means of a handle controlling a gas piston.
H 55 cm to 73 cm (21 in to 28 in)
Manufacturer: De Padova, Italy

87 KISHO KUROKAWA
Armchair, *Edo Series Part II*
Wood frame and legs; frame finished with green, vermilion and black lacquer. Legs finished with aluminium paint. Brass connectors. Seat covered with black leather. Designed for small-batch production and first used in the lobby of the Roppongi Prince Hotel in Tokyo.
H 62.6 cm (24 in). W 76 cm (29 in). L 66.4 cm (26 in)
Manufacturer: Tendo Co, Japan

87

88

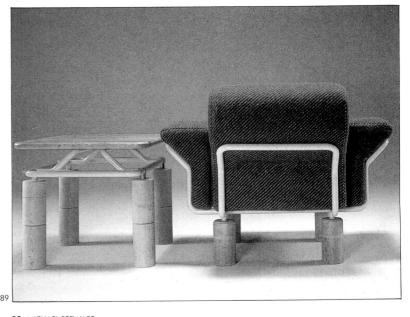

89

88 MICHAEL STEWART
Armchair and stool, *Lexicon*
Steel tube, baked enamel finish, cast aluminium, solid wood, polyurethane foam. The three differently shaped tube parts can be assembled to form a chair or stool frame, or can be extended into a sofa. Tubing is fixed by means of a cast aluminium connector; cushions are supported by the frame and the seat cushion by rubber webbing.
H 71 cm (28 in). D 91 cm (36 in). L 81 cm (32 in)
Manufacturer: Ambiant Systems, Canada

89 MICHAEL STEWART
Glass top table, *Lexicon*
Steel tube, solid wood, tempered glass. The frame can be extended horizontally to form a larger table by simply adding more tube parts and aluminium connectors.
H 36 cm (14 in). W 122 cm (48 in). L 122 cm (48 in)
Manufacturer: Ambiant Systems, Canada

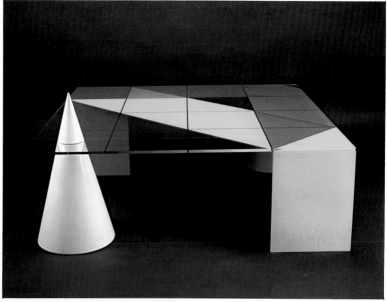

90

91

■ Four playful tables: one whimsical by Rita Taskinen; the others geometric acrobatics by John Smith that recall 1970s pop.

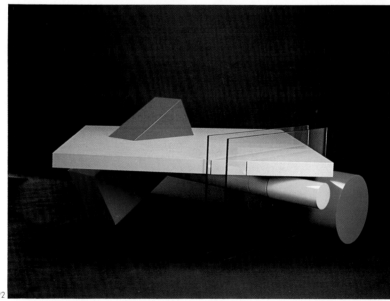

92

93 RITA TASKINEN
Chair, *Ballerina*
Birch, plywood and leather.
H 80 cm (32 in). D 42 cm (17 in)
Table, *Pythagoras*
Birch, steel and glass
H 72 cm (29 in). D 125 cm (50 in)
Manufacturer: Proforma, Finland

90 JOHN SMITH
Table, *Colourblock*
Painted timber, MDF board, PVC and glass top. One-off. Asymmetrical juxtaposition of solid coloured elements whose primary forms are derived from the square, triangle and circle.
H 40 cm (15 in). W 90 cm (35 in). L 180 cm (70 in)
Manufacturer: Design in the Round, Australia

91 JOHN SMITH
Table, *Colourband*
Painted MDF board and PVC, painted glass. One-off. Interplay of primary forms, with bands of primary colours projected across a grid underneath the glass; secondary colours appear where the bands overlap.
H 40 cm (15 in). W 124 cm (49 in). L 124 cm (49 in)
Manufacturer: Design in the Round, Australia

92 JOHN SMITH
Table, *Sliced Slab*
Colorcore Formica, painted MDF board, PVC and glass. One-off. The pink table-top hovers above two horizontal yellow and blue cylinders and is sliced by two vertical planes of glass. A red rectangular box, penetrated by the yellow cylinder, intersects the table plane.
H 40 cm (15 in). W 122 cm (48 in). L 122 cm (48 in)
Manufacturer: Design in the Round, Australia

93

■ Demountable furniture. The two chairs produced by the Italian firm, Numeri, are part of a larger collection called *Insieme Ordinato di Aste*. This is a range of seats and tables that are sold in kit form. The Z-shaped chair is plainly a Rietveld variant, but because of the sturdy components and sharp colours, has a toy-like appearance. Bernt's demountable chair has a quieter, obviously Scandinavian appearance. Despite its austerity it is surprisingly comfortable, the slats being carefully calculated to provide springiness.

94 DE PAS, D'URBINO AND LOMAZZI
Chair, *Palmira*
Legs of black-lacquered beech. Seat of stiff polyurethane covered with cowhide; back of cowhide. Colours: black, Russian red, natural, white, light grey, brown.
H 89 cm (35 in). Seat H 46 cm (18 in).
W 41 cm (16 in). L 51 cm (20 in)
Manufacturer: Zanotta, Italy

95 MARCO BALZAROTTI, MASSIMO FUSCO AND ROBERTO GANGEMI
Chair Three
Nylon grey structure reinforced with fibreglass. Polypropylene elements in white, grey, red, yellow, green, blue.
H 89 cm (35 in). D 51 cm (20 in). W 39 cm (15 in)
Manufacturer: Numeri, Italy

96 BERNT
Knock-down chairs, *CH 71, CH 72*
Beech and plywood.
CH 71 H 76 cm (29 in). W 48 cm (18 in). L 45 cm (17 in)
CH 72 H 73 cm (28 in). W 64 cm (25 in). L 64 cm (25 in)
Manufacturer: Carl Hansen and Son, Denmark

97 MARCO BALZAROTTI, MASSIMO FUSCO AND ROBERTO GANGEMI
Chair, *Insieme Ordinato di Aste*
One of a range of pieces of furniture made up of the same few parts. Made of grey nylon shafts and white spacers, the furniture is sold in kit form and is easy to assemble. It is hardwearing and suitable for interior and exterior use.
H 85 cm (33 in). Seat H 45 cm (17 in). D 40 cm × 45 cm (15 in × 17 in)
Manufacturer: Numeri, Italy

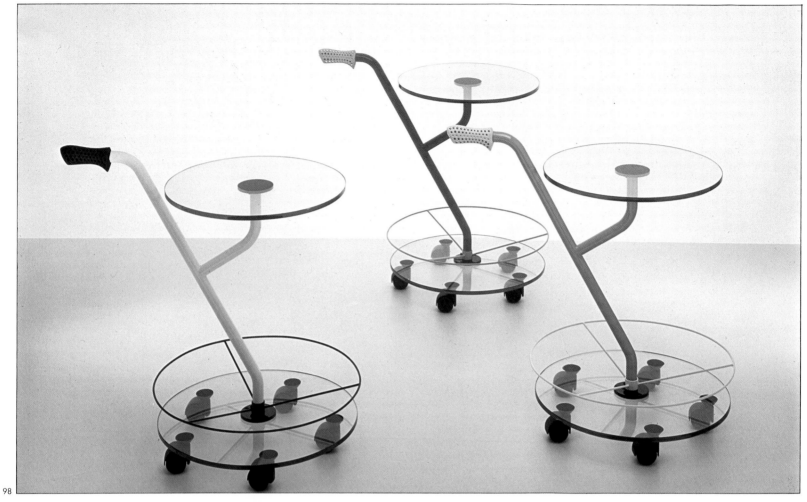

98

■ Post-Modernist intrusion into the glass-and-steel aesthetic has produced – to borrow from Charles Jencks – Slick Tech; though Regondi's trolley, with its canti-levering and angled handles evokes Eileen Gray. Remember her *Occasional Table* of 1927? The castors, however, invisibly fixed to the glass plate above, invoke Gae Aulenti.

99

98 GABRIELE REGONDI
Trolley, *Dixi*
Thick transparent crystal, polished metal tube and plastic.
H 75 cm (29 in). D 76 cm (30 in). L 52 cm (20 in)
Manufacturer: Rimadesio, Italy

99 MINALE, TATTERSFIELD AND PARTNERS
Split Level Table
Epoxy-coated tubular steel, natural-timber drawer, glass top. The split-level table is suitable for small living areas. Dining and coffee table are combined and the object can be adapted to take a television, telephone and other domestic equipment. The drawer can be an open steel tray. *Split Level Table* is available in a wide range of bright colours.
H 75 cm (29 in). W 100 cm (39 in)
Manufacturer: Cubic Metre Furniture, UK

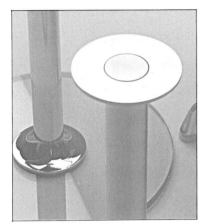

100

101

100, 101 PETER DRAENERT
Table, *1013*
Glass and steel.
H 70 cm or 72 cm (27 in or 28 in).
L 180 cm (70 in)
Manufacturer: Draenert Studios GmbH,
West Germany

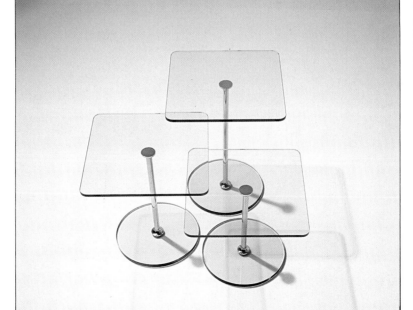

102

102 PETER DRAENERT
Table, *1011*
Glass and steel.
H 40 cm, 50 cm or 60 cm (15 in, 19 in or
23 in). 50 cm × 50 cm (19 in × 19 in)
Manufacturer: Draenert Studios GmbH,
West Germany

■ Despite attempts by critics to make the Memphis tendency go away, it has not done so, and indeed it has affected every aspect of design. Memphis objects are much prettier in reality than the photographs suggest, which has something to do with scale and their finite quality. While playful, they are strangely totemic, conforming to Sottsass' description of his own works as 'monuments which only go by themselves'. 'They don't,' he added at the time, 'even manage to create style. Nobody buys them apart from the odd collector or desultory Hollywood film star.' Since Memphis opened its showroom in Milan with a collection designed in riotous manner by an international group of designers, it has settled down, its objects becoming increasingly refined to the point where – despite Sottsass' observation – one can talk about the Memphis style. It has to do with a dream-like quality; the over- or under-sized elements; the toy colours suggesting the surrealism of the child. But the elephantine quality of much of the furniture evokes De Brunhoff's Babar (the elephant) rather than *Alice in Wonderland*.

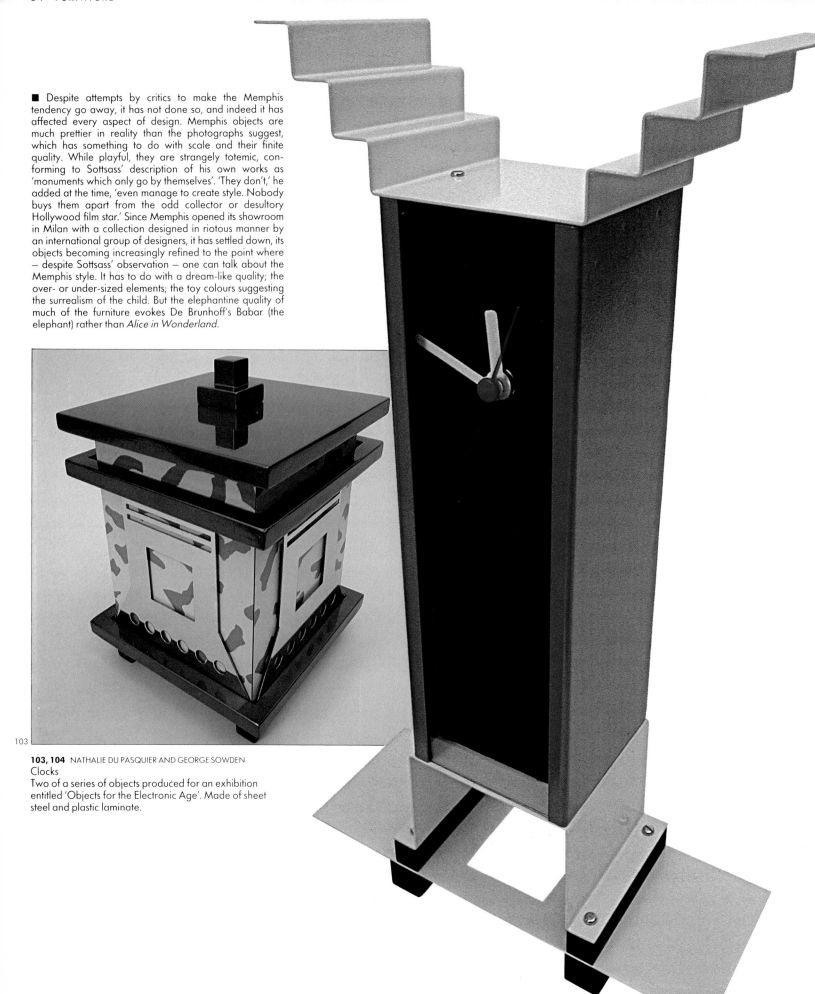

103

103, 104 NATHALIE DU PASQUIER AND GEORGE SOWDEN
Clocks
Two of a series of objects produced for an exhibition entitled 'Objects for the Electronic Age'. Made of sheet steel and plastic laminate.

104

105, 106 KEITH GIBBONS
Wooden block clock
Painted wood.
H 25 cm (9¾ in). D 16 cm (6¼ in). L 6 cm (2 in)
Manufacturer: Products, UK

107 ARQUITECTONICA
Table, *Madonna*
Lacquered wood.
H 74 cm (29 in). W 244 cm (96 in).
D 137 cm (53 in)
Manufacturer: Memphis, Italy

105

106

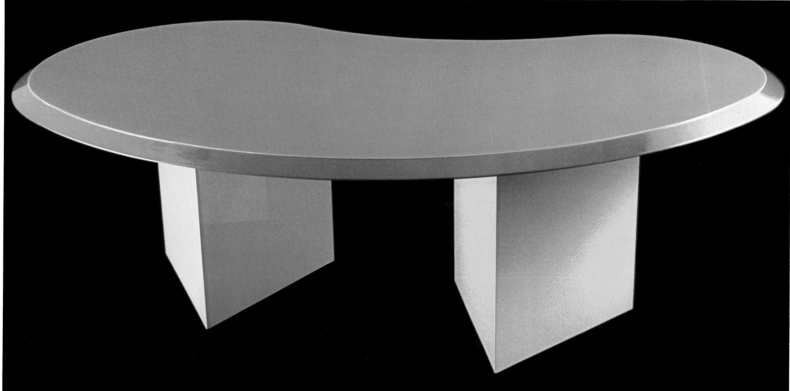

108

109

108 MICHELE DE LUCCHI
Small table, *Poplar*
Plastic laminate and lacquered wood.
H 40 cm (15 in). W 70 cm (27 in). D 35 cm
(13 in)
Manufacturer: Memphis, Italy

109 ETTORE SOTTSASS
Mirror, *Diva*
Plastic laminate.
H 108 cm (42 in). W 76 cm (29 in). D 5 cm
(2 in)
Manufacturer: Memphis, Italy

110 MARCO ZANINI
Armchair, *Lucrezia*
Aluminium frame upholstered and covered
in fabric by Ettore Sottsass, manufactured
by Rainbow.
H 77 cm (32 in). W 55 cm (21 in). D 60 cm
(23 in)
Manufacturer: Memphis, Italy

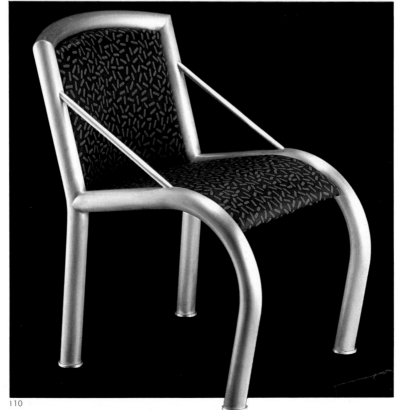

110

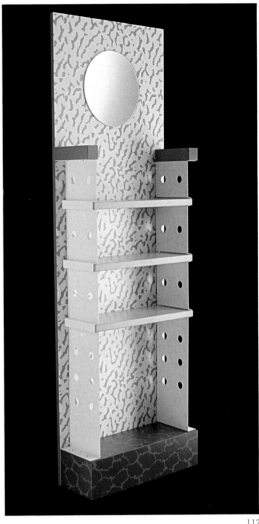

112 NATHALIE DU PASQUIER
Shelves, *Coral*
Metal and plastic laminate.
H 185 cm (72 in). W 60 cm (23 in). D 22.5 cm (9 in)
Manufacturer: Memphis, Italy

111 CARLO FORCOLINI
Dressing table, *Buñuel*
Iron frame, pink granite base, white polyethylene top with black-lacquered wooden drawers. Mirrors and halogen lamp mounted on flexible tubes covered with black rubber.
H 105 cm (42 in). W 73 cm (29 in)
Manufacturer: Alias, Italy

113, 114 MICHELE DE LUCCHI
Table, *Mist*
Lacquered timber and glass. Part of the
Morphos Collection.
H 72 cm (28 in). W 80 cm (31 in). L 180 cm
(70 in)
Manufacturer: Acerbis, Italy

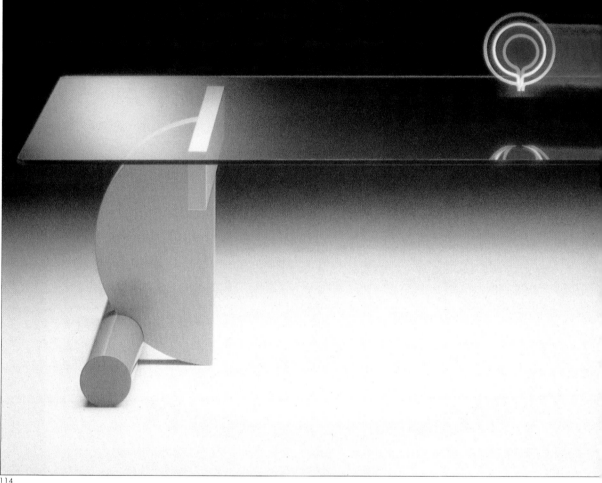

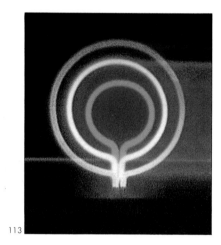

113

114

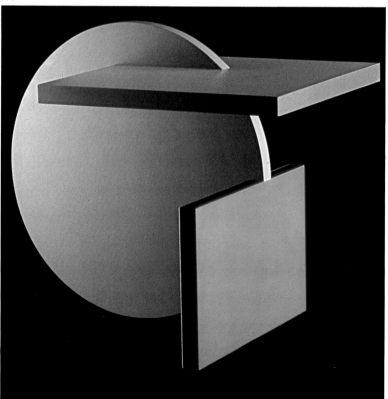

115 MICHELE DE LUCCHI
Side table, *Continental*
Plastic laminate and timber.
H 60 cm (23 in). W 60 cm (23 in).
L 90 cm (34 in)
Manufacturer: Memphis, Italy

115

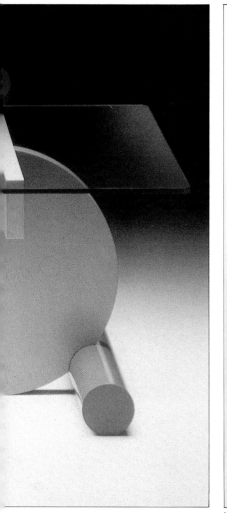

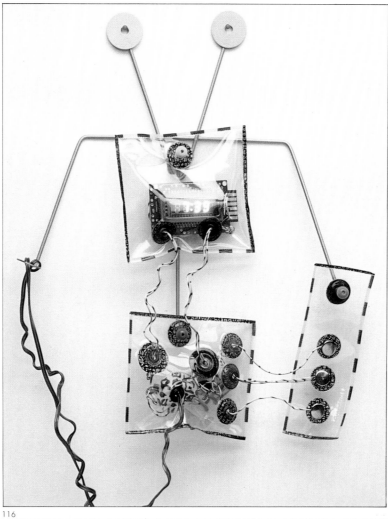

116

116, 117 DANIEL WEIL
Radio fm/am, *Andante*
Part of the Anthologie Quartett Collection.
H 30 cm (11 in). L 30 cm (11 in). D 4 cm
(1 ½ in)
Manufacturer: Quartett, West Germany

117

118

118 MICHELE DE LUCCHI
Kitchen furniture system, *RB 214*
Laminated timber, lacquered doors.
Designed to a 15 cm (5 in) module
Manufacturer: RB Rossana, Italy

119

119 CARLO FORCOLINI
Table, *Apocalypse Now*
Top in corten sheet steel, varnished or in marble. Legs in
steel tube, chromed or zinc coated. Adjustable 100w,
28v halogen light, chromed.
H 45 cm (17 in). D 120 cm (47 in). L 120 cm (47 in)
Manufacturer: Alias, Italy

120

120 HANS EBBING AND TON HAAS
Mirror GS 60
Glass, timber, metal. The mirror, rising through a lacquered
shelf, floats free of the wall and is held in place by an
invisible metal bracket. Available in red, white, and black.
H 60 cm (23 in). D 15 cm (5½ in). L 100 cm (39 in)
Manufacturer: Skizo, Netherlands

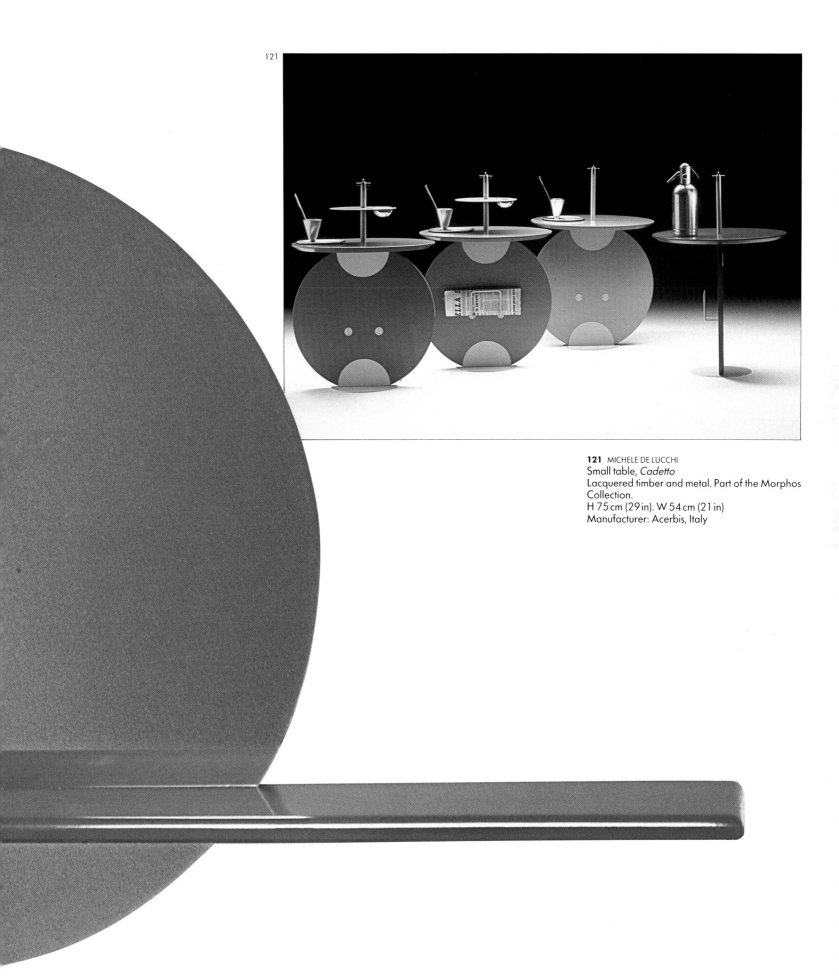

121

121 MICHELE DE LUCCHI
Small table, *Cadetto*
Lacquered timber and metal. Part of the Morphos
Collection.
H 75 cm (29 in). W 54 cm (21 in)
Manufacturer: Acerbis, Italy

■ Studio Alchimia (illustrations 122 to 126) is the other Milanese anti-functionalist protest group, set up like its counterpart, Memphis, to explore colour, form and decoration. Seen within the tribally divided and excitable Milanese design community, Alchimia seems the more austere, cerebral of the two. The objects it produces are totemic, as are those by Memphis, but one responds to them rather with the intellect than the senses. References have been esoteric, varying from Eileen Gray and Seurat, to, in this collection, vaguely megalithic art; and the group seems more attuned to introspective study than extroverted games. Post-post-Modernism perhaps? Since its inception in 1976 it has been involved in seminars and experimental theatre, and has published books such as Alessandro Mendini's inscrutably entitled *Il Progetto Infelice*. It also has links with the recently established Domus Academy in Milan. It has recently joined forces with the furniture firm, Zanotta, which has put its products into commercial production.

122

122 ALESSANDRO MENDINI AND BRUNO GREGORI
Table/chair, *Zabro*
Fold-down top in decorated timber. Seat in leather and painted timber.
Table H 70 cm (27 in). D 92 cm (36 in)
Chair H 137 cm (53 in). W 45 cm (17 in). L 92 cm (36 in)
Manufacturer: Zabro, Italy

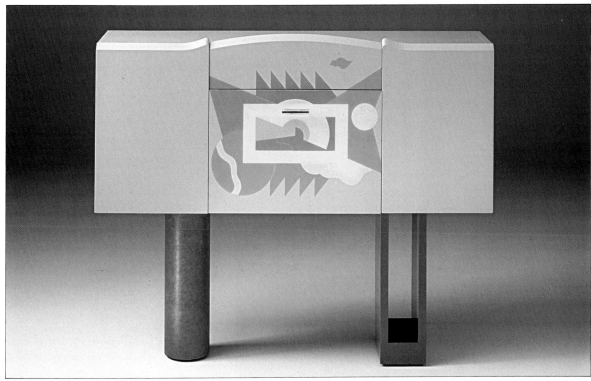

123

123 ALESSANDRO MENDINI AND BRUNO GREGORI
Chest of drawers, *Cantaride*
Decorated timber, handles in silver-plated metal.
H 90 cm (35 in). D 55 cm (21 in). L 120 cm (47 in)
Manufacturer: Zabro, Italy

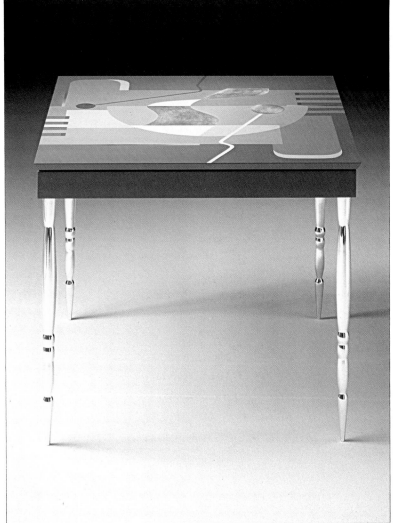

124 ALESSANDRO MENDINI AND BRUNO GREGORI
Card table, *Atropo*
Top in multicoloured painted timber. Legs of silver-plated turned aluminium.
H 71 cm (28 in). D 85 cm (33 in). L 85 cm (33 in)
Manufacturer: Zabro, Italy

124

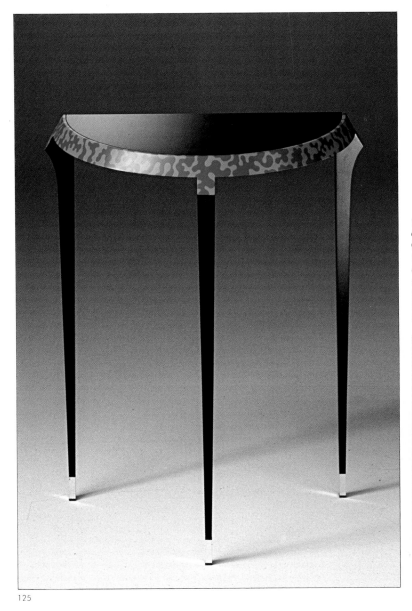

125

125 ALESSANDRO MENDINI AND BRUNO GREGORI
Console, *Agrilo*
Black-painted timber with border decoration in two colours. Glass top and silver ferrules.
H 90 cm (35 in). D 40 cm (15 in). L 79 cm (31 in)
Manufacturer: Zabro, Italy

126

126 ALESSANDRO MENDINI AND BRUNO GREGORI
Standard lamp, *Atomaria*
Sky-blue and grey-painted timber, silver pennants and tiny lights.
H 186 cm (73 in). D 42 cm (16 in). L 51 cm (20 in)
Manufacturer: Zabro, Italy

27

127 NEMO
Chair, *Faizz*
Epoxy finished metal frame with grey seat and back. Flexible back.
H 48 cm (18 in). L 100 cm (39 in). D 37 cm (14 in)
Prototype

128 NEMO
Chair, *Blue Lagoon*
Red seat and back with metal frame.
H 80 cm (31 in). L 70 cm (27 in). D 55 cm (21 in)
Prototype

129 NEMO
Reclining chair, *Molitor*
Metal frame, with elastic PVC body, transparent.
H 70 cm (27 in). L 150 cm (59 in). W 80 cm (31 in)
Prototype

129

■ However dangerous it is to make sweeping generalizations, there are undoubtedly national characteristics in design: the British are either cautious or mad, the Scandinavians sober, the Italians refined, sometimes to the point of preciousness; and so on. Could these chairs, in their exaggerations and brashness, be anything other than French? Look at the exaggerated frame of the *Faizz* chair; or the undulations of *Molitor*, set within a pennanted and metal frame. One is somehow reminded of those extraordinary new French towns, such as Marne La Vallée (outside Paris); architecturally so extreme, they are fantasy — or, depending on your viewpoint, nightmare — made manifest.

■ Swedfun, as the name suggests, seems to be the Swedish version of Memphis. The fun is somewhat heavy-handed and lacks the lightness of touch of the Italians.

130

130 HANS GUNNARSSON
Chaise longue, *Chezz Long*
H 140 cm (55 in). L 112 cm (44 in)
Manufacturer: Swedfun, Sweden

131 MARGARETA ABERG
Cupboard, *Salabim*
H 165 cm (65 in). W 90 cm (35 in). D 45 cm (17 in)
Manufacturer: Swedfun, Sweden

131

132 PELLE FRENNING
Rocking chair
H 125 cm (49 in). W 75 cm (29 in). D 90 cm (35 in)
Manufacturer: Swedfun, Sweden

■ The Finns, with their increasingly pared-away structures, seem to be approaching the outer edge of visibility. For firms like Vivero, Avarte and Inno, Finnish Minimalism is the keynote: Minimalist forms and minimal concessions to Post-Modernism, with references to Rietveld and early Eames. Yrjo Kukkapuro's seating, and his table for Avarte, contain a hint of Post-Modernism crossed with Aalto. Coloured decorative elements made of thinnish birch are combined with standard seats. Inno is a relatively young company selling products made of epoxy-coated steel tubing. Harri Korhonen's couch-cum-easy chair, with its attenuated light, is a witty comment on adaptability; but the aesthetic, conscious or not, harks back to Richard Schultz's 'leisure collection'.

133

134

134 YRJO KUKKAPURO
Settee, *Experiment 801*
Timber, and chrome-plated and black steel
tube. Glides made of black polyamide;
upholstery of PR foam and Dacron
wadding. Standard colours of the
component joining seat and backrest are
white, black or yellow.
H 68 cm (26 in). Back H 36 cm (14 in).
Seat W 77 cm (30 in). L 194 cm (76 in)
Table, *Experiment 601*
Top of white melamine-laminate-coated
birch plywood. Standard colour of edge
yellow. Screw-on legs are chrome-plated
steel tube.
H 43 cm (16 in). W 78 cm × 78 cm ×
106 cm (30 in × 30 in × 41 in)
Manufacturer: Avarte, Finland

135

133, 135 HARRI KORHONEN
Couch-chair, *Flip*
Chromed or epoxy-coated steel and
painted-timber frame, cotton upholstery.
By adjusting the cushions, *Flip* can be used
as a chair, couch or spare bed and is
equipped with wheels for easy movement.
H 75 cm (29 in). W 65 cm (25 in). L 195 cm
(76 in)
Manufacturer: Inno-tuote, Finland

■ The Norwegians, like the Swedes, seem preoccupied with ergonomics. At the 1984 Scandinavian Fair in Copenhagen, Norwegian stands featured curiously shaped objects for slumping against and for propping up various parts of the body. The Studio Hag piece evokes dental and gynaecological memories; but it in fact really does refresh tired limbs. Less ergonomically sophisticated, and somewhat untidily English, is the *Astride* chair by Minale Tattersfield, designed for sprawling around on.

136

137

136,137 MINALE, TATTERSFIELD AND PARTNERS
Chair, *Astride*
Dufalyte honeycomb and plywood core, extruded rubber edging, woven fabric upholstery. As the name suggests, the occupant sits astride this chair as if in a saddle.
H 90 cm (30 in). W 80 cm (31 in). L 100 cm (39 in)
Manufacturer: Cubic Metre Furniture, UK

138, 139 SVEIN ASBJØRNSEN AND JAN LADE
Ergonomic seat, *Split Returner*
Laminated beech, black stained, coloured upholstery. A switch-operated and silent electric motor, run off the mains, permits adjustment to individual requirements. The designers point out that 'legs above heart level stimulates the blood circulation'.
H 100 cm (39 in). W 67 cm (26 in).
L 195 cm (76 in)
Manufacturer: Hag AS, Norway

138

139

■ 'The furniture was designed for the Summer Room of a London house and hence has symbolic ornament which underscores this theme. The Sun Table has a solar disc in the centre, a *trompe l'oeil* in orange and based on photographs of sun spots and solar explosions. Nine planets run up the table leg to another sun, while nebulae and spiral galaxies are represented in the wood graining of the top. The fan shape of the top repeats that of the chairs, and when the table is in its smallest position, for four to six people, shows space and timber curving back at the edge of the universe. In the expanded position, seating ten to fourteen people, the fan trumpets out and forms floral petals of a sunburst. The Sun Chairs have similar imagery, and functionally, a back and seat which follow the body's curves.' Charles A. Jencks.

140

141

140, 141, 142, 143 CHARLES A. JENCKS
Sun Table and *Chairs*
MDF painted and glazed.
Table H 77 cm (30 in). Small 132 cm (52 in).
Expanded 183 cm (72 in)
Chair H 97 cm (38 in). W 61 cm (24 in).
L 44 cm (17 in)
Manufactured specially for the designer, available from Max Protech Gallery, New York

142

143

144

■ Looking at Venturi's humorous play on the treasured traditions of Queen Anne, Chippendale and Empire (illustrations 144 to 146), one is struck by the thought that one way of dealing with a psychological yearning for the past is to make light of it. On the other hand, those traditions in Europe are bound up with class affiliations and snobbishness; and it is exactly that American combination of disrespect and deference that is refreshing. Queen Anne de-natured, made out of something that looks like nougat and fitted with an 'optional fixed seat pad of polyester and foam' and nylon gliders? One has to admire it.

■ Compared with the Americans, the Italians' expression of nostalgia at its most refined level is altogether shyer and more delicate. The danger is lack of vigour and a certain degree of preciousness. Astori's most refined designs verge on the effete but are rescued by literacy and the high quality of the craftmanship.

144, 145, 146 ROBERT VENTURI
Chairs and tables, *Venturi Collection*
Venturi Chairs available in three styles –
Queen Anne, Chippendale or Empire.
Frame of bentwood laminations, laminate or wood-veneer face; optional fixed seat pad of polyester and foam; fixed nylon glides. Finishes: veneers can be natural maple or bird's-eye maple stained dark grey; laminates are surf white, grandmother floral pattern, black, yellow or burgundy.
Queen Anne: Seat H 46 cm (17½ in). Back H 96 cm (38½ in). L 67 cm (26¼ in)
Chippendale: Seat H 46 cm (17½ in). Back H 92 cm (37 in). L 64 cm (25½ in). D 59 cm (23¼ in)
Empire: Seat H 46 cm (17½ in). Back H 52 cm (32½ in). L 61 cm (24¼ in)
Venturi Tables are rectangular with double-urn base, or square with cabriole leg. Rectangular table top of wood veneer with matching 2 cm (1⅛ in) edge; base of wood laminations faced with wood veneer or laminate, capped with zinc toes in black or polished chrome. Veneer finishes are natural maple or bird's-eye maple stained dark grey. Laminate finishes are yellow or harlequin black and burgundy.
H 68 cm (28½ in). L 336 cm (120 in)
Square table top also available in solid granite. Base and veneer finishes as above. Laminate finishes in surf white, floral pattern, black, yellow or burgundy.
H 62 cm (28½ in). L 122 cm, 138 cm or 152 cm (48 in, 54 in or 60 in)
Manufacturer: Knoll International, USA

145

146

147 ANTONIA ASTORI
Wardrobe, *Aforismi: Acale*
Part of a series of cupboards. Made of metallic laminated panels, fitted with shelves or drawers, pull-out writing surface and/or record-holder in metallic blue-lacquered wood. Clothes rung in chrome-metal tubing, secretaire in metallic blue-lacquered wood and violet-coloured drawers. Various mouldings available in metallic blue, violet or silver-grey-lacquered wood. Rolling shutters of grey plastic. Part of the Aleph Collection.
H (excluding moulding) 181 cm (71 in).
D 62 cm (24 in). L 65 cm (25 in)
Manufacturer: Driade Diffusione, Italy

149

148 ANTONIA ASTORI
Dressing table, *Aforismi: Dione*
Top and pilasters of Abet Print laminate, white speckled with grey or with orange-peel finish. Chest of drawers of metallic laminate, cylindrical handles of grey plastic. Frame and mirror supports of chromed metal. 'A metaphysical piece of furniture', says the designer, the top rests on three pilasters at one end, and on a revolving chest of drawers at the other. The mirror set slightly askew has movable wings. Part of the Aleph Collection.
Overall H 132 cm (52 in). Table H 72 cm (28 in). D 72 cm (28 in)
Manufacturer: Driade Diffusione, Italy

149, 150 WENDY ROBIN AND ALAN STANTON
Range of office furniture
Wood and wood products, melamine, lacquer. Prototypes.
Manufacturer: Société Jacques Parisot, France

■ The Wendy Robin and Alan Stanton partnership was one of two British finalists in the international competition for the design of office furniture, organized in 1984 by the French Government. Its design is the antithesis of the coldly functional furniture of the modern office. Underlying it is the idea that the individual should be able to create his personal territory. There are three basic elements: portal, yoke and box. A great deal of thought has been devoted to the grouping of the elements: so that walls, at 168 cm (66 in) height, ensure both privacy and that views are between elements rather than over them; while the lighting-towers, with uplighters reflecting off a conical diffuser, are used as punctuation points.

■ Compared with the Americans, the Italians' expression of nostalgia at its most refined level is altogether shyer and more delicate. The danger is lack of vigour and a certain degree of preciousness. Astori's most refined designs verge on the effete but are rescued by literacy and the high quality of the craftmanship.

150

■ The Formica Corporation's promotion of its new material, Colorcore™, has involved the talents of some of the best-known architects and designers in America, Britain and France. 'Surface and Ornament' was a competition designed to explore the sculptural and ornamental potential of the material. The work of the winners was combined with that of nine American architects and designers into an exhibition that received world-wide attention. Certainly the works are quite extraordinary. Subsequently, London's Victoria and Albert Museum's 'Boilerhouse Project' invited Formica to expand the exhibition with furniture by well-known French and British designers.

Those exhibitions were followed by a touring one called 'Material Evidence', co-sponsored by Formica and The Gallery Workbench. It consisted of works by nineteen leading fine woodworkers in America, including such well-known furniture makers as Mitch Ryerson and Rick Wrigley. The project began with a seminar at which Formica's design team demonstrated Colorcore's potential and explained the tools and finishing techniques required.

Formica's selling point is that unlike conventional laminates, Colorcore™ is of uniform hardness, is durable, is available in twenty good colours, and is coloured through its depth. The material can therefore be bevelled, sandblasted, subjected to controlled chipping and tearing, inlaid and layered in colours, because there is no unsightly edge.

As can be seen, the participants in the various projects responded to Formica's challenge with enthusiasm, and the results of their enthusiasm are for the most part virtuoso exercises: sometimes fantastic, invariably ingenious.

151 JOHN CEDERQUIST
Chest of drawers, *The Great Art Deco Furniture Explosion*
Colorcore combined with maple, sycamore and birch ply. Part of the 'Material Evidence Exhibition'.
H 32 cm (12 in). W 101 cm (40 in).
L 152 cm (60 in)
Manufacturer: Formica Corporation, USA

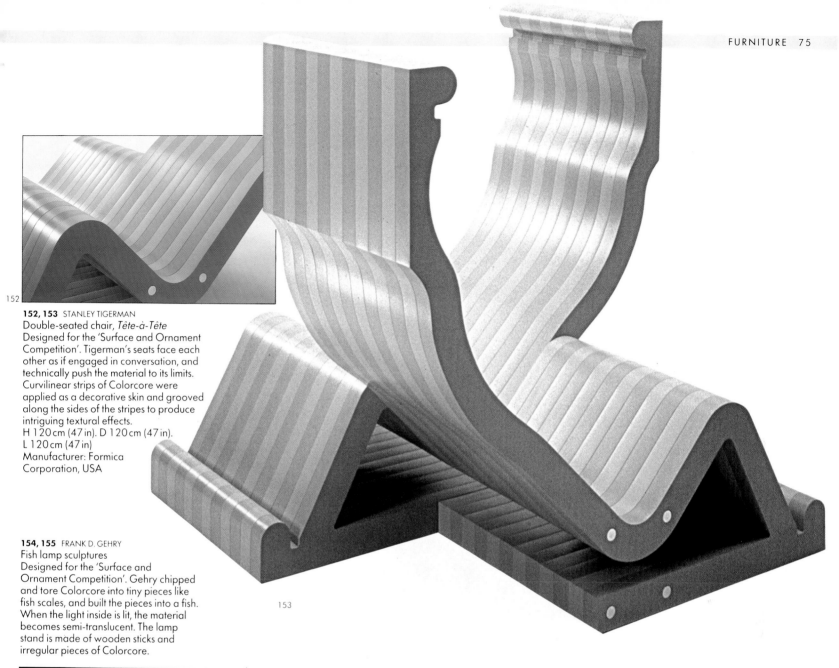

152

152, 153 STANLEY TIGERMAN
Double-seated chair, *Tête-à-Tête*
Designed for the 'Surface and Ornament
Competition'. Tigerman's seats face each
other as if engaged in conversation, and
technically push the material to its limits.
Curvilinear strips of Colorcore were
applied as a decorative skin and grooved
along the sides of the stripes to produce
intriguing textural effects.
H 120 cm (47 in). D 120 cm (47 in).
L 120 cm (47 in)
Manufacturer: Formica
Corporation, USA

154, 155 FRANK D. GEHRY
Fish lamp sculptures
Designed for the 'Surface and
Ornament Competition'. Gehry chipped
and tore Colorcore into tiny pieces like
fish scales, and built the pieces into a fish.
When the light inside is lit, the material
becomes semi-translucent. The lamp
stand is made of wooden sticks and
irregular pieces of Colorcore.

153

154

155

156, 157 VENTURI, RAUCH AND SCOTT BROWN
Mirror frame, *Mirror in the Greek Revival Manner*
Colorcore. Designed for the 'Surface and Ornament Competition'. The material has been layered and carved in a manner that reinterprets Classical ornamentation.
H 75 cm (29 in). W 75 cm (29 in)
Manufacturer: Formica Corporation, USA

156

157

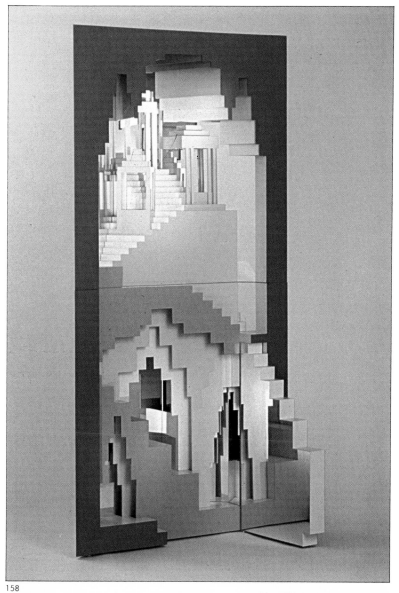

158

158, 159 CHARLES MOORE
Corner Cupboard
Colorcore. Designed for the 'Surface and
Ornament Competition'. Moore used
the material to express his preoccupation
with Classical decorative motifs.
H approx. 183 cm (72 in)
Manufacturer: Formica Corporation, USA

159

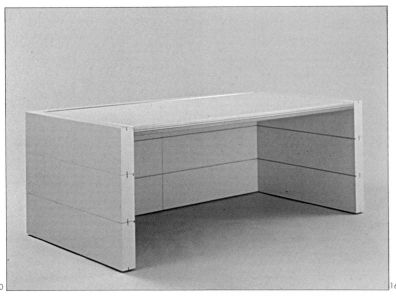

160

161

160 EMILIO AMBASZ AND GIANCARLO PIRETTI
Desk, *L-System*
Colorcore. Part of a modular system
based on a structurally stable L-shaped
unit. Designed for the 'Surface and
Ornament Competition'.
Manufacturer: Formica Corporation, USA

161 BRIAN FAUCHEUX
Table draped with a 'tablecloth' of
Colorcore
Designed for the 'Surface and Ornament
Competition'. Faucheux layered pink and
white Colorcore and chipped the layers to
create the impression of fabric. The main
body of the table is emphasized by
horizontal grooves and pink Colorcore
stripes.
H 60 cm (23½ in)
Manufacturer: Formica Corporation, USA

162 JAY STANGER
Drinks cabinet, *Dress Her*
Designed in the shape of a curvacious
turn-of-the-century woman. Corsetted top
of loosely bundled Colorcore slats, skirt of
vertical pieces of beefwood. Colourful bar
inside. Part of the 'Materal Evidence
Exhibition'.
H 183 cm (72 in). W 99 cm (39 in). L 64 cm
(25 in)
Manufacturer: Formica Corporation, USA

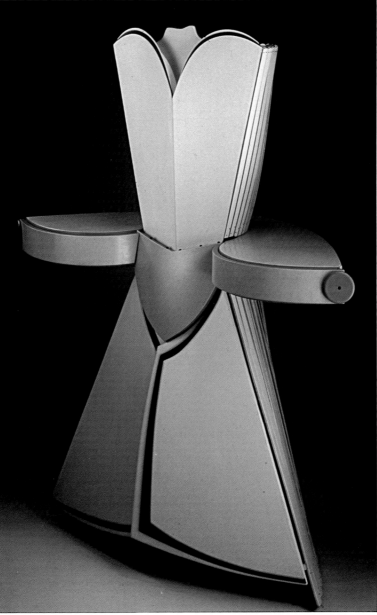

162

163

163, 164 LEWIS AND CLARK
Chair, *Temple*
Designed for the 'Surface and Ornament
Competition'. Designed as a fantasy, the
chair won first prize. 'For a deity who sits
enthroned while tiny imaginary
worshippers perform exotic rituals.'
H 150 cm (59 in). D 120 cm (47 in).
L 120 cm (47 in)
Manufacturer: Formica Corporation, USA

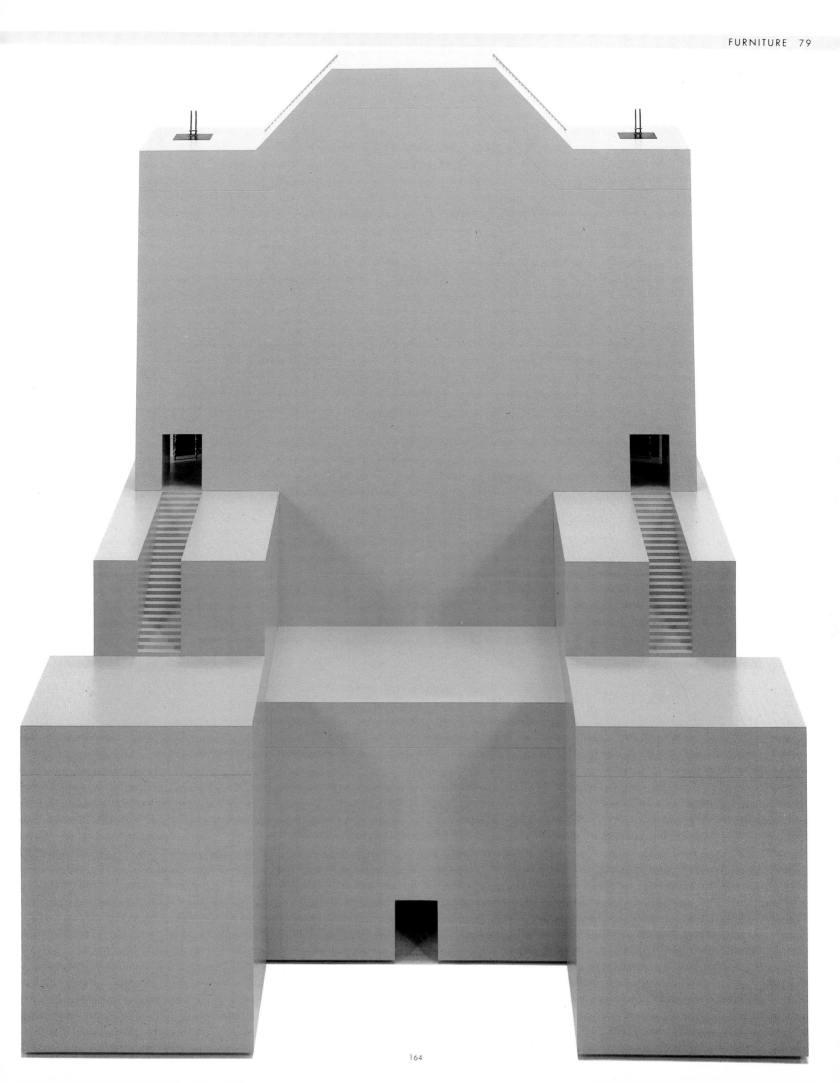

165, 166 PAUL CHIASSON
Classical Cabinet
Colorcore. Designed for the 'Surface and Ornament Competition'. The outline forms a perfect square, the square repeated throughout the design. Layering and routing techniques exploit the material's potential.
H 220 cm (86½ in). D 60 cm (23½ in).
L 220 cm (86½ in)
Manufacturer: Formica Corporation, USA

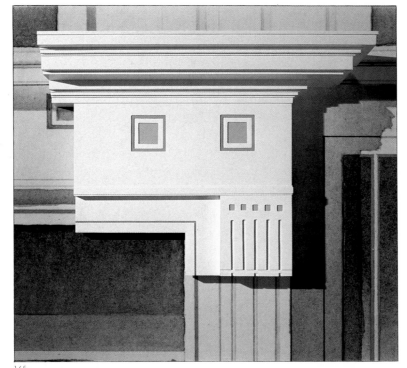

165

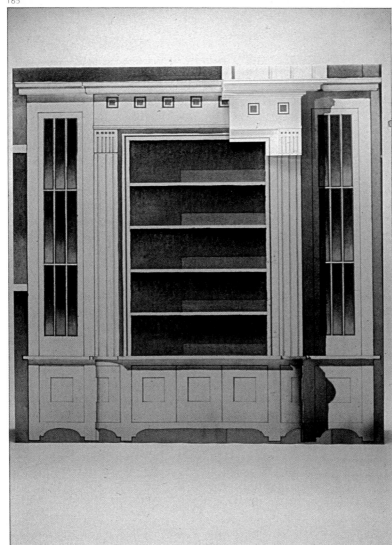

166

167 RICK WRIGLEY
Armoire
Colorcore, aromatic cedar and maple.
Base Colorcore brickwork. Upper section
made of routed Colorcore. Part of the
'Material Evidence Exhibition'.
H 244 cm (96 in). D 82 cm (32 in).
L 138 cm (54 in)
Manufacturer: Formica Corporation, USA

168 MITCH RYERSON
Hall furniture
Colorcore, latticed, the design based on that of a traditional 19th-century American hall piece. Part of the 'Material Evidence Exhibition'.
H 178 cm (70 in). D 44 cm (17 in).
L 117 cm (46 in)
Manufacturer: Formica Corporation, USA

169 JOHN MCNAUGHTON
Table, *Classic pairs*
Colorcore, Classical detailing. Part of the
'Material Evidence Exhibition'.
H 69 cm (27 in). D 41 cm (16 in). L 143 cm
(56 in)
Manufacturer: Formica Corporation, USA

170 WARD BENNET
Trolley, *Cart-Mobile*
Multicoloured layers of Colorcore form
the body; the two handles are layers of
Colorcore with a circular hole cut out. A
rainbow is exposed on the interior and
exterior edges. Designed for the 'Surface
and Ornament Competition'.
Manufacturer: Formica Corporation, USA

169

170

171

171 JOEL FOURNIER
Console, *Console Néo-Classique*
Colorcore surfacing used to create the
effect of simple mass. Part of the 'New
British and French Colorcore Exhibition'.
H 90 cm (35 in). W 40 cm (16 in).
Manufacturer: Formica Corporation, USA

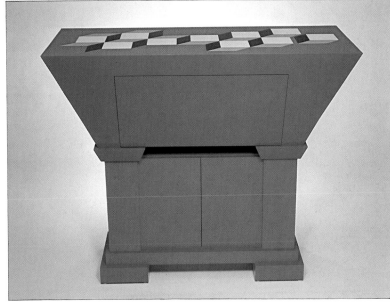

172

173

172 DAVID VICKERY
Sideboard
Top surfaced in Surf Colorcore with inlaid glass panel lit from underneath. Cupboard door and drawer faces in Black Colorcore, edged with Tawny Blush. Designed for Formica's 'New British and French Colorcore Exhibition'.
H 85 cm (33½ in). D 43 cm (16½ in).
L 152 cm (59½ in)
Manufacturer: Michael Reed for Formica Ltd, UK

173 RORY MCCARTHY
Sideboard/secretaire
Colorcore marquetry. Part of the 'Material Evidence Exhibition'.
H 112 cm (44 in). D 56 cm (22 in).
L 127 cm (50 in)
Manufacturer: Formica Corporation, USA

174 ALAIN MARCOT
Table, *Echiquier*
Colorcore worked by traditional marquetry techniques. Part of the 'New British and French Colorcore Exhibition'. Designed in the Classical style, the table has corner boxes that can be used either for displaced chessmen or as ashtrays.
D 90 cm (36 in). L 90 cm (36 in)
Manufacturer: Formica Corporation, USA

174

175 WENDY MARUYAMA
Chest of drawers, *Highgirl*
Colorcore routed and stippled with black
paint. Part of the 'Material Evidence
Exhibition'.
H 173 cm (68 in). D 46 cm (18 in). L 59 cm
(23 in)
Manufacturer: Formica Corporation, USA

176 PETER GLYNN SMITH
Low table
Colorcore with zinc tray. Specially
commissioned for Formica's 'New British
and French Colorcore Exhibition'.
H 35 cm (13½ in). D 100 cm (39½ in)
Manufacturer: Raymond Cole of Formica
Ltd, London

178 RODNEY KINSMAN
Dressing table and screen
Colorcore. Commissioned for Formica's
'New British and French Colorcore
Exhibition'.
Screen H 150 cm (59 in). W 50 cm (20 in).
L 85 cm (33½ in)
Dressing table H 147 cm (58 in). W 57 cm
(34½ in). L 120 cm (47 in)
Manufacturer: Kenneth Dobbin of Formica
Ltd, London

177 SITE (JAMES WINES AND ALISON SKY)
Door
Colorcore. Designed for the 'Surface and
Ornament Competition'. It is intended to
convey decaying New York architecture.
H 228 cm (90 in). W 142 cm (56 in).
Manufacturer: Formica Corporation, USA

176

177

178

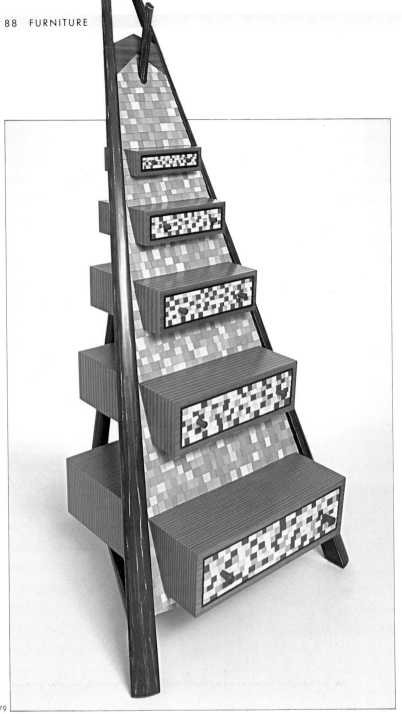

179

180

181

179 TOM LOESER
Chest of drawers
Colorcore combined with birch, poplar, bubinga and enamel. Pyramidal in shape, the chest of drawers' decoration with decorative ladder forms and saw tooth patterns evokes American folk art. Part of the 'Material Evidence Exhibition'.
H 155 cm (61 in). D 84 cm (33 in). L 82 cm (32 in)
Manufacturer: Formica Corporation, USA

180 YONEL LEBOVICI
Light, *Obelix*
Colorcore column supporting a nickel-plated brass reflector. Part of the 'New British and French Colorcore Exhibition'.
Manufacturer: Formica Corporation, USA

181 EVA JIRICNA
Folding table and chair
Made of Colorcore, routed and perforated. Part of the 'New British and French Colorcore Exhibition'.
Table H 60 cm (25½ in). D 90 cm (36 in)
Chair H 41 cm (16½ in). D 36 cm (14½ in)
Manufacturer: TAG Design Partnership for Formica Ltd, UK

182

■ The crafts in Britain are very much alive and flourishing. One of their most important proponents is the furniture-maker John Makepeace, whose school for cabinet-makers is at Parnham House. The Parnham workshops specialize in fulfilling commissions for private, commercial and public clients.

The woods used vary enormously in character and origin. Practically no soft woods are used, except for cedar of Lebanon as a scented lining for drawers; the hardwoods include the classic English timbers, oak, ash, cherry, walnut and burr elm, but also the less common robinia, holly, yew and laburnum. Exotic timbers like rosewood, ebony, paldao and satinwood have to be used more sparingly. All are sawn in planks, spaced with sticks and left to season naturally over a number of years. Trees are selected for their quality, colour and grain; natural phenomena like burrs are chosen for their unusual character. Occasionally other materials — burnished lacquer, gold leaf, leather, ivory, silver and stainless steel — are incorporated.

The chair and table shown here are by Makepeace and made in his workshops. Makepeace's furniture is frequently romantic, tending to exploit in virtuoso manner the inherent structure and nature of the particular timber used.

182 JOHN MAKEPEACE
Breakfast table
Carved burr and laminated English oak. The irregular top is made of consecutive but reversed veneers, with a solid edge cut from the adjoining board. The 'trunks' are built up of layers, freely shaped and abraded to emphasize the grain. The base, of knotty burr and reminiscent of roots, spreads to form a clump.
H 72 cm (28 in). L 105 cm (41 in)
Manufacturer: Andrew Millwards for John Makepeace, UK

183 JOHN MAKEPEACE
Chair
One of a set of chairs in English oak with leather upholstery.
H 97 cm (37 in). D 60 cm (23 in). L 55 cm (21 in)
Manufacturer: John Makepeace, UK

183

■ Apart from John Makepeace's school, other colleges in Britain, including the postgraduate Royal College of Art in London, continue to turn out fine cabinet-makers, though the emphasis tends to be on design, rather than, as with Makepeace, on craft.

Lucie McCann's piece was made while she was a student at Kingston Polytechnic. Martin Grierson and Ashley Cartwright on the other hand are established furniture makers with their own workshops, turning out beautifully finished objects.

184 ASHLEY CARTWRIGHT
Pair of chests of drawers, left and right Sycamore and cedar.
H 120 cm (47 in). W 38 cm (15 in).
D 40 cm (16 in)
Manufacturer: Tim Wells, UK

185 MARTIN GRIERSON
Desk, *Partner*
Natural and brown oak with black stringing. Constructed in three interlocking parts. Centre drawer takes AO plans. A one-off piece, made for exhibition and sale.
H 71 cm (28 in). D 100 cm (39 in).
L 190 cm (74 in)
Manufacturer: Martin Grierson, UK

186 MARTIN GRIERSON
Chair, *Chinese*
Macassar ebony, seat and back splat in American black walnut.
H 80 cm (31 in). W 60 cm (23 in). L 120 cm (47 in)
Manufacturer: Martin Grierson, UK

187 LUCIE MCCANN
Settee, *Bacchus*
Walnut frame, feather-filled pigskin cushions. Can be made in teak for garden use.
H 91 cm (33 in). W 65 cm (25 in). L 179 cm (69 in)
Manufacturer: John Coles, UK

LIGHTING

Lighting design can readily be divided into two classes — light fittings and lighting systems. Those in the former category range in character from the Modernist — often making reference to precision-engineering practice — to the purely decorative. Here the influence of Memphis, and to a lesser extent of Studio Alchimia, has been profound. Both studios protest against functionalism and call for individual expression, colour, warmth and even irrationality.

Decorative lights lend themselves to plant-like forms. Designers such as Vico Magistretti, Perry King and Santiago Miranda have evolved shapes that are infinitely delicate, subtly evocative, and yet economical. Their lamps seem botanically inspired — whether the snaking, multi-coloured glass stems of Fraser's lamp for Stilnovo; the sun-burst petal of Buti's lamp for the appropriately named Stars; or the drooping head of Jiran's table lamp.

Light systems, on the other hand, like the high-technology architecture with which their development is associated, have become specialized affairs. Governed by a complex technology, the light system involves an extensive, and sometimes bewildering range of equipment: downlighters; uplighters; tubes and spotlights; low-voltage, halogen and HID lamps; systems that can be built into the structure of the building with concealed light sources, or mounted on separate movable substructures. Various elements can be combined into flexible systems for any kind of building, domestic or public. Lighting design has been influenced by the work of architects fixated with high-technology like Norman Foster and Richard Rogers. It has also been influenced by the increasing sophistication of building structures and the need for greater flexibility. For firms like the internationally successful West German company, Erco Lighting, which specializes in architectural lighting, this has meant a conflict between a desire to produce the custom-made on the one hand, and to comply with production targets on the other. Now, it seems, the problem is solved by means of computers. (For the first time last year the company's investment in computer software exceeded that in new machinery and equipment.)

Lighting lends itself to division by function, so apart from lights by King and Miranda, and by Kurokawa, which seemed naturally to fall into their own sections, it has been divided into table, wall, standard and pendant lamps, and light systems.

■ Inventors and designers have been devoting attention to desk lights for the last one hundred and fifty years. The Anglepoise – excellent though it is and *de rigueur* in any Modernist architect's office in the 1930s – was not the definitive desk light. There has been recent progress. The designs shown in illustrations 188 to 196 have an economy of form which accords with the sophistication of the electronic elements themselves.

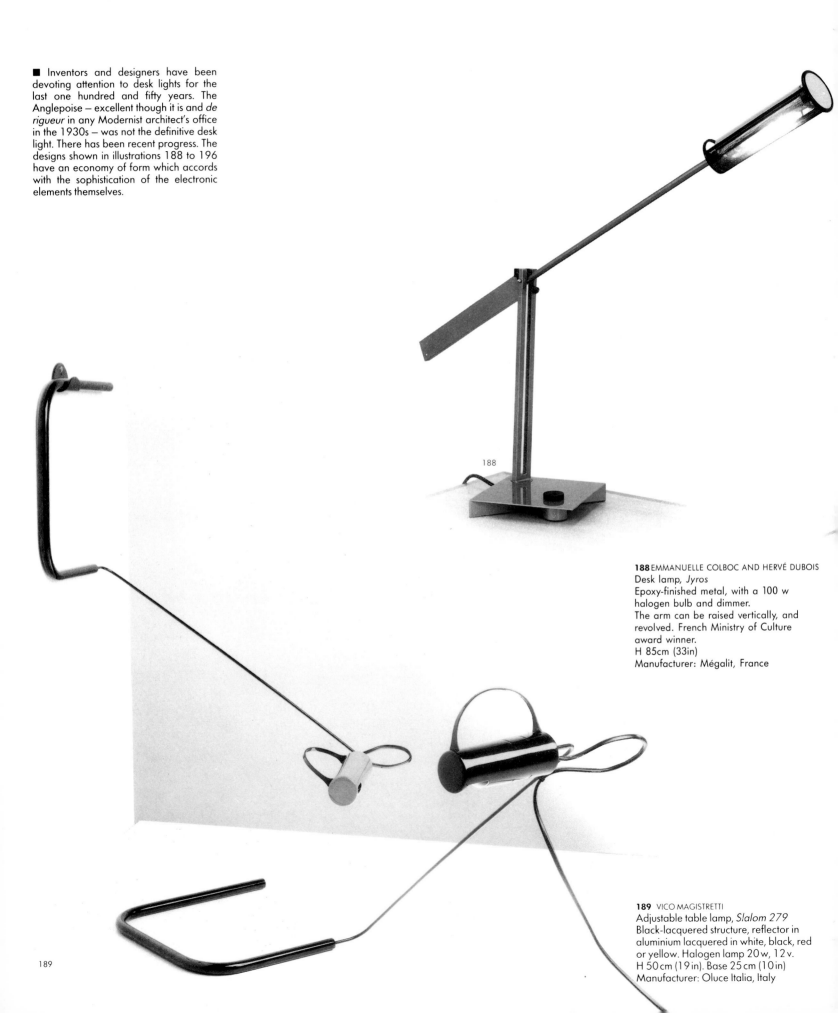

188 EMMANUELLE COLBOC AND HERVÉ DUBOIS
Desk lamp, *Jyros*
Epoxy-finished metal, with a 100 w halogen bulb and dimmer.
The arm can be raised vertically, and revolved. French Ministry of Culture award winner.
H 85cm (33in)
Manufacturer: Mégalit, France

189 VICO MAGISTRETTI
Adjustable table lamp, *Slalom 279*
Black-lacquered structure, reflector in aluminium lacquered in white, black, red or yellow. Halogen lamp 20w, 12v.
H 50cm (19in). Base 25cm (10in)
Manufacturer: Oluce Italia, Italy

193 SYLVAIN DUBUISSON
Light, *Lita*
The flat, angled support for the light is
designed to hold A-4 sized documents.
The light itself can be adjusted and is
composed of two plastic parts: a
cylindrical reflector and fixing. French
Ministry of Culture award winner.
H 51 cm (20 in)
Manufacturer: Lita, France

190 SACHA KETOFF
Desk Lamp, *Aluminor WEO*
The aluminium arm can be raised vertically,
left horizontal, or turned through 360°, so
that direct and indirect lighting is possible.
The shade is of macrolon. French Ministry
of Culture award winner.
H 74 cm (29 in). W of shade 28 cm (11 in)
Manufacturer: Aluminor, France

191 MARTINE BEDIN
Desk lamp, *Mégalit*
Aluminium and copper, covered with a
double coat of metallic paint and with a
low-tension halogen bulb. The arm is held
in place by the friction of the wheel
against the bracket. French Ministry of
Culture award winner.
H 58 cm (22 in). W of base 50 cm (19 in)
Manufacturer: Mégalit, France

192 NEMO
Desk lamp, *Megano*
Epoxy-finished metal, with an 18 w
fluorescent lamp. French Ministry of
Culture award winner.
H 51 cm (20 in)
Manufacturer: Mégalit, France

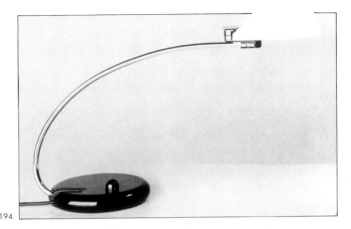

194 BRUNO GECCHELIN
Table lamp, *Dogale 512*
Adjustable with controlled light intensity.
Chromium plated arc, hand-blown Murano
glass diffuser, in opal or green. Halogen
bulb 50 w, 12 v.
H 45 cm (17 in). W 65 cm (25 in). D 22 cm
(9 in)
Manufacturer: Oluce Italia, Italy

194

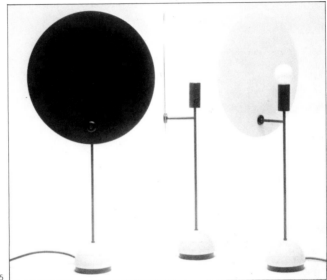

195 VICO MAGISTRETTI
Table lamp, *Kuta 250*
Base in white marble, aluminium-lacquered
plate, black chromium-plated structure.
Base H 60 cm (23 in). D 10 cm (4 in). Shade
D 30 cm (11 in)
Manufacturer: Oluce Italia, Italy

195

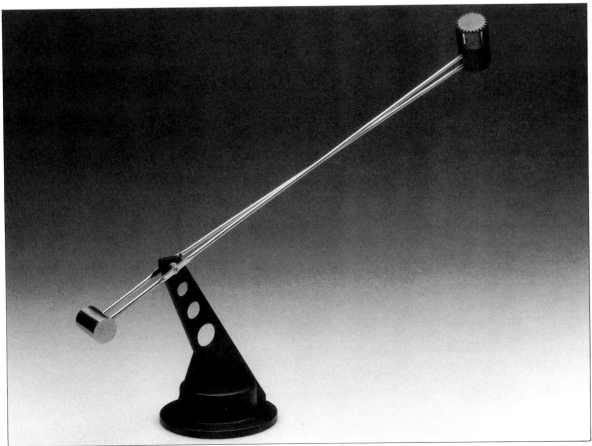

196 RAMON BIGAS BAUCELLS, PEP SANT
Halogen lamp kit, *Altalena (Tecno)*
Halogen light, 20 w. Aluminium, nylon.
H 40 cm (15 in). W 15 cm (6 in). L 64 cm
(25 in)
Manufacturer: Luxo Italiana, Italy

196

■ The organically-inspired fantasies of Frans van Nieuwenborg and Martijn Wegman — in this case, the glassfibre cloth light, *Delight* — is at the low-tech end of the lighting spectrum, and recalls Mario Bellini's *Area* lamp of 1974 — a translucent foil twisted over a light bulb.

197

197 FRANS VAN NIEUWENBORG, MARTIJN WEGMAN
Light, *Delight*
Glassfibre cloth over a lightbulb. Can be suspended or made to stand upright.
H 75 cm × 75 cm (29½ in × 29½ in)
Manufacturer: Ingo Maurer, West Germany

■ The somewhat formal lamps in illustrations 198 to 200 are appropriate impedimenta of the drawing room or the dining room, seeming almost to be elegant paraphrases of the designs of an earlier, utterly secure, bourgeois culture. The triple light by Sergio Asti has a certain bio-morphic, fin-de-siècle quality about it.

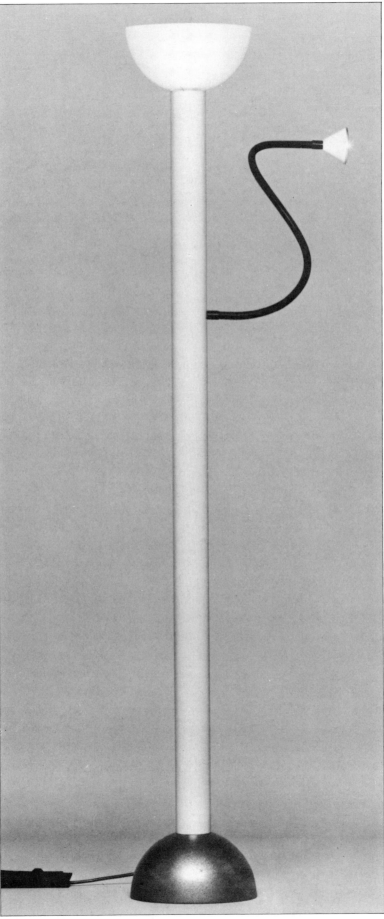

198 SERGIO ASTI
Standard lamp with flexible arm, *Commercial Strip*
Designed for Alice's Collection.
L 180 cm (71 in)
Manufacturer: Eleusi, Italy

199 SERGIO ASTI
Wall lamp, *MMC or Middle Middle Class*
Designed for Alice's Collection.
Disk D 50 cm (19 in). Arm L 180 cm (71 in)
Manufacturer: Eleusi, Italy

200 SERGIO ASTI
Standard or table lamp, *Middle Class*
Designed for Alice's Collection.
L 80 cm (30 in)
Manufacturer: Eleusi, Italy

201 ISAO HOSOE
Table lamp, *Picchio*
Upright support in ABS with built-in ballast. ABS lamp head with inner reflector in polished aluminium. Naturcolor fluorescent bulb. Colours: red, black and white.
H 41.5 cm (16 in). W 9 cm (3½ in). L 38 cm (15 in)
Manufacturer: Luxo Italiana, Italy

201

202 ALBERTO FRASER
Halogen lamp, *Jack*
The arm is a transparent, flexible plastic strip. The lamp is fitted with accessories for fixing where required. Colours: white, black, red, yellow.
W 7 cm (2¾ in)
Manufacturer: Stilnovo, Italy

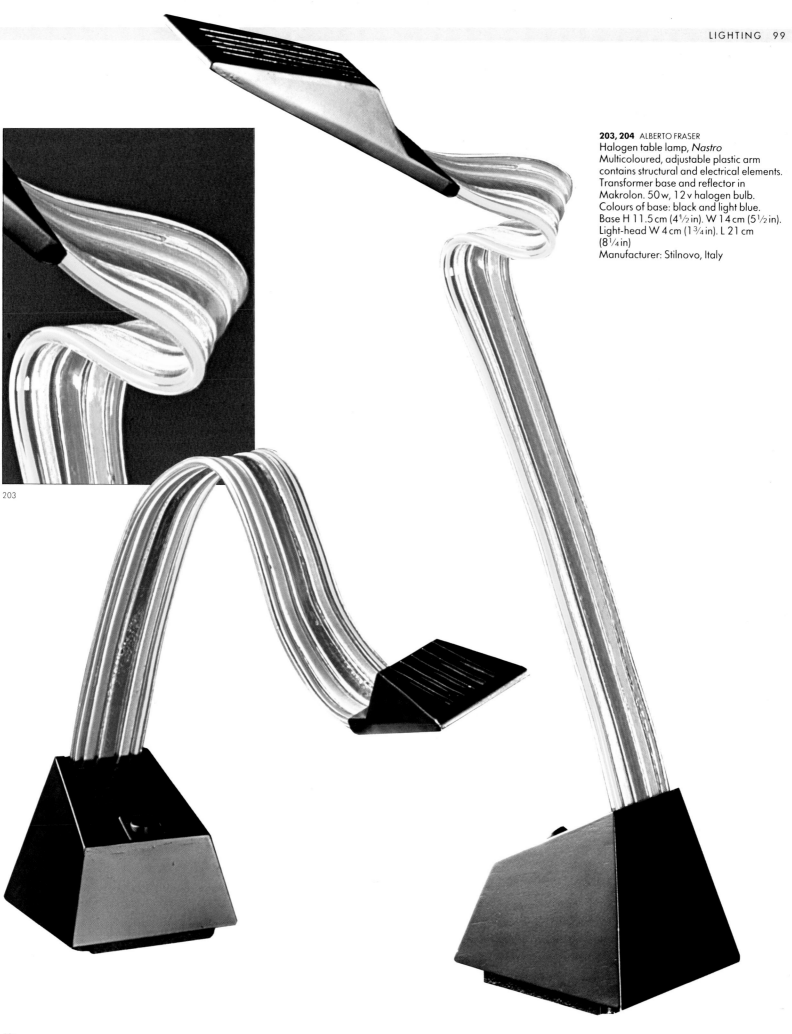

203

204

203, 204 ALBERTO FRASER
Halogen table lamp, *Nastro*
Multicoloured, adjustable plastic arm
contains structural and electrical elements.
Transformer base and reflector in
Makrolon. 50 w, 12 v halogen bulb.
Colours of base: black and light blue.
Base H 11.5 cm (4½ in). W 14 cm (5½ in).
Light-head W 4 cm (1¾ in). L 21 cm
(8¼ in)
Manufacturer: Stilnovo, Italy

205, 206 CARLO A. URBINATI-RICCI AND
ALESSANDRO VECCHIATO
Halogen table lamp, *Rolli Tavolo*
Glass dish with stripes in green/blue/
aquamarine; yellow/blue/aquamarine; or
red/aquamarine/grey. Stem and base in
black lacquered metal; decorations in
metallicized red, blue or grey.
H 75 cm (29 in)
Manufacturer: Foscarini, Italy

207 DAVIDE MERCATALI AND PAOLO
PEDRIZZETTI
Lamp, *Basket*
Iron and aluminium, enamelled finish,
double light-intensity switch. Available in
black and yellow, or black and red.
H 64 cm (25 in). W 38 cm (15 in)
Manufacturer: Eleusi, Italy

206

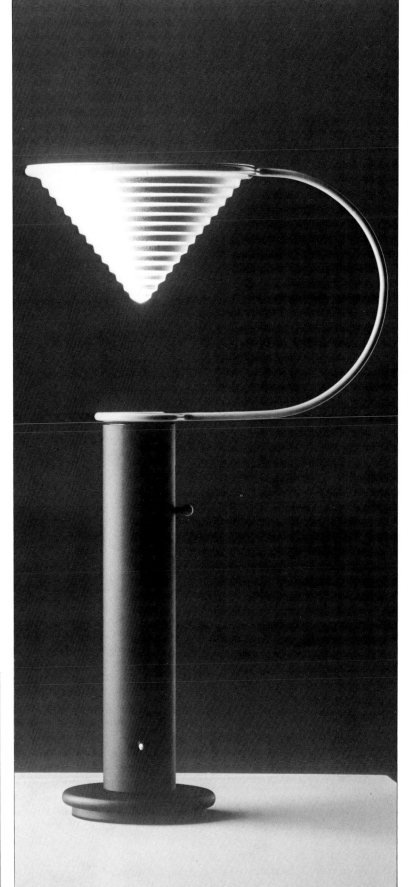

207

208

208, 211 REMO BUTI
Lights, *Stars*
Tubular elements in polycarbonate with
special micro-bulbs. Can be sunburst-
shaped clusters of stems, single stems, or
stems bent into an arc.
Manufacturer: Stars (Targetti Sankey),
Italy

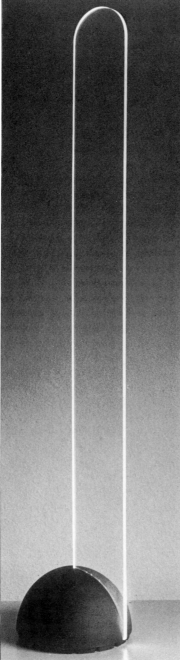

209, 212 FRANCO ALBERTO BERG
Light sculptures, *Argon, Radon, Xenon*
Base in grey cast iron; panels in hardened
acrylic.
D 24 cm (9 in). H 124 cm (48 in)
Manufacturer: Berg Licht and Objekt,
West Germany

209   210

211

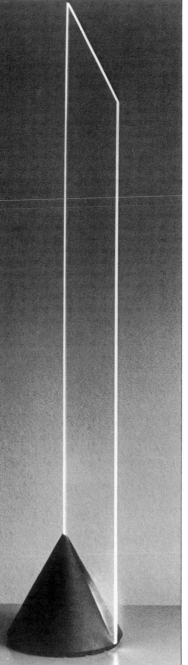

210 ANTONIN JIRAN
Table lamp, *Brandweerman*
All metal with swivelling head and 40 w
reflector bulb. Finished in silver or
anthracite.
H 50 cm (19 in). W 22 cm (9 in)
Manufacturer: Cortina VOF, Netherlands

212

■ Without being in any way historicist, these lights (illustrations 213 to 217) tell of the continuity and stability of lighting design. But, as with the bicycle, the essential form can be varied almost infinitely.

213

213 GIOVANNI OFFREDI
Pendant lamp, *Diskos*
Red ABS with translucent disc. Equipped with fluorescent
2D Thorn tube 16w or 28w; light intensity equal to that of
an incandescent bulb 100/150w.
H 7.5 cm (3 in). W 60 cm (23 in). L 67 cm (26 in)
Manufacturer: Sirrah, Italy

214 HANS EBBING, TON HAAS
Hanging lamp, *KL 45*
In white, black or grey. It has a standard
lamp version.
D 45 cm (17 in)
Manufacturer: Skizo, Netherlands

215 HANS EBBING, TON HAAS
Hanging lamp, *Schaallamp SL 56*
Aluminium. In white, black or grey.
H 14 cm (5 in). D 56 cm (22 in)
Manufacturer: Skizo, Netherlands

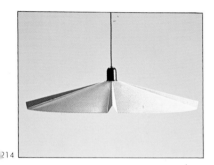

214

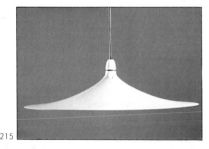

215

216

216 INGO MAURER
Pendant light, *Willydilly*
White cotton canopy, translucent over
fluorescent bulb.
In three lengths: 30 cm, 50 cm, 70 cm
(11¾ in, 19 in, 27 in)
Manufacturer: Ingo Maurer

217 DIEPERINK-KRECHTING
Suspended halogen lamp, *Saturn*
Aluminium. 50 w, 12 v bulb. In grey, black,
white and red; with red, grey or black wires.
H up to 300 cm (118 in). W 50 cm (19 in)
Manufacturer: Profilight, Netherlands

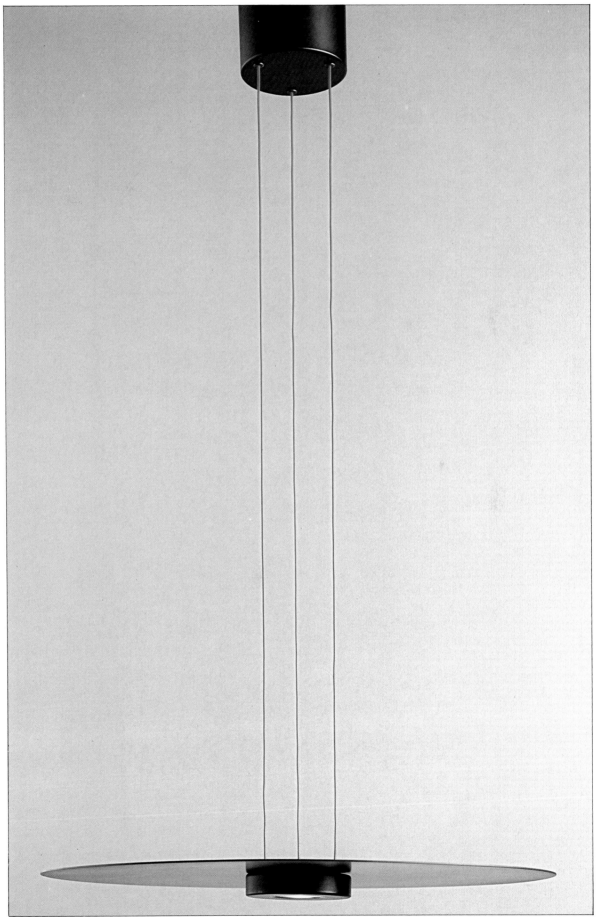

217

■ The standard lamps in illustrations 218 to 224 are examples of an assertive, if not aggressive, attitude towards technology. One is reminded a little, perhaps, of the approach taken by Peter Behrens in his seminal designs for electrical equipment for AEG in the first decade of the present century.

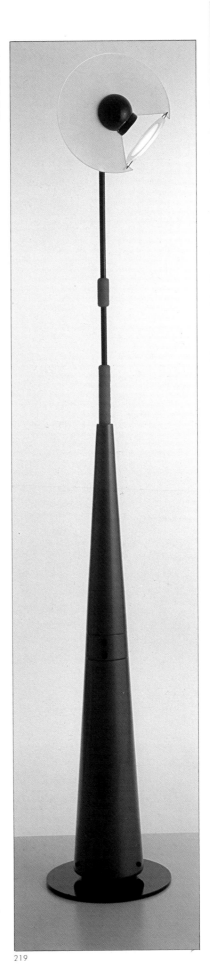

218 HANS ANSEMS
Standard lamp, *Stringa*
Part of a family of products whose design is based on a system of pivots and bent tubes. Colours: white, black, burgundy or ivory. Halogen bulb 250w, 220v, 4200 Lumen.
Maximum extension: 220 cm vertically (86 in). 61 cm horizontally (24 in)
Manufacturer: Luxo Italiana, Italy

219 P.G. RAMELLA
Standard lamp, *Club*
Stem in painted metal with a coloured rubber handgrip. Height of stem and angle of metacrylate diffuser are adjustable. Painted metal base incorporates two switches to regulate brightness.
H 130 cm to 160 cm (51 in to 63 in)
Manufacturer: Arteluce, Italy

220 PHILIPPE MICHEL
Light, *Strip*
Steel.
H 186 cm (73 in)
Prototype

221 MARTINE BEDIN
Standard lamp, *Charleston*
Aluminium, halogen bulb 500w.
H 207 cm (81 in). D 40 cm (15 in)
Manufacturer: Memphis, Italy

222, 223, 224 EMILIO AMBASZ
Adjustable halogen lamp, *Agamennone*
Body in extruded, painted aluminium. The base is in black-coated metal.
H 200 cm (78 in). D 46 cm (18 in)
Manufacturer: Artemide, Italy

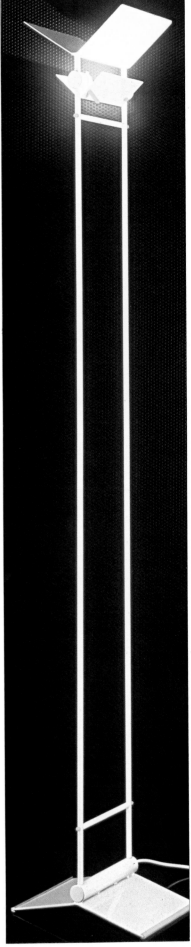

218

219

220

221

222

223

224

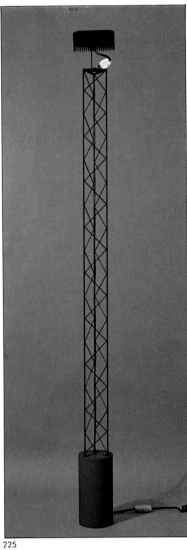

225

226

225 ANDREW HOLMES
Flood Light
Mild-steel rod.
H 200 cm (78 in). W 15 cm (6 in). Base
15 cm × 30 cm (6 in × 12 in)
Manufacturer: MEC Engineering, Concord
Lighting, Oval 31, Andrew Holmes, UK

226 ANDREW HOLMES
Crane Light
Stove-enamelled mild-steel rod.
H 68 cm (26 in). Base D 15 cm (6 in).
L 75 cm (29 in)
Manufacturer: MEC Engineering, UK

227 ASAHARA SIGHEAKI
Halogen standard lamp, *Palomar*
Body and reflector of lacquered metal.
White, black and grey.
H 180 cm (70 in). W 40 cm (15 in)
Manufacturer: Stilnovo, Italy

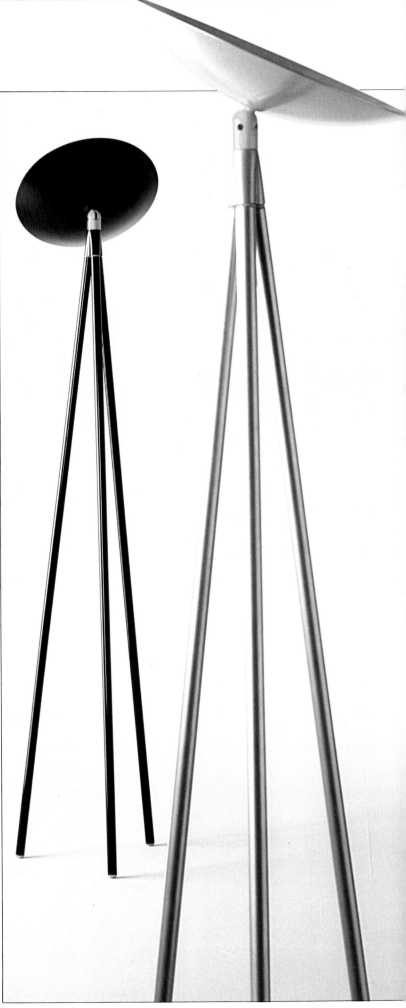

227

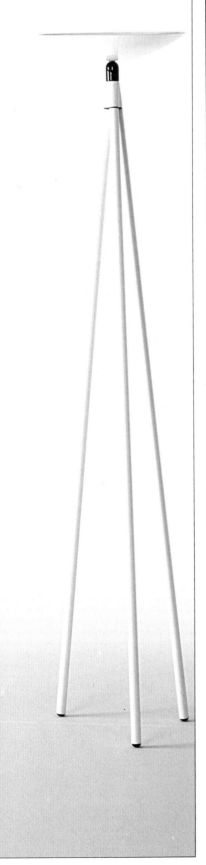

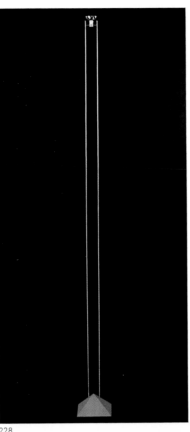

228

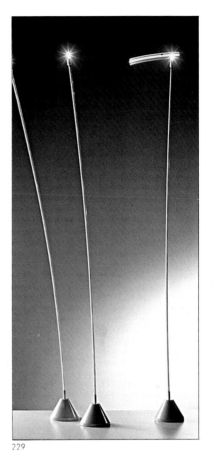

229

228 VOLKER WEINERT
Standard lamp, *LE 5/84*; Hanging
lamp *LE 6/84*
Low-voltage halogen bulbs, 55 w, with
cool light mirror; the standard lamp has a
dimmer.
H 175 cm (68 in). W 15 cm (6 in). L 15 cm
(6 in)
Manufacturer: Sektor 3, West Germany

229 REMO BUTI
Lights, *Stars*
Tubular elements in polycarbonate with
special micro-bulbs. This tiny pinprick of
light on a tall stem is an extension of the
same system as the sunburst-shaped table
lamp shown earlier.
Manufacturer: Stars (Targetti Sankey), Italy

230 HANS EBBING, TON HAAS
Standard lamp with buckled shade, *KL 45*
Cast-iron base, iron stand, in white, black
or grey.
H 192 cm (75 in)
Manufacturer: Skizo, Netherlands

231 INGO MAURER
Rocking standard lamp, *Ilios*
Metal and glass, insulation red fluorescent.
Halogen bulb 12 v, 50 w. Supplied with
transformer.
H 190 cm (74 in). Base 18 cm × 18 cm
(7¼ in × 7¼ in)
Manufacturer: Ingo Maurer, West
Germany

230

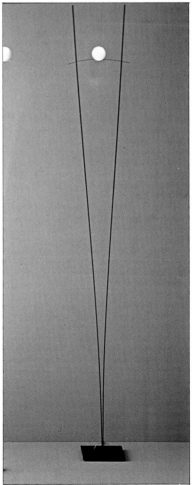

231

■ The wall-mounted light – which has the bracket candle-sconce as its ancestor – was particularly popular in the 1920s and 1930s. The wall-light lends itself especially well to a decorative treatment, and is consequently associated more with the 'Moderne' – popular Modernism – than with the work of the principal architects of the Modern Movement itself. The wall-light is once again respectable and popular.

232

232 REMO BUTI
Uplighter, *Iris*
Enamelled metal body, coloured grey, halogen lamp.
Manufacturer: Stars (Targetti Sankey), Italy

233 MART Z. VAN SCHIJNDEL
Wall lamp, *Shofloat*
Steel plate. High pressure multi-vapour lamp with transformer.
H 22 cm (8 in). W 28 cm (11 in). L 31 cm (12 in)
Manufacturer: Martech, Netherlands

233

234 TOBIA SCARPA
Wall light, *Oti*
Screen in white ceramic and reflector in anodized metal. Halogen bulb, 60 w.
W 26 cm (10¼ in); reflector D 20 cm (7¾ in). H 6 cm (2½ in)
Manufacturer: Flos, Italy

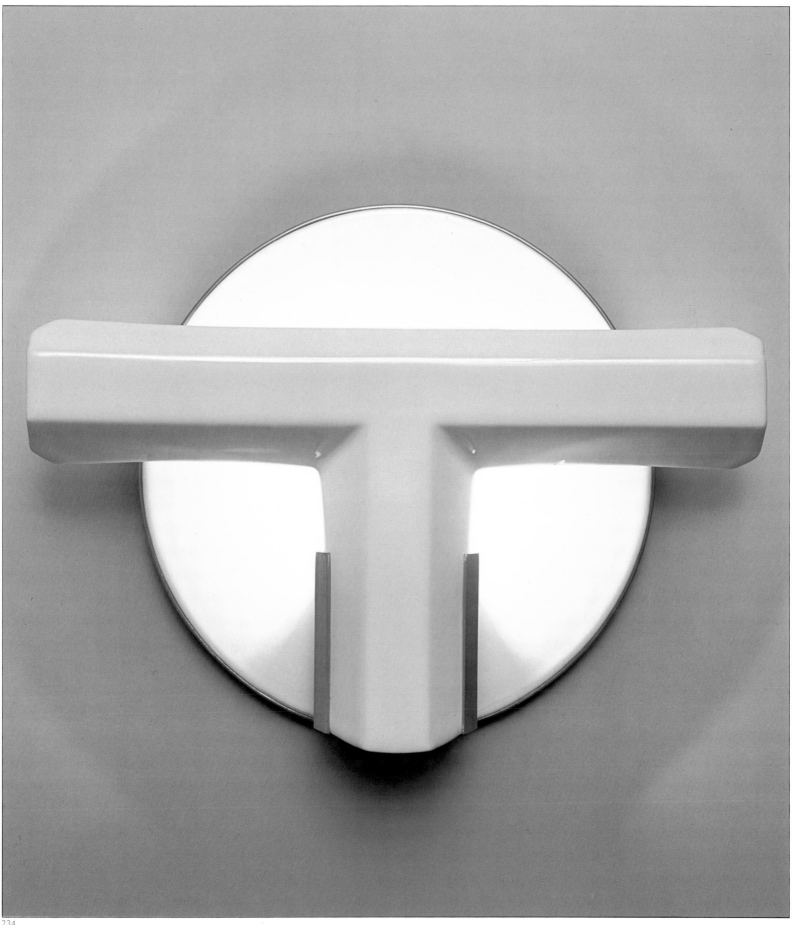

235

236

237

235 BRUNO GECCHELIN
Wall lamp, *Perla 750*
Opaline diffuser glass, white lacquered metal structure.
Diffuser W 50 cm (20 in)
Manufacturer: Oluce, Italy

236 CHRIS HIEMSTRA
Light, *Planeta*
Injection-moulded plastic. Energy-saving fluorescent bulb
9 w; part of a small range of lights designed on similar
principles.
H 25.5 cm (10 in). W 22 cm (8¾ in). L 8.5 cm (3½ in)
Manufacturer: Luminance, Netherlands

237 DIEPERINK-KRECHTING
Wall-mounted light, *Lotus*
Steel and glass. In white and grey. Integrated pull-switch.
D 30 cm (11 in). W 12 cm (4 in)
Manufacturer: Profilight, Netherlands

238 KAZUHIDE TAKAHAMA
Wall or ceiling lamp, *Kumo*
White opaline glass shade.
H 18 cm (7 in). W 34 cm (13 in). L 15 cm (6 in)
Manufacturer: Sirrah, Italy

238

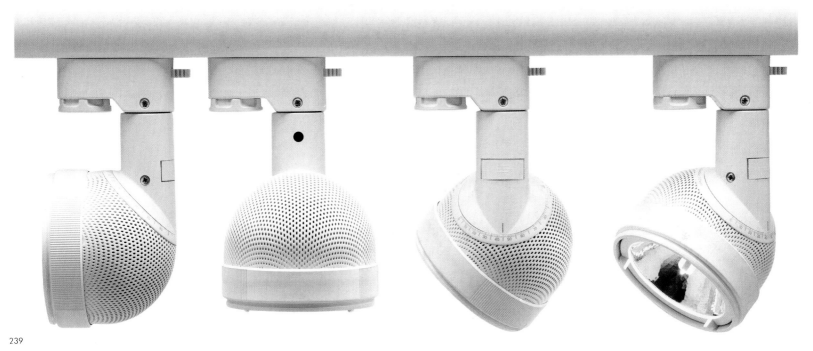

239

240

241

239 EMILIO AMBASZ AND GIANCARLO PIRETTI
Low-voltage spotlight, *Oseris*
Perforated steel plate, black or white
powder coated, and thermoresistant
thermoplast. The spotlights can be
mounted on a three-circuit track, with a
mechanical adapter and a separate
transformer, or on a special low-voltage
track fed by a separate external
transformer. Light can be varied by using
glass colour filters, flood lenses and
sculpture lenses. Special fixing rings,
multigroove baffles and honeycomb anti-
dazzle screens concentrate the light.
H 15.6 cm (6 in). W 93 cm (36 in). D 9.4 cm
(3½ in)
Manufacturer: Erco Lighting,
West Germany

240 ERNESTO GISMONDI
Recessed spotlight, *Achille Par*
Painted aluminium and resin: grey.
Halogen lamp, 12 v, 50 w.
D 12 cm (4¾ in). Overhang minimum 6 cm
(2 in); maximum 12 cm (4 in)
Manufacturer: Artemide, Italy

241 DIETER WITTE
Light, *Circolux-El*
Glass, plastic, metal.
H 10 cm (4 in). D 21 cm or 17 cm (8 in or
6¾ in)
Manufacturer: Osram, West Germany

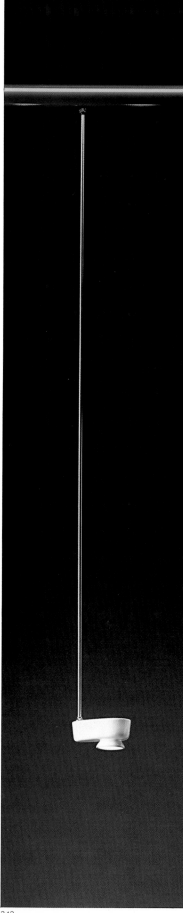

243

244 PERRY KING, SANTIAGO MIRANDA
Pendant lamp, *Aurora*
Three low-voltage halogen bulbs, and a
pair of diffusers in textured glass with a
blue metacrylate disc between. The
transformer is contained in the painted-
metal ceiling rose.
D 60 cm (23 in)
Manufacturer: Arteluce, Italy

242

244

245

242, 243, 245–252 PERRY KING, SANTIAGO MIRANDA
Lighting system, *Expanded Line (245–6)*: lamps with
dichroic spots, *Lucy (247–249)*, *Ra*; low-voltage halogen,
Spillo (242), *Pianetta (252)*, *Quintilla (250)*; mains-voltage
halogen, *Up-Do (251)*
The system is based on a 125 cm (49 in) module, and is
infinitely flexible, capable of being suspended in open
space at any height, or fixed to a ceiling or wall.
Manufacturer: Arteluce, Italy

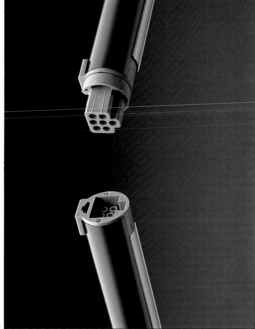

246

247

248

249

250

251

252

■ Kurokawa's lights are peculiarly his own. Extraordinarily diverse, they range from an evocation of the old rise-and-fall light, to a table lamp like a small penguin, a nippled, breast-like lamp, and a series of architectural lights designed to be fitted diagonally across the corners of rooms (illustrations 253 to 262).

253 MASAYUKI KUROKAWA
Lighting fixture, *Kite*
Painted steel. Can be surface mounted, recessed or pendant.
H 33.5 cm (12 in). D 72 cm (28 in)
Manufacturer: Yamagiwa Corporation, Japan

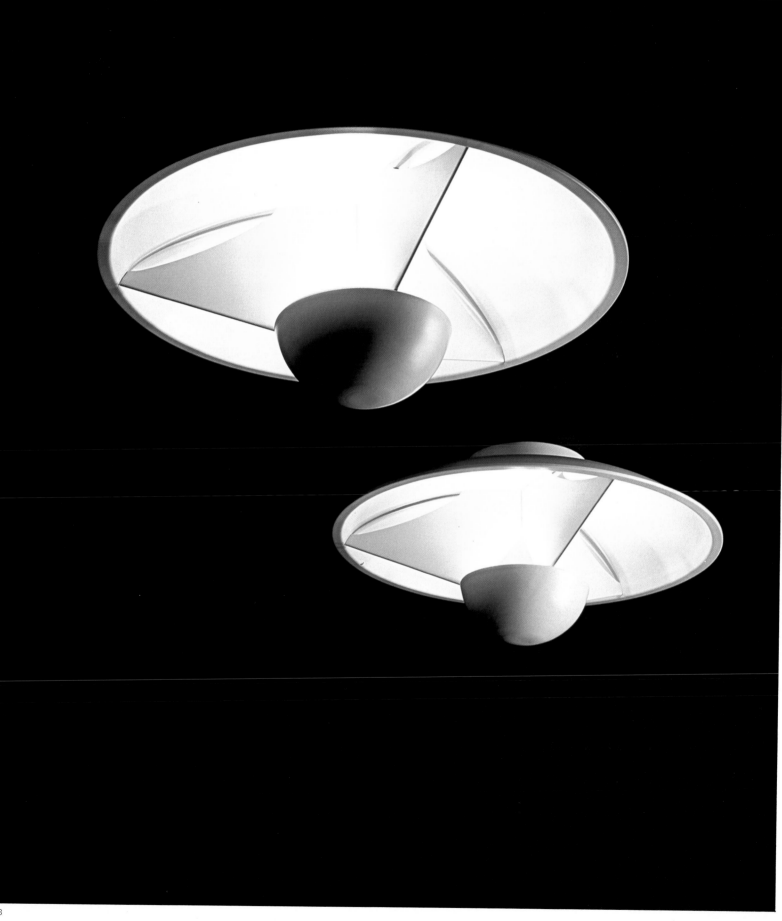

254

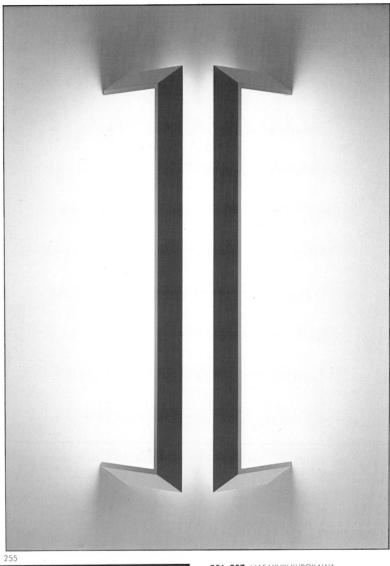

255

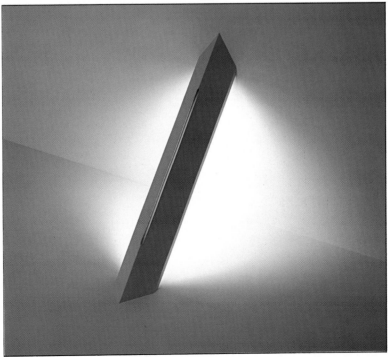

256

254, 255 MASAYUKI KUROKAWA
Lighting fixture, *Angolo Slit T Bar*
Painted steel.
W 11.6 cm (4½ in). L from 77 cm to 91 cm
(30 in to 35 in)
Manufacturer: Yamagiwa Corporation,
Japan

256, 257 MASAYUKI KUROKAWA
Lighting fixture, *Angolo*
Painted steel.
W 11.6 cm (4½ in). L from 77 cm to 91 cm
(30 in to 35 in)
Manufacturer: Yamagiwa Corporation,
Japan

258

259

260

261

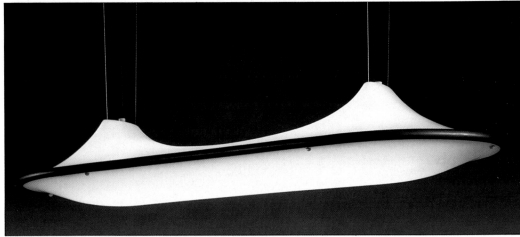

262

258 MASAYUKI KUROKAWA
Pendant light, *Donna*
Painted aluminium. Ivory or dark grey.
H 36 cm (14 in). D 39 cm (15 in)
Manufacturer: Matsushita Electrical
Works, Japan

259 MASAYUKI KUROKAWA
Lighting fixture, *Ombra*
Painted steel, glass. Surface-mounted light,
which can be mounted on a wall bracket,
or used as a table light.
H 22.3 cm (9 in). D 32 cm (12 in)
Manufacturer: Yamagiwa Corporation,
Japan

260 MASAYUKI KUROKAWA
Spotlight, *Farfalla*
Painted aluminium, painted steel, in pearl
white, blue or pink. Can be surface
mounted, or mounted on a track. Cool-ray
reflectors.
H 21.3 cm (8½ in). W 14 cm (5½ in).
L 9.5 cm (3¾ in)
Manufacturer: Matsushita Electrical
Works, Japan

261 MASAYUKI KUROKAWA
Table light, *Gufo*
Plastic, acrylic. Dark grey, silver or brown.
H 35.5 cm (14 in). W 17.5 cm (7 in).
L 41 cm (16½ in)
Manufacturer: Matsushita Electrical
Works, Japan

262 MASAYUKI KUROKAWA
Pendant light, *Fumo-Pen*
Acrylic, painted steel, rubber.
H from 26.5 cm to 28.5 cm (10½ in to
11 in), W from 60 cm to 71.2 cm (23 in to
28 in). L from 100 cm to 159.7 cm (39 in to
63 in)
Manufacturer: Yamagiwa Corporation,
Japan

CERAMICS & GLASS

The potter is both artisan and artist. The potter can make pots for everyday use, miniature art works or even small-scale sculpture. Sometimes the potter succeeds in investing the most mundane object with an unassailable, almost metaphysical perfection — as did the Chinese and Japanese.

As with all the other crafts, pottery is undergoing a considerable revival. But potters, like other contemporary craftsmen, seek their own artistic identity, rather than serve a hallowed tradition. The austere gospel of Bernard Leach, one of the greatest of twentieth-century potters, seems, for the moment, unfashionable. Peter Ting's pots, for example, appear to be at first sight almost anti-ceramic statements.

Post-Modernism has made decoration once again respectable — Loos', Le Corbusier's or Gropius' anathemas have now become intellectual curiosities. Margaret McCurry's, Richard Meier's and Stanley Tigerman's designs for Swid Powell establish that a Post-Modern decorative style is in the making. The style is eclectic, vigorous and, above all, enjoyable.

Gallé and Lalique took their art to the heights of virtuosity, without always sympathizing, one feels, with the true nature of glass as a material — infinitely tractable, ductile. Contemporary glassmakers eschew virtuosity as an end in itself and hold fast to a tradition of restraint. Even Memphis glass is diffident.

263

264

■ A return to past forms of decoration for ceramics has been evident for some time. Implied is nostalgia for the stately manners of the past; a nostalgia particularly evident among the American architects represented here. Influences range from the Vienna Secession present in Gwathmey's Hoffmannesque pieces (illustrations 277 and 278); to 1920s Woolworths in Tigerman's and McCurry's cheerful plates (illustrations 273 and 274); and the 1930s in those by Meier (illustrations 263 to 265). Stern's plate is Maxims, de-luxe (illustration 275); while Spear has evidently been struck by the delights of *nouvelle cuisine* (illustration 272). Trim's plates (illustration 279) – looking curiously like Chinese coolie hats – have the feeling of fabric weave about them. Both the Hinchcliffe and Barber team (illustration 276) and Pearcey-Cobbold (illustrations 266 to 271) have in their separate ways turned to lyricism and garden traditions for inspiration.

265

263 RICHARD MEIER
Plate, *Joseph*
Ceramic.
D 30 cm (12 in)
Manufacturer: Swid Powell, USA

264 RICHARD MEIER
Plate, *Peachtree*
Ceramic.
D 30 cm (12 in)
Manufacturer: Swid Powell, USA

265 RICHARD MEIER
Plate, *Anna*
Ceramic.
D 30 cm (12 in)
Manufacturer: Swid Powell, USA

266

267

268

269

270

271

266–271 CHRISSIE PEARCEY-COBBOLD
Tiles
Ceramic tin-glazed with oxides. Hand-painted designs based on those of traditional French tiles of southwest France.
W 13 cm (5 in)
Manufacturer: Chrissie Pearcey-Cobbold, France

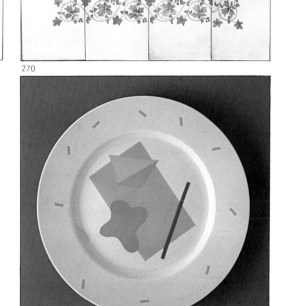

272

272 LAURINDA SPEAR
Plate, *Miami Beach*
Ceramic.
D 30 cm (12 in)
Manufacturer: Swid Powell, USA

273 STANLEY TIGERMAN AND MARGARET MCCURRY
Plate, *Heaven*
Ceramic.
D 30 cm (12 in)
Manufacturer: Swid Powell, USA

274 STANLEY TIGERMAN AND MARGARET MCCURRY
Plate, *Sunshine*
Ceramic.
D 30 cm (12 in)
Manufacturer: Swid Powell, USA

275 ROBERT A.M. STERN
Plate, *Majestic*
Ceramic.
D 30 cm (12 in)
Manufacturer: Swid Powell, USA

273

274

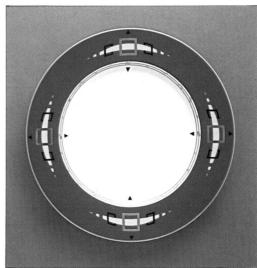

275

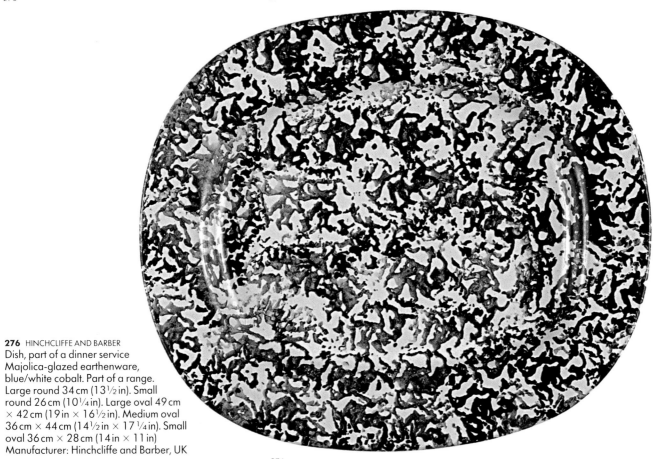

276 HINCHCLIFFE AND BARBER
Dish, part of a dinner service
Majolica-glazed earthenware,
blue/white cobalt. Part of a range.
Large round 34 cm (13½ in). Small
round 26 cm (10¼ in). Large oval 49 cm
× 42 cm (19 in × 16½ in). Medium oval
36 cm × 44 cm (14½ in × 17¼ in). Small
oval 36 cm × 28 cm (14 in × 11 in)
Manufacturer: Hinchcliffe and Barber, UK

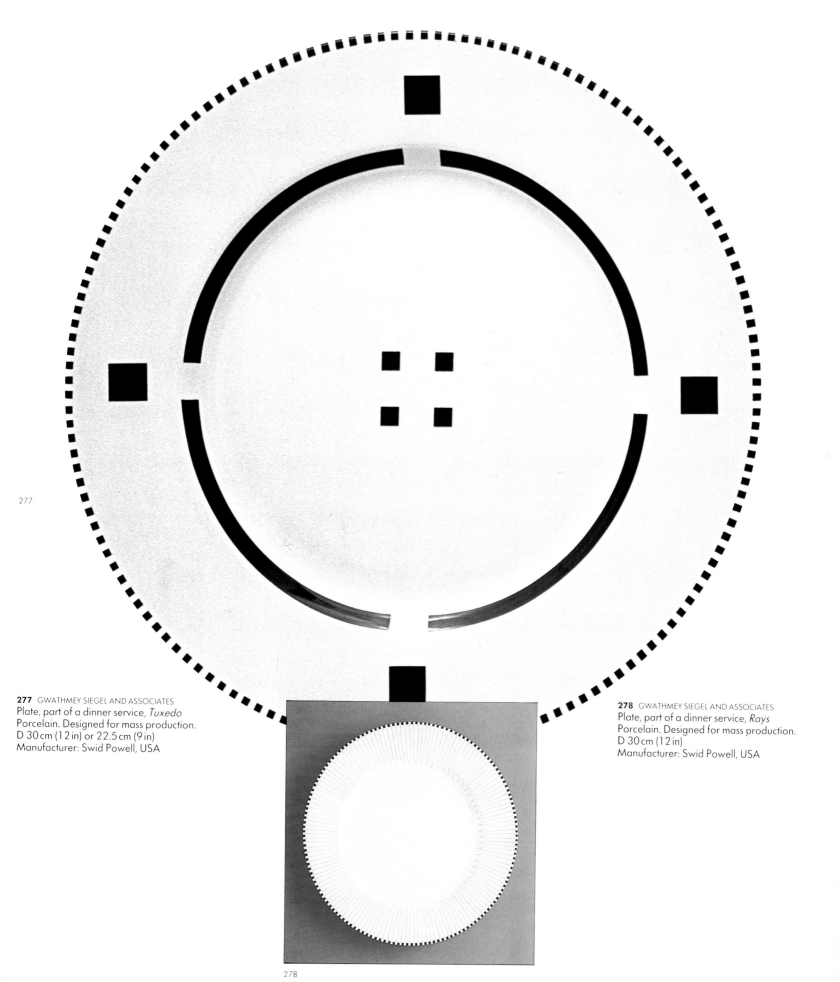

277

277 GWATHMEY SIEGEL AND ASSOCIATES
Plate, part of a dinner service, *Tuxedo*
Porcelain. Designed for mass production.
D 30 cm (12 in) or 22.5 cm (9 in)
Manufacturer: Swid Powell, USA

278 GWATHMEY SIEGEL AND ASSOCIATES
Plate, part of a dinner service, *Rays*
Porcelain. Designed for mass production.
D 30 cm (12 in)
Manufacturer: Swid Powell, USA

278

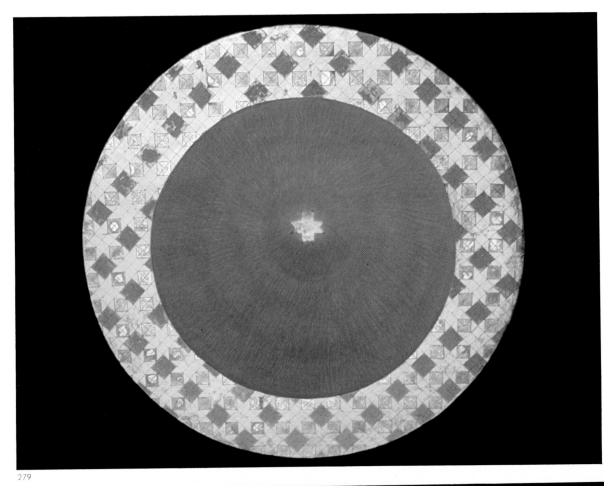

279

280 JUDITH TRIM
Sun Bowl
Burnished lustred clay.
H 20 cm (8 in). D 61 cm (24 in)
Manufacturer: Judith Trim, UK

279 JUDITH TRIM
Large Star Bowl
Lustred burnished stoneware clay.
H 15 cm (6 in). D 61 cm (24 in)
Manufacturer: Judith Trim, UK

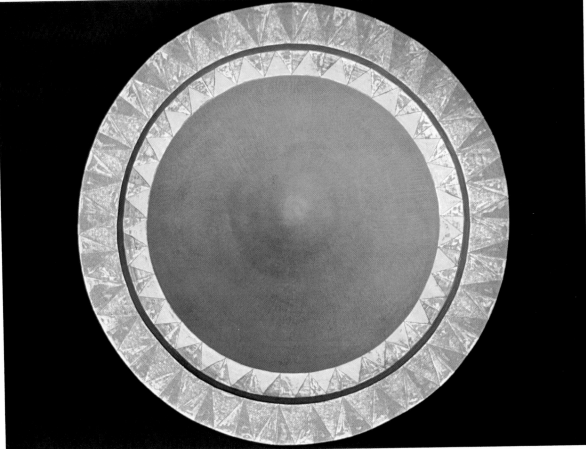

Both Penny Smith's decorative pottery (illustrations 285 to 291) and Peter Ting's ceramics (illustrations 281 to 284) belong firmly to the crafts. Smith's tea sets and dinner services have a 1930s look about them, and also the feeling of fabric design. Ting's objects, on the other hand, look almost animated, as if they were objects for strange rituals.

281

282

283

284

281–284 PETER TING
Decorative ceramics
Manufacturer: Peter Ting, UK

285, 286 PENNY SMITH
Mix and Match Tea Sets
Slip-cast stoneware, coloured casting clays and multiple moulds. Clear glazed.
Teapots H 18 cm (7 in). W 7 cm (2 in).
L 25 cm (9 in)
Manufacturer: Design in the Round, Australia

285

286

287

287–291 PENNY SMITH
Pottery, *Mix and Match Dinner Service*
Soup bowls D 16/17 cm (6 in). H 6 cm (2 in).
Side plates D 19 cm (7 in). Dinner plates
D 25 cm (9 in)
Manufacturer: Design in the Round, Australia

288

289

290

291

■ Anthologie Quartett appears to be the West German equivalent of the Italian Memphis group. Indeed it shares some of the same designers, notably Ettore Sottsass and Matteo Thun, so it is hardly surprising if its objects occasionally look similar. Here, Thun's *Extravergine* oil-and-vinegar set has an organic aspect; while Alessio Sarri makes passing reference to the now modish Vienna Secession.

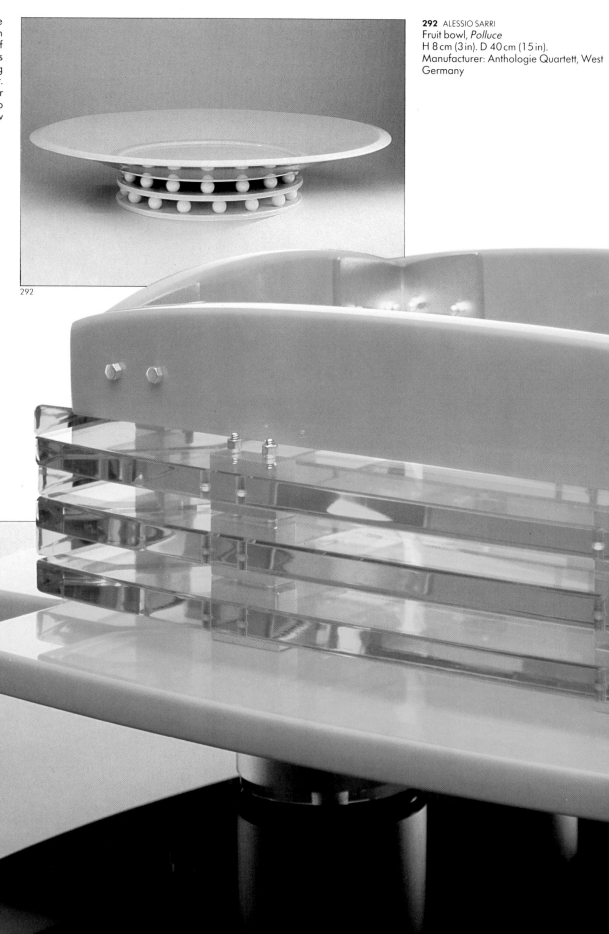

292 ALESSIO SARRI
Fruit bowl, *Polluce*
H 8 cm (3 in). D 40 cm (15 in).
Manufacturer: Anthologie Quartett, West Germany

292

293

293 LINDA MACNEIL
Plate Glass Vessel
Plate glass, fabricated brass, gold plated.
The glass is cut, ground, drilled and
polished.
H 20 cm (8 in). D 15 cm (6 in). L 33 cm (12 in)
Manufacturer: Dailey Glass, USA

294 MATTEO THUN
Container for oil and vinegar, *Extravergine*
H 20 cm (8 in). W 6.5 cm (2½ in).
L 19.5 cm (7½ in)
Manufacturer: Anthologie Quartett, West
Germany

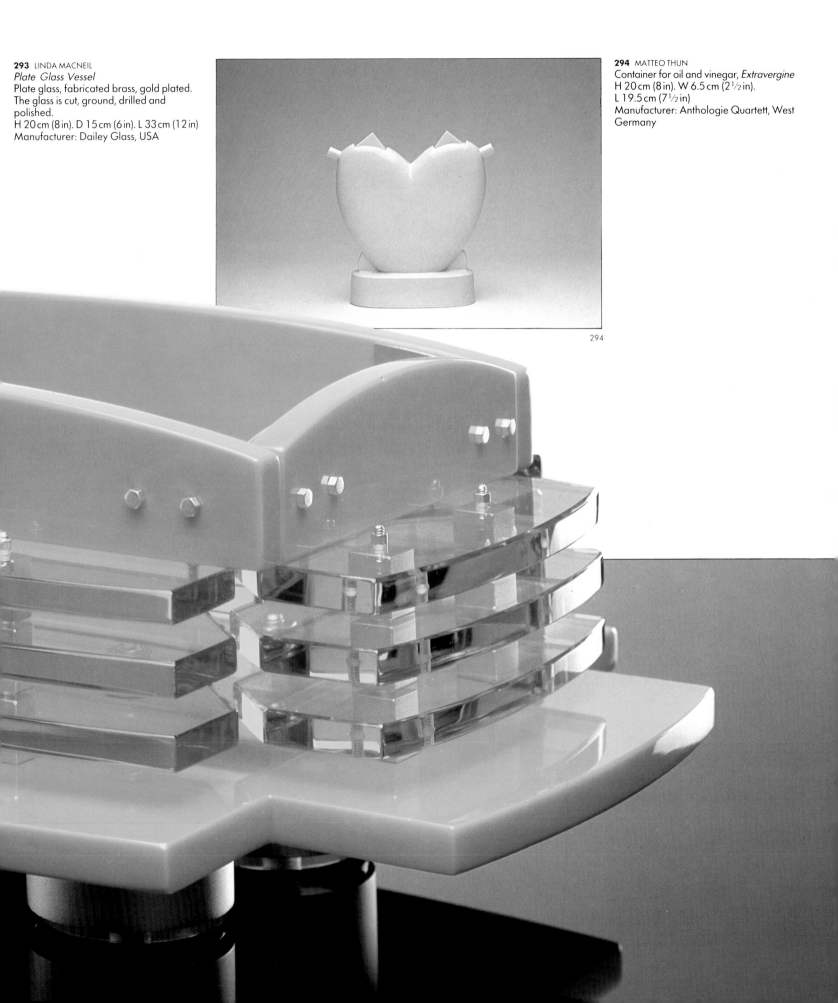

294

■ 'Design,' says Achille Castiglioni, 'is an art in so far as it invents a function and translates it into a form.' His own forms are invariably elegant, frequently spidery thin, attenuated and taut. An ability to extemporize and invent can transform mistakes. The goblet shown here was the result of the glassblower misjudging the force required to form the vase originally designed. It now consists of two cones joined to form a waisted hourglass.

295

295 ACHILLE CASTIGLIONI
Set of glasses and carafe, *Ovio*
Full-lead crystal glass, hand-blown and ground. Tulip-flower shaped, with a cylindrical base surmounted by a continuous horizontal groove to house the ring which marks the grip-line for the fingers.
Liqueur glass H 7.5 cm (2¾ in). D 5 cm (2 in). Whisky glass H 7.5 cm (2¾ in). D. 10 cm (4 in). Wine glass H 10 cm (4 in). D 7 cm (2½ in). Water glass H 12 cm (4¾ in). D 7 cm (2½ in). Champagne glass H 17 cm (6½ in). D 5 cm (2 in). Carafe H 29.5 cm (11½ in). D 7 cm (2¾ in)
Manufacturer: Danese, Italy

296 ACHILLE CASTIGLIONI
Goblet, *Paro*
Full-lead crystal glass, hand-blown and ground. The glass can be reversed according to use.
H 20 cm (7¾ in). D 8 cm (3 in)
Manufacturer: Alessi, Italy

■ Carlo Moretti's delicate cones of glass are the refined products of an encounter between ancient Murano glass tradition and a modern designer. Their flower-like quality is echoed in Nick Mount's fluted and flower-like glasses with grey stems. In a somewhat different, more prosaic category, are Richard Meier's series of robust decorated glasses for bars, and his more fragile long-stemmed glasses.

297

297, 298   CARLO MORETTI
Glasses, vases, *Cartoccio*
Hand-blown, hand-finished glass, the method of manufacture maintaining the ancient Murano glass tradition.
Glasses H 13.4 cm, 16 cm, 19 cm (5 in, 6 in, 7 in). W 70 cm, 84 cm, 60 cm (27 in, 33 in, 23 in)
Vases H 36.8 cm, 53 cm (14 in, 20 in). W 13 cm, 16 cm (5 in, 6 in)
Manufacturer: Vetreria Carlo Moretti, Italy

298

299   NICK MOUNT
Jug with swizzle stick, olive bowl and glass, *Martini Set*
Blown glass.
Jug H 12 cm (5 in). Glass H 15 cm (6 in). Bowl H 5 cm (2 in)
Manufacturer: Nick Mount, Australia

300   RICHARD MEIER
Set of bar glasses, *Spiral*
Manufacturer: Swid Powell, USA

301   RICHARD MEIER
Tall-stemmed glasses, *Lattice*
Manufacturer: Swid Powell, USA

299

300

301

302 RICHARD MEIER
Set of bar glasses, *Professor*
Manufacturer: Swid Powell, USA

302

TEXTILES

It is very hard to think of a time when textile design has been wholly in the doldrums. Even when the Modern Movement was at its zenith, textile design seemed to flourish. Walter Gropius anathematized decoration, but under his very gaze at the Bauhaus, Anni Albers, Gunta Stadler Stölzl and Gertrud Kadow produced woven textiles which were as delightfully insouciant as the miniatures of Paul Klee. In Britain, artists associated with the Modernism of the early post-war years — like Henry Moore, Ben Nicholson and Graham Sutherland — designed textiles which, if not precisely conforming to the prevailing popular taste, were not unsuccessful commercially.

The current revival of interest in decoration has produced textiles which are as vital as they have been at any time in this century. Nevertheless, no really distinct school of decorative design has yet come into being. Post-Modernism is too diffuse ideologically to have inspired its own decorative school. Memphis, however, has produced some quasi-vernacular, would-be populist patterns which have had a good deal of influence. Antoinette de Boer, with her restrained cerebral geometry, proves that the salient values of the Modern Movement still have a powerful authority.

In contrast with the minimalism of de Boer's work there is another school that produces textiles which evoke the decoration-saturated Bohemian interiors of Vuillard or Bonnard, or those in the photographs of Atget. Such textiles, by such designers as Sarah Campbell, Susan Collier, Lillian Delevoryas, Nathalie Gibson or Annagrete Halling-Koch, seem appropriate to intimate rooms in which objects are gathered, not as trophies of culture but for their associative qualities. Good taste is cast aside in favour of a delightful clutter of loved objects. The influence of Laura Ashley, or Miss Marple, is no doubt present in these nostalgic, escapist designs.

303

■ With the exception of the one-off pieces by British designer, Wendy Jones, the textiles on pages 138 to 141 are the products of well-known firms — Knoll in America, Stuttgarter Gardinenfabrik in West Germany, Cassina in Italy, Gabriel in Denmark, and Marks Pelle Vävare in Sweden. All have a well-deserved reputation for quality and make use of designs by some of the most famous names in the field. Discreetly luxurious, and without showy opulence, the textiles are intended for the discerning end of the market. Cassina is, of course, a furniture firm that stages its collections by famous designers with panache. It recently added Jack Lenor Larsen's name to its galaxy of stars. Wendy Jones's blankets have been included here for their quality, and for the same feeling of discreet luxury.

Textiles made of Greenland wool are a speciality of the Danish firm, Gabriel. Sheep were bred in Greenland by Eric the Red as early as AD 1000, but not until the beginning of this century was there a distinctive Greenland sheep. Greenland wool is difficult to process, but once woven, unmistakable.

303 JHANE BARNES
Furnishing fabric, part of the Knoll Line
Silk, wool, linen, rayon, cotton, polyester.
W 138 cm (54 in)
Manufacturer: Knoll International, USA

304 ANTOINETTE DE BOER
Furnishing fabric, *Dirili 2668*
75 per cent polyester, 25 per cent cotton.
W approx. 132 cm (52 in)
Manufacturer: Stuttgarter Gardinenfabrik, West Germany

305 ANTOINETTE DE BOER
Furnishing fabric, *Media 2116*
100 per cent cotton.
W approx. 126 cm (49 in).
Manufacturer: Stuttgarter Gardinenfabrik, West Germany

304

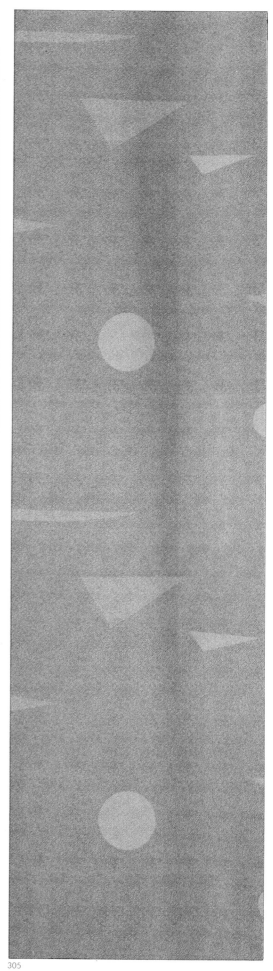

305

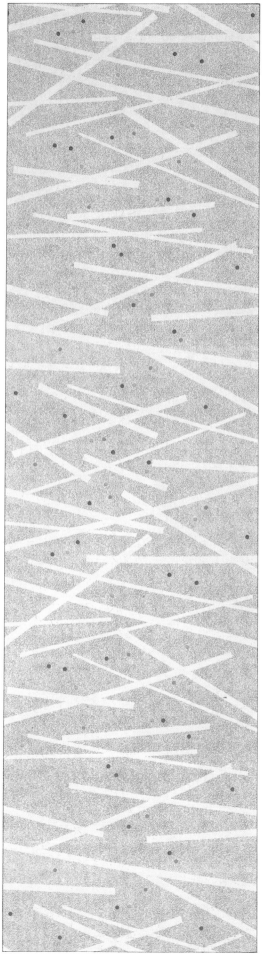

306

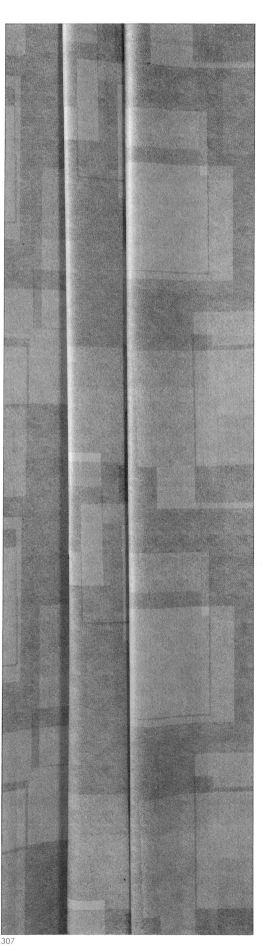

307

308

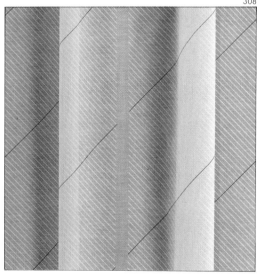

309

306 ANTOINETTE DE BOER
Furnishing fabric, *Klio 2113*
100 per cent cotton.
W approx. 126 cm (49 in)
Manufacturer: Stuttgarter Gardinenfabrik, West Germany

307 ANTOINETTE DE BOER
Furnishing fabric, *Sintra 2118*
100 per cent cotton.
W approx. 126 cm (49 in)
Manufacturer: Stuttgarter Gardinenfabrik, West Germany

308 TINA HAHN
Furnishing fabric, *Monza 2117*
100 per cent cotton.
W 124 cm (48 in)
Manufacturer: Stuttgarter Gardinenfabrik, West Germany

309 TINA HAHN
Furnishing fabric, *Piron 2667*
75 per cent polyester, 25 per cent cotton.
W approx. 132 cm (52 in)
Manufacturer: Stuttgarter Gardinenfabrik, West Germany

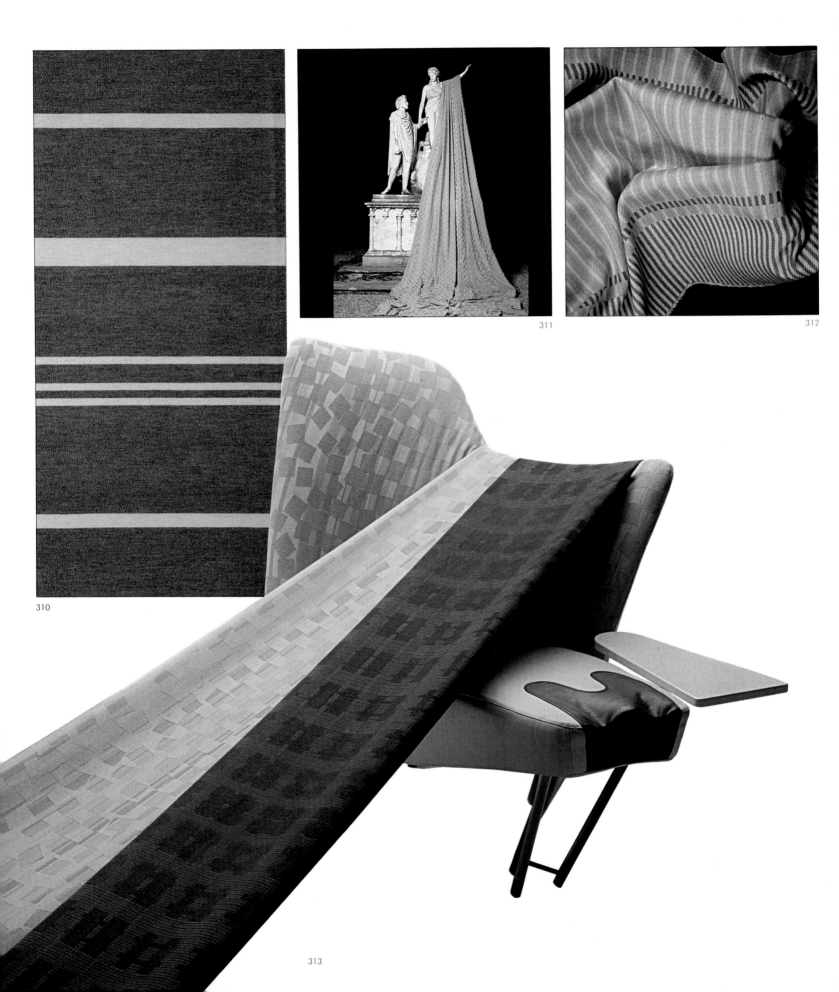

310

311

312

313

314

315

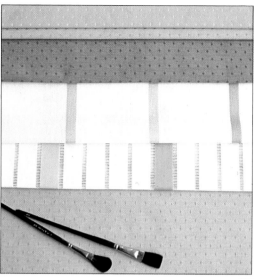
316

317

318

319

310 TOVE KINDT LARSEN
Blanket (travelling rug), *Savak*
140 cm (55 in) × 220 cm (86 in)
Manufacturer: Gabriel Boligtextiler, Denmark

311, 313 JACK LENOR LARSEN
Architectonic furnishing fabrics
Manufacturer: Cassina, Italy

312 WENDY JONES AND LESLEY BURKENSHAW
Blanket/throw, *Doubleweave*
One of a range in double-twill weave, 100 per cent
worsted. W 114 cm (45 in). L 182 cm (72 in)
Manufacturer: Wendy Jones, UK

314 ANN LARSSON-KJELIN
Furnishing fabrics, *Yes, Alright, Box, Palett, Pastell, Akvarell*
100 per cent cotton chenille, soft and hardwearing.
W 150 cm (59 in)
Manufacturer: Marks Pelle Vävare AB, Sweden

315 MONICA HJELM
Furnishing fabrics, *A Japanese Breeze, Yosu, Chidori, Mikado, Kiri*
100 per cent cotton.
W 150 cm (59 in)
Manufacturer: Marks Pelle Vävare AB, Sweden

316 MONICA HJELM
Furnishing fabrics, *A Japanese Breeze, Nikko, Ito, Fuji, Nikko*
100 per cent cotton.
W 150 cm (59 in)
Manufacturer: Marks Pelle Vävare AB, Sweden

317 WENDY JONES AND LESLEY BURKENSHAW
Doublecloth Blanket/Throws: Doubleweave
Double plain weave, commercially finished. 100 per cent
worsted, reversible design.
W 114 cm (45 in). L 182 cm (72 in)
Manufacturer: Wendy Jones, UK

318 MONICA HJELM
Furnishing fabrics, *A Japanese Breeze, Kyoto, Chidori, Kiri, Mikado*
100 per cent cotton.
W 150 cm (59 in)
Manufacturer: Marks Pelle Vävare AB, Sweden

319 MONICA HJELM
Furnishing fabrics, *A Japanese Breeze, Yosu, Mikado*
100 per cent cotton.
W 150 cm (59 in)
Manufacturer: Marks Pelle Vävare AB, Sweden

320

321

322

■ Some of the most exciting and richly architectural fabrics issued recently have been produced by the Swiss firm, Mira-X. Their quality is scarcely surprising when one sees some of the names associated with the firm: one of them is the Danish architect, and founder member, Verner Panton. The other names are also of renown: H-design members, Trix and Robert Haussmann, and Alfred Hablützel. Similarly, the designers responsible for the collections of *trompe l'oeil* fabrics have assured this firm the regular coverage they enjoy in architectural magazines all over the world: German textile designer, Freia Prowe; as well as the most recent member, the Swiss painter and textile designer, Elisabeth Strässle.

H-design's architectural patterns, their *faux marbres* and *faux bois*, create the illusions of stone or wood; of walls and wood panelling draped or dissolving into silken folds. The *Mira-Terrazzo* collection shown here suggests the 'surfaces of terrazzo floors, distorted and crumpled paper and something similar to parchment: paper with damp stains'. Prowe's *Mira-Diadem* collection in soft harmonies is subdued, elegant and silky; while Strässle's, at times evoking late Monet, is reminiscent of pastel chalks and watercolours. Here, feeling for colour ranges from the delicate to the strongly accentuated. Underlying Panton's work is a preoccupation with movement and colour, expressed in animated surfaces and plastic form. His *Mira-Rubin* mosaic, part of the new *Diamond Collection*, has a flashing jewel-like brilliance.

320, 321 FREIA PROWE
Furnishing fabric, *Mira-Diadem, Strié, Chiné, Dessiné*
90 per cent Acrylic, 10 per cent Ramie.
W 140 cm (51 in)
Manufacturer: Mira-X, Switzerland

322 ELISABETH STRÄSSLE
Furnishing fabric, *Botanica Collection*
Clockwise from top left: *Mira-Toccata, Mira-Adagio, Mira-Vivace, Mira-Pastorale, Mira-Prelude, Mira-Sinfonia, Mira-Sonata, Mira-Cantata*
100 per cent cotton chintz.
W 130 cm (51 in)
Manufacturer: Mira-X, Switzerland

323

323 TOSO AND MASSARI
Furnishing fabric, *Selene*
Part of the *Mosaico Collection*
Manufacturer: L. Marcato, Italy

324 H-DESIGN
Furnishing fabric, *Mira-Terrazzo 10,
Mira-Terrazzo 30*
Former of 100 per cent cotton; latter 59
per cent Polyester, 41 per cent cotton.
W 130 cm (51 in)
Manufacturer: Mira-X, Switzerland

325 H-DESIGN
Furnishing fabric, *Mira-Terrazzo 20,
Mira-Terrazzo 40*
Former 59 per cent Polyester, 41 per cent
cotton; latter 100 per cent cotton
W 130 cm (51 in)
Manufacturer: Mira-X, Switzerland

324

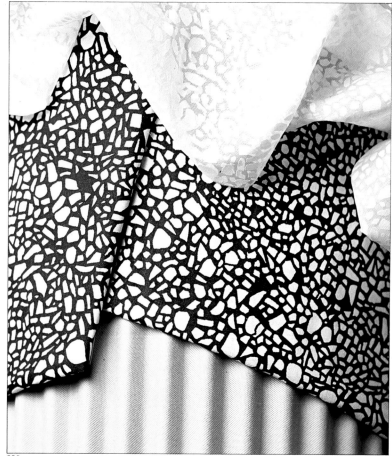

325

326 VERNER PANTON
Furnishing fabric, *Diamond Collection*
Plain fabric, *Mira-Plaza*; printed fabric, *Mira-Rubin*
100 per cent cotton chintz.
W 140 cm (55 in)
Manufacturer: Mira-X, Switzerland

326

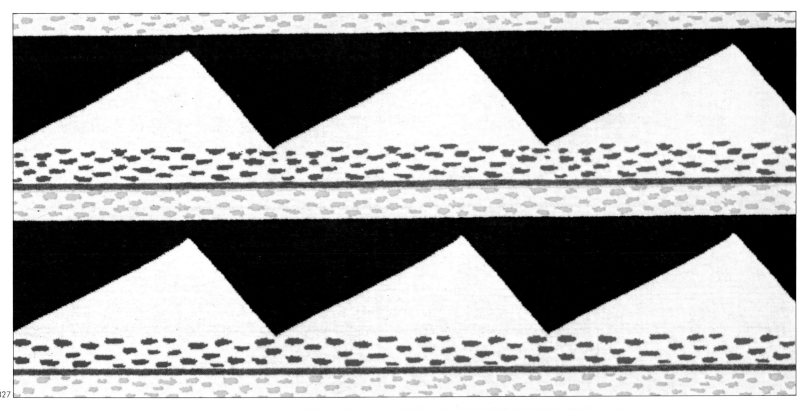

327

■ *Taival* and *Karhusaari* (illustrations 328 and 329) belong to Fujiwo Ishimoto's collection for Marimekko, called *Iso Karhu* (The Great Bear); and derive from the designer's interest in ikat weaving. To translate the feeling of handmade ikat cloth into a printed fabric, colours have been layered one upon another to give the impression of uneven brush strokes. The result has a considered folk-art quality; one that appears also in Marc Van Hoe's fabric for Ter Molst International (illustration 327), though here the influence appears again to have been south-east Asia.

328

329

327 MARC VAN HOE
Furnishing fabric, *Etnic*
Polyacryl-PC. W 140 cm (55 in)
Manufacturer: Ter Molst International, Belgium

328 FUJIWO ISHIMOTO
Fabrics, *Taival* (left), *Karhusaari* (right)
100 per cent cotton.
W 145 cm (58 in)
Manufacturer: Marimekko, Finland

329 FUJIWO ISHIMOTO
Fabric, *Taival*
100 per cent cotton.
W 145 cm (58 in)
Manufacturer: Marimekko, Finland

330

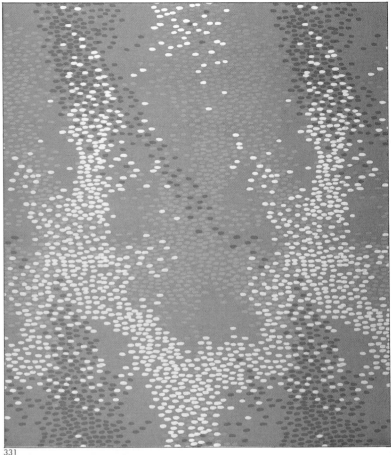

331

■ For some time now the 1950s has been making a come-back — a period most people old enough to remember clearly would choose to pass over quietly. Here are three designers from different countries: Anneli Airikka-Lammi from Finland, Helen Abson from Australia and Marta Moia who is Argentinian born, but who works in Britain: all of them exhibit a similar pre-occupation with texture expressed in pattern, and muddied colours; though Abson's designs show the influence of ethnic textiles.

332

330, 331, 332 HELEN ABSON
Furnishing fabrics, *Shimmer Collection*
100 per cent cotton, pigment printed. The base fabric is imported already dyed from Japan and is printed in Melbourne. Plain dyed and quilted fabric, coordinating with the prints, is also available. Five colourways.
W 120 cm (47 in)
Manufacturer: Zab Design, Australia

333 ANNELI AIRIKKA-LAMMI
Furnishing fabric, *Keikaus-Viesti*
100 per cent cotton. Printed.
W 150 cm (59 in)
Manufacturer: Tampella Habit, Finland

333

334 MARTA MOIA
Furnishing fabric, *Abstract – colourways 1
and 2*
100 per cent cotton, screen printed with
helizarin dyes, colourfast and washable.
W 127 cm (50 in)
Manufacturer: Marta Moia, UK

334

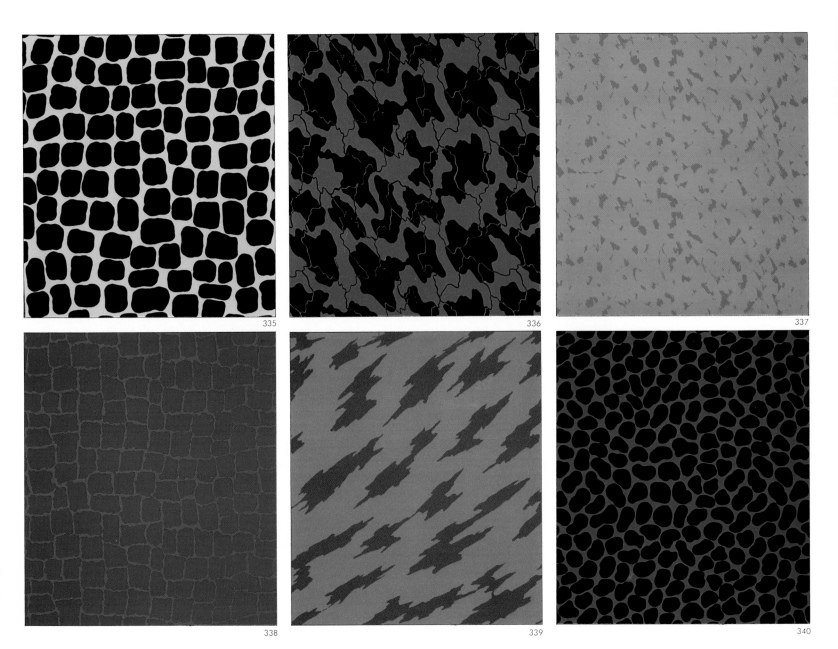

335

336

337

338

339

340

335–346 NATHALIE DU PASQUIER AND GEORGE SOWDEN
A collection of decorative surfaces, *Progetto Decorazione*
Silk-screen printed papers. 'For some time we have been
working on drawn surfaces,' say the designers. 'The
support material for the drawing is not important; it could
have been wood or silk, plastic, stone or stainless steel. In
this case it is paper because we wanted to do things
quickly; it is a convenient medium, and easy to move
about. What was important was the drawing on the paper
. . . the colours and shapes that evoke emotions and excite
curiosity; colours and shapes that form patterns,
transforming the material into swirling or agitated or
blinding surfaces.'
Manufacturer: Werk Galerie Steinemann, Switzerland

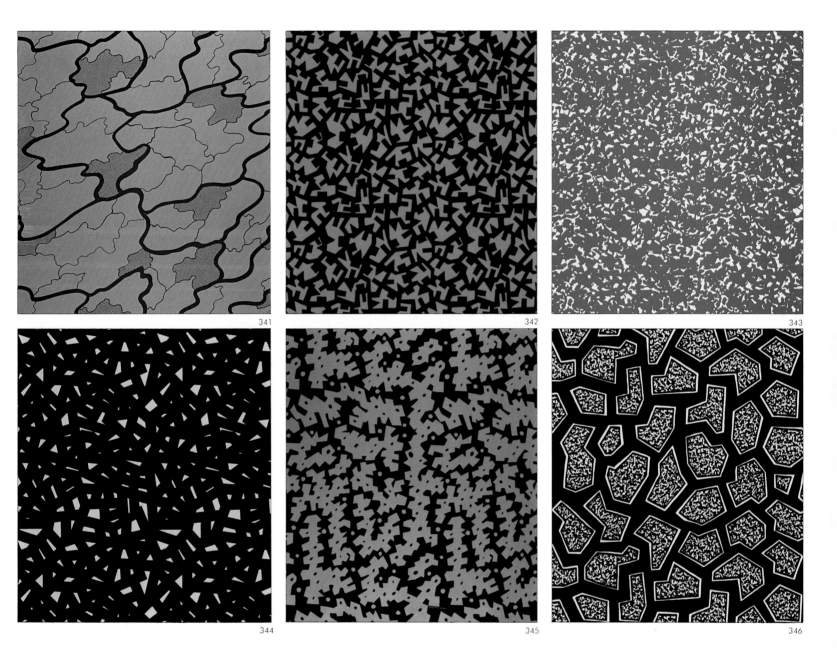

341

342

343

344

345

346

■ Several of the textiles included here appear to have been conceived as paintings rather than designs. Collier Campbell's *6 Views* collection for Fischbacher — part of which is represented here — won the 1984 British Design Council award and the Duke of Edinburgh's award for outstanding achievement in design. The painterly quality of Collier Campbell's rich and varied textile designs makes them recognizable whether sold by Habitat, Cacherel, Jaeger or Martex.

347

347 COLLIER CAMPBELL
Sofa in *Havanna* (colour 14)
Curtains in *Cote d'Azur* (colour 14)
Manufacturer: Collier Campbell, UK

348 COLLIER CAMPBELL
Blind in *Spice Route* (colour 16)
Manufacturer: Collier Campbell, UK

348

349

351 COLLIER CAMPBELL
Sofa in *Caravan*: *Toy Mix* (colour 212)
Wallcovering in *Bazaar*: *Multi Exotic*
(colour 533)
Curtain in *Bedouin Stripe*: *Aubergine Mix*
(colour 112)
Reverse of curtain in *Caravan*: *Multi*
(colour 215)
Lampshade in *Okra*: *Lantern Red* (colour
22)
Tablecloth in *Okra*: *Jet* (colour 15)
Manufacturer: Collier Campbell, UK

350 COLLIER CAMPBELL
Curtains and window-seat small cushions
in *Bedouin Stripe*: *Sahara Rose* (colour
114)
Blinds and window seat cushions in
Caravan
Tablecloth and small cushions in *Okra*:
Lantern Red (colour 22)
Large cushions on floor and suspended
ceiling fabric in *Bedouin Stripe*: *Aubergine
Mix* (colour 112)
Manufacturer: Collier Campbell, UK

349 COLLIER CAMPBELL
Curtain in *Cote d'Azur* (colour 11)
Table cloth in *Spice Route* (colour 18)
Duvet cover in *Silk Passage*
This duvet cover is part of a set of bed
linen produced with Martex, USA.
Manufacturer: Collier Campbell, UK

350

351

352

353

354

352 COLLIER CAMPBELL
Sofa in *Spice Route* (colour 14)
Tablecloth and cushions in *Romany*
(colour 15)
Lampshade in *Cote d'Azur* (colour 15)
Manufacturer: Collier Campbell, UK

■ Natalie Gibson applies her passion for birds and beasts, fans and flowers to almost anything that comes to hand. Her colours are as fresh and delicate as those of an Oriental watercolour. In Arts and Crafts style she has designed wallpapers and furnishing fabrics for Heals, silk scarves for Liberty's, tin trays and fabrics for Conran and lavatories for Adamsez. Her beautiful cobwebby embroideries produced for dress designer Janice Wainwright became an inseparable part of the Wainwright look, machines stitched from the basic pattern onto the clothes. Her most recent work includes hand-painted silk screens and scarves for private commissions.

The Japanese influence appears again in a less spontaneous way in fabrics designed for the commercial market by Danish designer Annagrete Halling-Koch (illustrations 353 and 354). Her subjects too are Oriental: fans, birds and flowers.

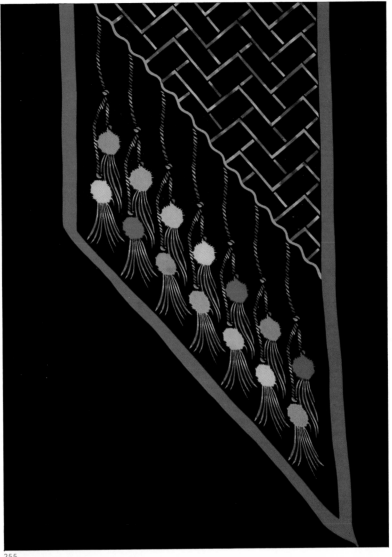

355

353 ANNAGRETE HALLING-KOCH
Furnishing and dress fabrics, *Fantasi: Vifter*
W 140 cm (55 in)
Manufacturer: Pausa, Denmark

354 ANNAGRETE HALLING-KOCH
Furnishings and dress fabrics, *Fantasi: Fugle*
W 140 cm (55 in)
Manufacturer: Pausa, Denmark

355 NATALIE GIBSON
Screen print
Crepe de chine. Designed for Liberty's,
London
Manufacturer: Natalie Gibson, UK

356

356 NATALIE GIBSON
Trellis design handpainted on silk satin
with appliquéd flowers
Manufacturer: Natalie Gibson, UK

357

358

359

357, 358, 359 NATALIE GIBSON
Detail of screen
Handpainted on silk.
Manufacturer: Natalie Gibson, UK

360 NATALIE GIBSON
Handpainted silk
Manufacturer: Natalie Gibson, UK

360

■ Two wall hangings, one by an American designer, the other English. *Nicotiana Bouquet* by Lillian Delevoryas is nostalgic and pastoral, in an Arts-and-Crafts manner. One can almost breathe in the perfume. Pauline Burbidge's hangings, on the other hand, are highly architectural, but paradoxically crafted in romantic fashion with pieces of Honan silk (illustrations 362 to 365).

361

361 LILLIAN DELEVORYAS
Small carpet or wallhanging, *Nicotiana Bouquet*
Chainstitched embroidery on canvas. Accompanying
cushion covers, bed covers and tablecloths available.
L 172 cm (68 in). W 122 cm (48 in)
Manufacturer: Divertimenti, UK

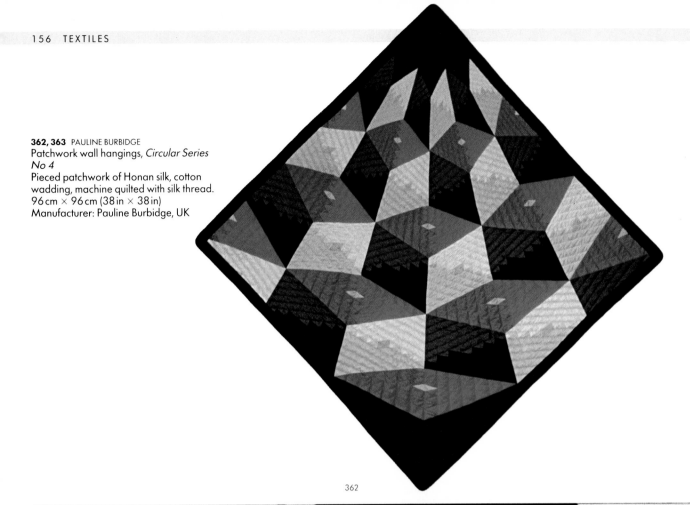

362, 363 PAULINE BURBIDGE
Patchwork wall hangings, *Circular Series
No 4*
Pieced patchwork of Honan silk, cotton
wadding, machine quilted with silk thread.
96 cm × 96 cm (38 in × 38 in)
Manufacturer: Pauline Burbidge, UK

362

363

364

365

364, 365 PAULINE BURBIDGE
Patchwork wall hangings, *Circular Series No 5*
Pieced patchwork of Honan silk, cotton wadding, machine quilted with silk thread.
96 cm × 96 cm (38 in × 38 in)
Manufacturer: Pauline Burbidge, UK

■ Charles Gwathmey's hanging is an abstract play on geometry: the golden section, square and circle, with implied diagonals and the intersection of curve and line.

Of his rug, called *Dinner at Eight*, Robert Stern says: 'The phrase Dinner at Eight invokes a certain genre of Hollywood film comedy that combined disingenuous innocence with metropolitan sophistication. This rug seeks to recapture the mood of those films – their heightened sense of romance, their use of theatrical convention, and of exquisitely ambiguous euphemism.

'It presents a highly formalised image within a proscenium-like frame of classical columns and theatrical drapes. The curtains are drawn, the doors about to open and music about to play as the comedy begins.'

367 CHARLES GWATHMEY
Tapestry, *Soleil Couchant*
Wool. Design based on 'the golden section, square and circle, real and implied diagonals and cubist form'.
H 153 cm (60 in). W 214 cm (84 in)
Manufacturer: V'Soske Shops Inc, USA

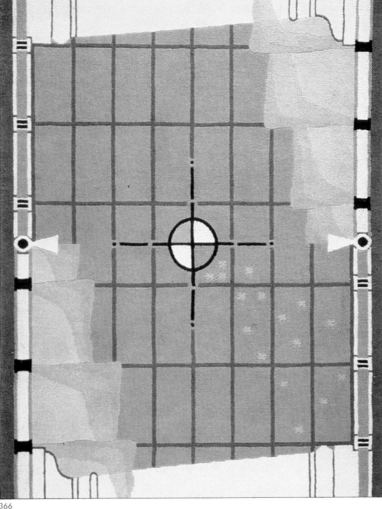

366

366 ROBERT A.M. STERN
Rug, *Dinner at Eight*
100 per cent wool, handmade in Spain. Commissioned, designed and produced for Furniture of the Twentieth Century, USA.
H 165 cm (65 in). W 250 cm (99 in)

367

■ Ulf Moritz's geometrically patterned carpets, at first glance abstract and modern, acquire on closer inspection the presence of objects of antiquity. It is an impression heightened by the names: *Pharao, Carrara, Obelisque*. Some of the geometries have strong archaeological associations. The pieces are set like jewels against sombre back-grounds.

369 ULF MORITZ
Carpet, *Pharao*
H 200 cm (78 3/4 in). D 200 cm (78 3/4 in)
Manufacturer: Detlef Rosen, West Germany

370 ULF MORITZ
Carpet, *Obelisque*
H 145 cm (59 in). D 145 cm (59 in)
Manufacturer: Detlef Rosen, West Germany

371 ULF MORITZ
Carpet, *Carré*
H 185 cm (73 in). D 185 cm (73 in)
Manufacturer: Detlef Rosen, West Germany

368 ULF MORITZ
Carpet, *Circle*
D 200 cm (78¾ in)
Manufacturer: Detlef Rosen, West
Germany

372 ULF MORITZ
Carpet, *Carrara*
H 200 cm (78¾ in). D 200 cm (78¾ in)
Manufacturer: Detlef Rosen, West
Germany

373 ULF MORITZ
Carpet, *Triada*
H 220 cm (86½ in). D 220 cm (86½ in)
Manufacturer: Detlef Rosen, West
Germany

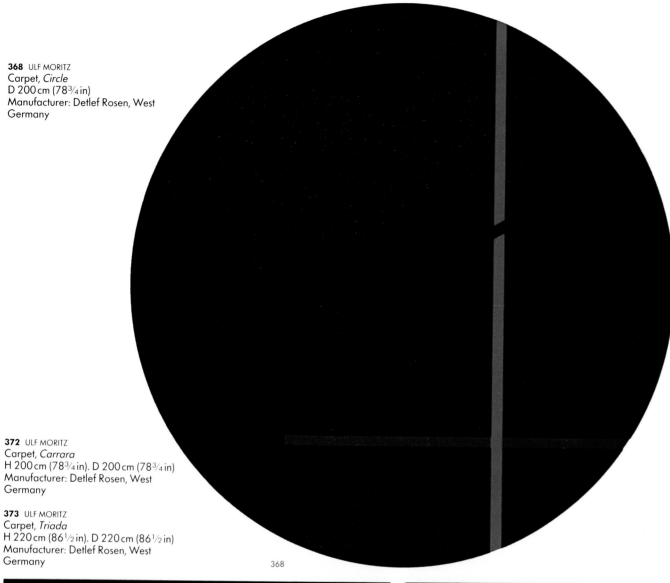

368

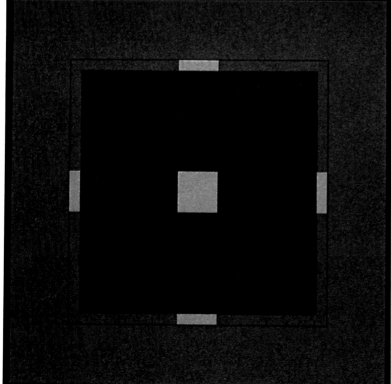

369

370

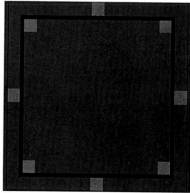

371

372

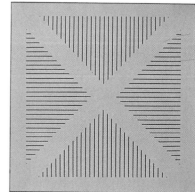

373

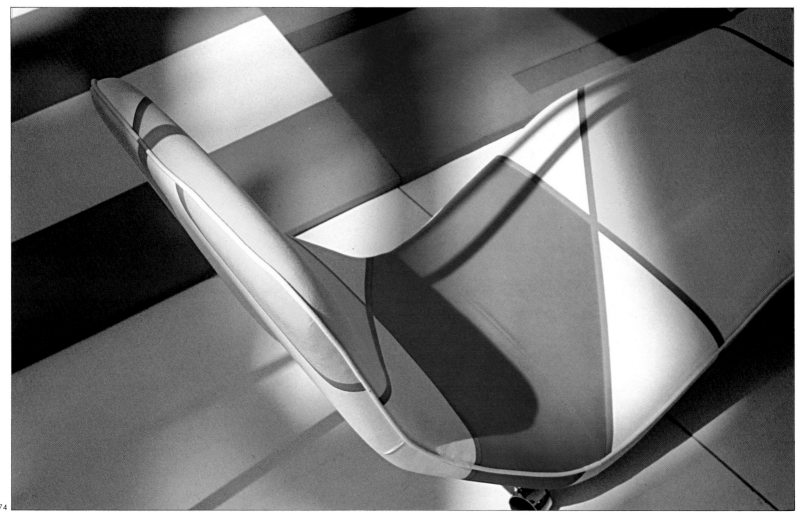

374

■ Two examples of the free and joyous use of colour, that reflect their northern and southern origins respectively. Vuokko's new oranges-and-lemons fabric, here used to cover Antti Nurmesniemi's famous reclining chair, evokes Finnish clarity; while the hot kaleidoscopic designs for Saporiti's *Miamina* folding chair suggest more southerly latitudes.

374 VUOKKO
Cotton furnishing fabric
Manufacturer: Vuokko, Finland

375 SALVATI-TRESOLDI
Chair, *Miamina*
Manufacturer: Saporiti, Italy

375

PRODUCTS

We are fortunate to be able to illustrate a series of coffee services, designed by eleven influential architects, which were commissioned by Alessi, the Italian stainless-steel manufacturer. Alessi have long patronized the most accomplished designers — including Sottsass himself and Sapper. Even Salvador Dali has designed for Alessi — admittedly a 'useless object', an object with a near-impossible topography. Alessi's selection of their architects could hardly have been more topical — for this is a most formidable Post-Modernist gathering.

The Alessi coffee services are as different as their designers. Post-Modernism is more a way of thinking than a style. But it indulges in frequent, perhaps too unselfconscious, historical asides. Perhaps the most powerful historical influence to be felt in the Alessi designs is that of Josef Hoffmann, whose metalwork for the Wiener Werkstätte, in the 1900s, successfully purveyed bourgeois *Gemütlichkeit* and an entirely palatable modernity at the same time. Other obvious influences are Jean Puiforcat — master of geometrical Art Déco — and Marianne Brandt of the Bauhaus. It is also possible to detect the influence of Christopher Dresser, that enigmatic nineteenth-century Proto-Modern. Of the Alessi coffee services the most unexpected is Charles Jencks' — poetic, but atavistic.

Alessi have shown us, in microcosm, the conscious and unconscious preoccupations of contemporary architects. This is an invaluable historical exercise. One cannot help thinking that a mere ten years ago the coffee services would have been more inhibited and much less delightful.

Richard Sapper's kettle — outwardly unassertive — will make the experience of making an ordinary cup of tea or coffee a romantic one, with its two-tone Chattanooga choo-choo whistle. Is this a rare example of audio kitsch?

The door furniture for Fusital by Gae Aulenti, Cini Boeri, Gregotti Associati and Marco Zanuso establishes that even in such a circumscribed area there can be endless and enjoyable variation. The same can be said of the door furniture of Davide Mercatali and Paolo Pedrizzetti and of Alan Tye's design for Allgood UK.

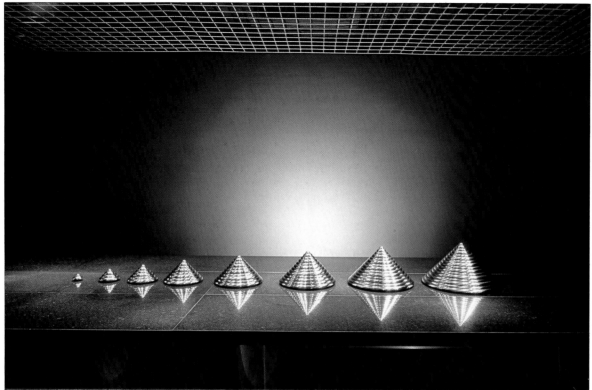

376

376, 377 MASAYUKI KUROKAWA
Tray set A, *Metal Wave: TR-A: 0–7*
Stainless steel, rubber.
H 3.3 cm (1¾ in). D from 5 cm to 40 cm
(2 in to 16 in)
Manufacturer: Daichi Co, Japan

377

■ Kurokawa is one of Japan's leading designers; and, as might be expected, his collection of objects for the desk — pen-holders, ashtrays, lighters and pins — consists of impeccably crafted miniature essays in architecture. The sculptural delicacy and the attention to detail, even in such small objects, have a particularly Japanese quality.

378

378 MASAYUKI KUROKAWA
Pushpin, *Metal Wave*
Stainless steel.
Type *A–J*: H 0.5 to 2.8 cm (¼ in to 1¼ in).
D 1 cm to 2 cm (¼ in to ¾ in). Three long
pins *J 1–3*: W 0.8 cm (¼ in). L 3.8 cm to
8.3 cm (1½ in to 3¼ in).
Manufacturer: Daichi Co, Japan

379 MASAYUKI KUROKAWA
Range of ashtrays, coasters and lighters,
Gom Collection
Rubber, stainless steel, plastic. These
objects are included in the permanent
collection of the Museum of Modern Art in
New York.
Clockwise from top left:
Square ashtrays H 4 cm to 4.5 cm (1½ in
to 1¾ in). W 7 cm to 10 cm (2½ in to
3½ in). L 7 cm to 10 cm (2½ in to 3½ in)
Round ashtray H 4 cm (1½ in). D 7 cm
(2½ in)
Coaster H 0.5 cm (¼ in). D 8 cm (3¼ in)
Square lighter H 4.2 cm (1½ in). W 7 cm
(2½ in). L 7 cm (2½ in)
Round lighter H 4.2 cm (1½ in). D 7 cm
(2½ in)
Centre left: ashtray H 4 cm (1½ in).
D 17.4 cm (7 in)
Centre right: ashtray H 3.2 cm (1¼ in).
D 13 cm (5½ in)
Manufacturer: Fuso Gomund Co, Japan

379

380

381

380 MASAYUKI KUROKAWA
Range of objects for desk or table, *Metal Wave*
Stainless steel, rubber.
Clockwise from top left:
Pen stand *PS 1–4*: H 9.1 cm (3½ in).
D 10 cm to 25 cm (3½ in to 9¾ in)
Round paperweight *PW 1–2*: H 3.3 cm
(1¼ in). D 5 cm and 10 cm (1¾ in and
3½ in)
Long paperweight: H 1.5 cm (¾ in).
W 2.5 cm (1 in). L 12.5 cm to 27.5 cm (5 in
to 11 in)
Tray set *A 0–7*: H 3.3 cm (1¼ in). D 5 cm
to 40 cm (2 in to 15 in)
Cigarette lighter which can be used with
the tray set: H 4.8 cm. D 10 cm (2 in to
3½ in)
Tray set *B 1–3*: H 2 cm (¾ in). D 10 cm to
20 cm (3½ in to 7 in)
Manufacturer: Daichi Co, Japan

381 MASAYUKI KUROKAWA
Gom Pushpin
Rubber, colours: black, brown, violet, red,
yellow, green. Mass produced.
Types A, B, C, D: H 1 cm to 1.2 cm (½ in to
¾ in)
Manufacturer: Fuso Gomund Co, Japan

382 ALESSANDRO MENDINI
Coffee and tea service of six pieces
Part of the Tea and Coffee Piazza series.
Silver.
Coffee-pot H 24 cm (9 in)
Teapot H 21.5 cm (8½ in)
Cream jug H 18 cm (7¼ in)
Sugar bowl H 8 cm (3¼ in)
Spoon L 11 cm (4½ in)
Tray D 45 cm (17 in)
Manufacturer: Alessi, Italy

383 RICHARD MEIER
Tea and coffee set
Part of the Tea and Coffee Piazza series.
Silver, ivory handles. The set comprises
a coffee-pot, teapot, milk jug, sugar bowl
and tray.
Coffee-pot H 22.5 cm (8½ in)
Teapot H 20.5 cm (7¾ in)
Milk jug H 9.5 cm (3¾ in)
Sugar bowl H 12.5 cm (4¾ in)
Tray D 36 cm (14 in)
Manufacturer: Alessi, Italy

■ The Tea and Coffee Piazza project was an experiment sponsored by Officina Alessi. Eleven well-known architects were invited to design a tea and coffee service. The group included an American contingent, Robert Venturi, Michael Graves, Richard Meier and Stanley Tigerman; the Italians Aldo Rossi, Paolo Portoghesi and Alessandro Mendini; and lone wolves like Hans Hollein, Charles Jencks, Oscar Tusquets and Kazumasa Yamashita.

The result of the experiment has been a series of intriguing architectural miniatures. The services in blue and silver by Hollein (illustration 394) and Rossi (illustrations 384 and 389) are essays in exquisite restraint. Hollein's tray alone is a masterpiece, shaped like an aircraft-carrier deck with the pieces designed and arranged according to elegant geometric logic. Rossi's enclosure, echoing his floating theatre project, seems a little arcane, but is irresistible; and his containers remind one of traditional tin vessels used for centuries by Arabs for boiling coffee.

The Wiener Werkstätte was evidently a rich source of inspiration. Portoghesi's handsome service (illustration 395) evokes Josef Hoffmann. It is the only one to exploit a decorative inlay. Late Wiener Werkstätte lingers around Graves' jolly, festive objects with their high-flying handles and festooning, columns and cupolas (illustration 393).

Late Wiener Werkstätte appears to have affected Mendini (illustration 382) as well, though here the over-riding impression is rather of a flock of alert one-legged creatures culled from Tenniel's classic illustrations for Lewis Carroll's *Alice in Wonderland*.

Two exercises in spatial illusion by Meier (illustration 383) and Yamashita (illustration 401) are made all the more interesting by being placed side by side. Meier is perhaps the only one to have really appreciated the richness of the material. Yamashita's by contrast seem two-dimensional, with attenuated handles and multifarious spouts. Venturi's containers with ebony handles have straightforward Georgian shapes (illustration 396).

The danger of making heavy witticisms in a costly material with stately associations is that they can seem merely ostentatious. Both Tigerman and Jencks run that risk, though it is interesting that Jencks has tried to bring back real detailing (illustrations 397 and 398).

Finally, there is the service by Oscar Tusquets (illustration 391), with its containers composed of welded shells. Tusquets professes a geometric logic. Other pieces of high design also fall within the category of Arts and Crafts. Two were designed for the eccentric Italian collector, Cleto Munari. One, by Mario Bellini (illustration 399), is a sumptuous and classically columned service in pink onyx and silver. Bellini, who has been responsible for some of the highest of high-technological objects, has a well-developed sense of history and a predilection for the operatic; here he has given rein to both. The other is an elegant teapot in silver and rosewood by David Palterer (illustration 392), that in its horizontality recalls Christopher Dresser.

Wiener Werkstätte influences — with exaggerations — appear again in Johannes Kuhnen's teapot in silver and anodized aluminium (illustration 400), and in a purer form in Meier's bowl, tray and candlesticks (illustrations 385 to 387). Stern's candlesticks, on the other hand, are pure Movietone Glamour (illustration 390).

The handsome kettle by Richard Sapper — and the manufacturer is once again Alessi — is conceptually Arts and Crafts; a piece of industrial sculpture that can indeed be made precious in the literal sense by being silver plated (illustration 388).

382

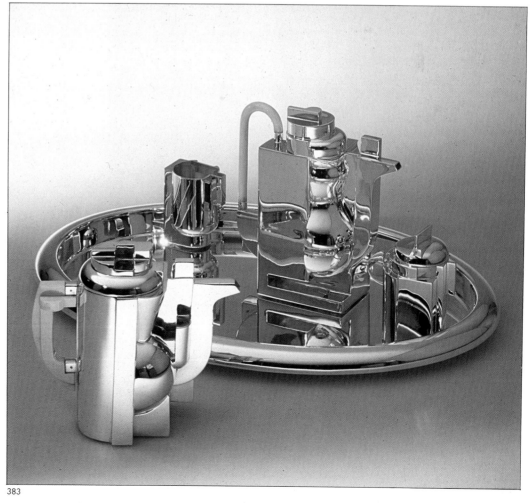

383

384, 389 ALDO ROSSI
Coffee and tea service in six pieces
Part of the Tea and Coffee Piazza series.
Coffee-pot: Silver. Truncated cone body
with upper cylindrical band in light blue
stoved enamel. H 26 cm (10 in)
Teapot: Silver H 22.5 cm (9 in)
Milk jug: Silver, cylindrical body H 8.5 cm
(3½ in)
Sugar bowl: Silver, domed lid with
terminal sphere in quartz. H 22.5 cm (9 in)
Spoon: Silver plate L 11.7 cm (4½ in)
Service container: boxed in black iron;
frame in brass section-door in hinged
glass; handleknob in quartz; pitched-roof
lid in copper; drum in light blue glazed
plate with battery clock.
H 64.5 cm (25 in)
Manufacturer: Alessi, Italy

385 RICHARD MEIER
Serving tray, *King Richard*
Silver plate.
D 138 cm (15 in)
Manufacturer: Swid Powell, USA

386 RICHARD MEIER
Bowl, *King Richard*
Silver plate.
D 26 cm or 36 cm (10 in or 14 in)
Manufacturer: Swid Powell, USA

387 RICHARD MEIER
Candlestick, *King Richard*
Silver plate.
H 24 cm (9¼ in)
Manufacturer: Swid Powell, USA

384

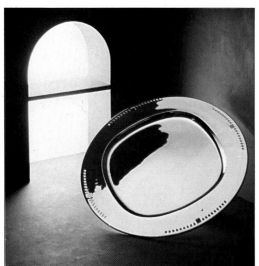

385

386

387

388

388 RICHARD SAPPER
Kettle with melodic whistle
Stainless steel with copper heat-diffusing
bottom, brass whistle, pitched notes E and
B, polyamide-covered handle. In two
sizes: 2 litre (70 oz) and 3 litre (106 oz).
Also available in silver-plated stainless
steel. The whistle reproduces the sound of
an American steam locomotive.
Manufacturer: Alessi, Italy

389

390 ROBERT A.M. STERN
Candlesticks
From left to right: *Century, Harmonic, Metropolitan*
Silver plate.
H 17 cm (6½ in), 16 cm (6 in), 31 cm (12¼ in)
Manufacturer: Swid Powell, USA

390

391

391 OSCAR TUSQUETS
Tea service of four pieces
Part of the Tea and Coffee Piazza series.
Teapot: silver, body formed by two welded shells with relief riveting along a tilted axis. The handle is attached to one shell and the spout to the other. Handle cover in ebony, glass lid. H 19 cm (7½ in)
Milk jug: silver, body formed by two welded shells with relief riveting along a tilted axis; the handle is attached to one shell, the spout to the other. H 12 cm (4¾ in)
Sugar bowl: silver, spherical body, glass lid. H 8 cm (3 in)
Tray: silver, trapezoidal with rounded sides and raised rims that become handles. H 6 cm (2¼ in)
Manufacturer: Alessi, Italy

392 DAVID PALTERER
Teapot, *Teiera*
Silver and rosewood. Designed for the collector Cleto Munari, and produced in a signed and limited edition.
H 12 cm (4¾ in)
Manufacturer: Rossi and Arcandi, Italy

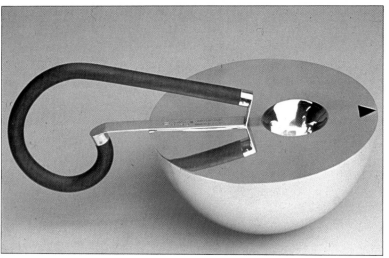

392

393 MICHAEL GRAVES
Tea and coffee service
Part of the Tea and Coffee Piazza series.
Silver container body, blue lacquered
aluminium spheres, feet in black bakelite;
truncated conical lid of four miniature
silver columns and semispherical cupola in
blue glazed aluminium; handle in mock
ivory. Spoon is silver with spherical knob
in blue lacquered aluminium. Tray, round
with glass surface, upper and lower
spheres in blue lacquered aluminium; ring
and columns of rim, and handle
connections in silver; handles in mock
ivory.
Coffee-pot H 24.5 cm (9½ in)
Teapot H 20.5 cm (8 in)
Cream jug H 10 cm (4 in)
Sugar bowl H 14.5 cm (5¾ in)
Spoon L 19.5 cm (7¾ in)
Tray H 7 cm (2¾ in). D 41 cm (16½ in)
Manufacturer: Alessi, Italy

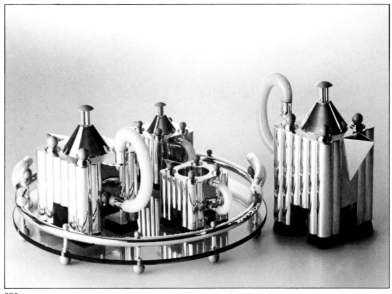

393

394 HANS HOLLEIN
Coffee and tea service with five pieces
Part of the Tea and Coffee Piazza series.
Coffee-pot: silver with blue metacrylate
handle; square section body with spout
and handle pivoted at the corners; lid
hinged on the spout side with concealed
hinge. H 17 cm (6¾ in)
Teapot: silver with feet and handle in blue
metacrylate; lid with internal central hinge
and opening next to the spout. H 18 cm
(7¼ in)
Milk jug: silver with handle in blue
metacrylate; cylindrical section body with
truncated conical base. H 13 cm (5¼ in)
Sugar bowl: silver, three quarters of a
circle section body; knob in blue
metacrylate. H 7 cm (2¾ in)
Tray: electro-plated brass; surface has a
satin-finished transversal band; shaped
like an aircraft-carrier deck, on which the
pieces have a precise position. H 4.5 cm
(2 in). L 92.4 cm (36 in). D 31 cm (12 in)
Manufacturer: Alessi, Italy

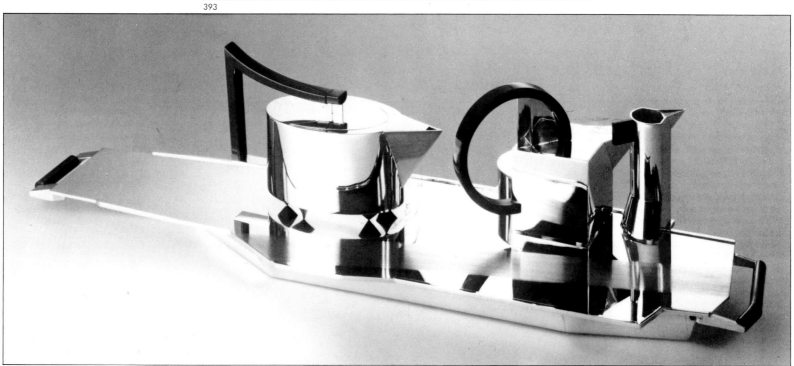

394

395

395 PAOLO PORTOGHESI
Coffee and tea service of six pieces
Part of the Tea and Coffee Piazza series.
Coffee-pot: silver; body with hexagonal
base and hexagonal pyramid lid and flat
knob; decorative band engraved and
enamelled in black and white; ebony
handle. H 16.5 cm (6½ in)
Teapot: silver. H 16.5 cm (6½ in)
Milk jug: silver. H 9.5 cm (3¾ in)
Sugar bowl: silver. H 11 cm (4¼ in)
Ashtray: silver. H 3 cm (1 in)
Tray: silver; irregular hexagonal shape
H 2 cm (¾ in). L 42.5 cm (16¾ in).
D 20.5 cm (8 in)
Manufacturer: Alessi, Italy

396

396 ROBERT VENTURI
Coffee and tea service of five pieces
Part of the Tea and Coffee Piazza series.
Coffee-pot: silver; ovaloid body with three
feet; line engraved on body and lid; Alessi
logotypes in gold plate; ebony handle.
H 21.5 cm (8¾ in)
Teapot: silver; ovaloid body with round-
based feet; flowers with petals in gold
plate, engraved stems and leaves cover
the piece; ebony handle. H 15 cm (6 in)
Milk jug: silver; truncated conical body,
flat handle; band of small gold-plated
rectangles. H 10 cm (4 in)
Sugar bowl: silver; oval shaped on round
foot; festooned band on the body and lid
in gold-plate; lines engraved on the base
and knob. H 13 cm (5¼ in)
Tray: silver; oval, decoration on the top
and on the gold-plated edge. H 1.5 cm
(¾ in)
Manufacturer: Alessi, Italy

397

397 STANLEY TIGERMAN
Coffee and tea service of five pieces
Part of the Tea and Coffee Piazza series.
Coffee-pot: silver; cylindrical body with
hinged lid; handle, spout and knob in lost-
wax casting. H 15.5 cm (6 in)
Teapot: silver. H 15.5 cm (6 in)
Milk jug: silver. H 11.5 cm (4¾ in)
Sugar bowl: silver; spherical body.
H 8.5 cm (3½ in)
Tray: silver; rectangular with brim and
rounded edges. H 4 cm (2 in). L 47 cm
(18½ in). D 34 cm (13 in)
Manufacturer: Alessi, Italy

399 MARIO BELLINI
Tea and coffee service
Designed for Cleto Munari in pink onyx
and silver.

398

399

398 CHARLES JENCKS
Coffee and tea service of five pieces
Part of the Tea and Coffee Piazza series.
Coffee-pot: silver; three Ionic volutes in cast silver alternate with three spouts and serve as handles; column base with square base, polygonal capital lid; the surface of the column is partly satin-finished. H 22 cm (8¾ in). Teapot: silver; column base with square base, polygonal capital lid.
H 22 cm (8¾ in)
Teapot: silver; lines engraved on the surface of the column for two-thirds of its height; two rams' heads in cast silver serve as handles. H 21 cm (8¼ in)
Milk jug: silver; sectioned column body with square base, which becomes round-sectioned at the top; lid with square capital; lines engraved on the surface of the column. H 14 cm (5½ in)
Sugar bowl: silver; sectioned column body with square base, which becomes round-sectioned at the top; lid with square capital; lines engraved on the surface of the column. H 14 cm (5½ in)
Tray: silver; rectangular shape; four shapes engraved on the tray's surface indicate the positions of the pieces. H 2 cm (¾ in). 45 cm × 18.5 cm (17 in × 6¾ in)
Manufacturer: Alessi, Italy

400

400 JOHANNES KUHNEN
Teapot
Sterling silver, anodized aluminium One-off, made in the designer's own workshop; now part of the Victoria State Craft Collection, Australia.
H 18 cm (7 in). D 15 cm (5½ in)

401 KAZUMASA YAMASHITA
Coffee and tea service of six pieces
Part of the Tea and Coffee Piazza series.
Coffee-pot: silver; rectangular section body; hinged lid; handle and spout made of double tubular segments; knob tubular, bent to form the initial C (coffee).
H 22.5 cm (9 in)
Teapot: silver; square section body; knob tubular, bent to form the letter T (tea).
H 19.5 cm (7½ in)
Milk jug: silver; rectangular section body, knob tubular, bent to form the letter S.
H 15 cm (6 in)
Tray: relief seams on surface determine the arrangement of the pieces. H 1.5 cm (¾ in). L 51 cm (22¼ in). D 16 cm (6¼ in)
Manufacturer: Alessi, Italy

401

402 LABBAR HOAGLAND, ALFONSO SOTO
SORIA AND PEDRO LEITES
Double-wall bowl
Sterling silver.
H 20 cm (8 in). W 16 cm (5½ in)
Manufacturer: Tane Orfebres, Mexico

402

403 LABBAR HOAGLAND, ALFONSO SOTO
SORIA AND PEDRO LEITES
Creamer and sugar bowl
Sterling silver.
H 7.5 cm (3 in). W 8.25 cm (3¼ in)
Manufacturer: Tane Orfebres, Mexico

403

404

404 LABBAR HOAGLAND, ALFONSO SOTO
SORIA AND PEDRO LEITES
Ice cooler
Sterling silver.
H 25.5 cm (10 in). W 17.8 cm (7 in)
Manufacturer: Tane Orfebres, Mexico

405

405 LABBAR HOAGLAND, ALFONSO SOTO
SORIA AND PEDRO LEITES
Container, *Centerpiece*
Sterling silver.
H 15 cm (6 in). D 25.5 cm (10 in)
Manufacturer: Tane Orfebres, Mexico

406 ERIK MAGNUSSEN
Jug with cover
BS plastic. The jug is sealed simply by turning the top clockwise.
H 23 cm (9 in). W 10.5 cm (3½ in)
Manufacturer: A/S Stelton, Denmark

406

■ The stainless-steel tea set and jug by Erik Magnussen is in the tradition of modern Scandinavian design: straightforward, unfussy and well-detailed. The stopper of the jug incorporates a rocking device which opens it automatically when the jug is tilted forward and closes it when the jug is upright.

407

407 ERIK MAGNUSSEN
Tea set
Stainless steel. The set includes a 1.5 litre teapot, 1 litre jug with lid, 250 c. litre creamer, 300 g sugar bowl/jam pot.
Manufacturer: A/S Stelton, Denmark

■ Cutlery must be functional, and cannot be over-designed. Even the cutlery of Hoffmann and Van de Velde, or of Mackintosh, for that matter, is surprisingly restrained. In addition, few people nowadays can afford the luxury of precious silverware and the butler to polish it. Of the various collections shown here, Andrée Putman's is the most decorative (illustration 412). The pieces have at first a traditional air, but then one notices the transparent handles. Those by Mellor (illustration 411) and by Mercatali and Pedrizzetti (illustration 408) are in the well-designed, sensible Modernist mould; while Sarpaneva's stainless-steel pieces are recognizably handsome and classic Scandinavian (illustrations 413 and 414). Though broadly Modernist, the designs by Asti (illustration 410) and Castiglioni (illustration 409) exhibit the authors' characteristic lightness of touch and wit.

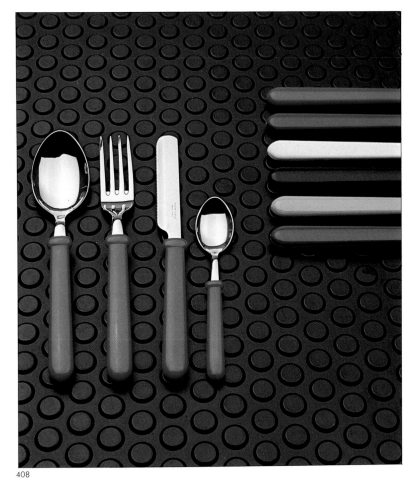

408

408 DAVIDE MERCATALI AND PAOLO PEDRIZZETTI
Cutlery, *Seltz*
Nylon and stainless steel.
Spoon L 20 cm (7½ in)
Knife L 20.8 cm (8 in)
Manufacturer: Cose Casa-Industrie Casalinghi Mori, Italy

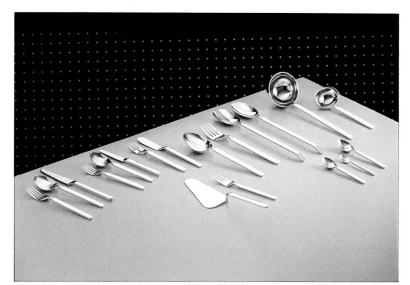

409 ACHILLE CASTIGLIONI
Cutlery, *Dry*
Produced in 18/10 stainless steel, silver-plated stainless steel and in 925/100 silver. The cutlery was awarded the XIIIth Compasso d'Oro in 1984.
Manufacturer: Alessi, Italy

409

410

411

410 SERGIO ASTI
Range of cutlery
Stainless steel.
Manufacturer: Hiromori, Japan

412

411 DAVID MELLOR
Cutlery, *Café*
Stainless steel. A robust set of everyday stainless-steel cutlery, designed ergonomically. The set consists of knife, fork, large spoon and small spoon, and is intended for large-scale production at an economical price.
Knife 20 cm (7½ in)
Large spoon 19 cm (7 in)
Fork 18.5 cm (6¾ in)
Small spoon 13.5 cm (5 in)
Manufacturer: David Mellor Design, UK

412 ANDRÉE PUTMAN
Cutlery for Siècle
France

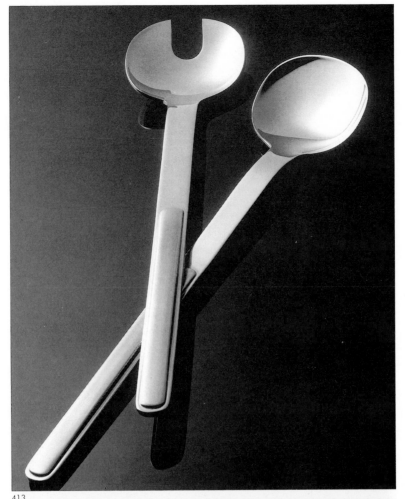

413

413 TIMO SARPANEVA
Stainless-steel salad set, *Suomi*
Manufacturer: Rosenthal, West Germany

414

414 TIMO SARPANEVA
Stainless-steel cutlery, *Suomi*
Manufacturer: Rosenthal, West Germany

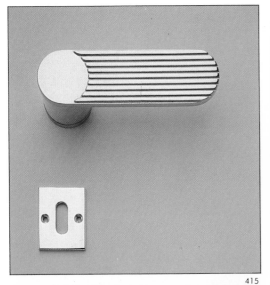

415

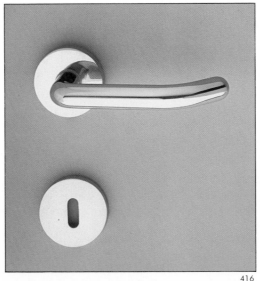

416

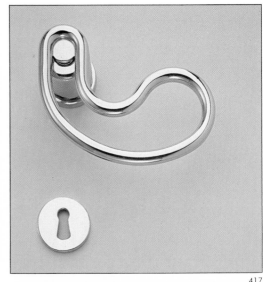

417

418

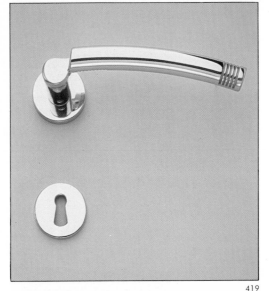

419

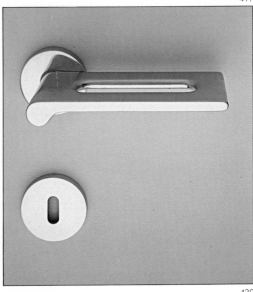

420

■ Door furniture traditionally expressed not only the character of the building with which it was associated, but invariably indicated the status or aspirations of the occupants. Modernism reduced individualism, while more recently upward mobility produced nostalgic kitsch. The Scandinavians and Italians, with their traditions of craft and eye for detail, continue to use the talents of their leading designers and architects for such incidental objects, lavishing great care on the design of a keyhole.

415 GREGOTTI ASSOCIATI
Door furniture, *Series Otto G*
Cast brass, coloured gold, black.
H 4 cm (2 in). W 15.1 cm (6 in)
Manufacturer: Fusital, Italy

416 GREGOTTI ASSOCIATI
Door furniture, *Series Due G*
Cast brass, coloured gold, red, grey, black.
H 5.2 cm (2 in). W 14.7 cm (5½ in)
Manufacturer: Fusital, Italy

417 GAE AULENTI
Door furniture, *Series Otto A*
Cast brass, coloured gold.
H 9.7 cm (3½ in). W 12.4 cm (5 in)
Manufacturer: Fusital, Italy

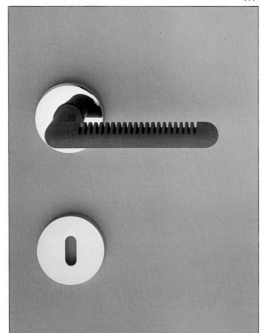

421

418 CINI BOERI
Door furniture, *Tre B*
Cast brass, coloured gold satin and black.
H 5.2 cm (2 in). W 14.3 cm (5½ in)
Manufacturer: Fusital, Italy

419 CINI BOERI
Door furniture, *Series Otto B*
Cast brass, coloured gold-nerox.
H 3.6 cm (1½ in). W 12.5 cm (5 in)
Manufacturer: Fusital, Italy

420 GAE AULENTI
Door furniture, *Series Tre A*
Cast brass, coloured gold.
H 5.2 cm (2 in). W 15.6 cm (5½ in)
Manufacturer: Fusital, Italy

421 MARCO ZANUSO
Door furniture, *Series Due Z*
Metal core with elastomer coating, coloured brick red, cement grey, ebony.
The series includes window pull, coathooks, switch-cover, key for door furniture, and furniture fittings.
H 5.2 cm (2 in). W 14 cm (5½ in)
Manufacturer: Fusital, Italy

422

423

422, 423 DAVIDE MERCATALI AND PAOLO PEDRIZZETTI
Door furniture, *Ping Pong*
Finished in polished brass; polished brass and ivory; or
amaranth red, dark green, black, or yellow, blue, red,
green, black. The range includes handles for doors and
windows, with various matching accessories.
W 7.6 cm (3 in). L 12 cm (4¾ in)
Manufacturer: Domus, Italy

424

425

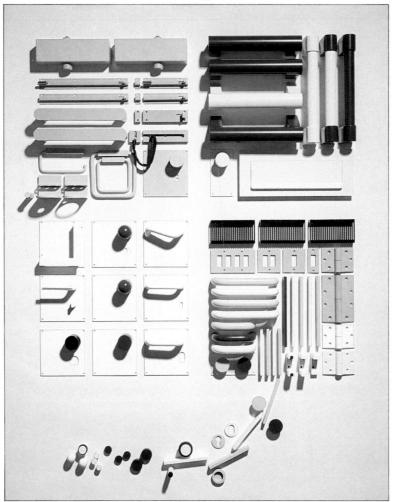

424 DAVIDE MERCATALI AND PAOLO
PEDRIZZETTI
Door furniture, *Bikini*
Nylon. Colours: black, black and white,
yellow, or red; or all-white, yellow and
red.
W 5.9 cm (2 in). L 13.3 cm (5½ in)
Manufacturer: Domus, Italy

425 DAVIDE MERCATALI AND PAOLO
PEDRIZZETTI
Door furniture, *Sfinge*
Nylon and aluminium. Colours: dull black,
red, green, yellow, white.
W 5.2 cm (2 in). L 13.6 cm (5½ in)
Manufacturer: Olivari, Italy

426 ALAN TYE DESIGN
Architectural ironmongery, *Modric Spectra*
Powder-coated aluminium or steel. Over
700 items in the range. A number of
colours can be combined as required.
Manufacturer: G & S Allgood, UK

426

REVIVALS

Reproduction furniture savours of petit-bourgeois insecurity, while facsimiles of the canonical pieces of modern furniture seem entirely respectable. Such furniture was originally made for mass-production, so goes the argument. Should we not talk about the survival — rather than the revival — of Thonet's bentwood pieces, Le Corbusier's metal furniture, or Breuer's cantilevered tubular chair? Many of William Morris' wallpapers and textiles have literally never been out of print. We should not worship — as relics — designs which were never thought of as unique works of art by those who conceived them.

Revivalism has a long history — the Romans copied Greek sculpture, Piranesi borrowed forms from the Egyptians, Schinkel took from the Greeks, Philip Webb and Burges were indebted to the Middle Ages, Norman Shaw found inspiration in vernacular and Queen Anne architecture, and a fine contemporary craftsman like Martin Grierson can nod deferentially to Hoffmann.

Why has the furniture of Hoffmann and his contemporary Mackintosh become so popular? Perhaps we have come to believe that the societies in which they lived were less frenetic than ours. But if, by association, Hoffmann and Mackintosh make us feel secure, what is our response to anti-traditionalists like Le Corbusier, Rietveld, Mallet-Stevens or Eileen Gray? Their works, though canonical, still possess the vitality and optimism of their era.

Our current revivals are not always slavishly correct in a strictly archaeological sense — an indication not of effrontery, but of confidence in our own judgment.

Reviving the designs of the Arts and Crafts period of the Modern Movement at its apogee is likely to become more widespread. We enjoy our recent history as no past era has done — we no longer require that works of art be sanctified by remoteness in time. Soon there will be, no doubt, facsimiles of Voysey's, Adolf Loos', Edgar Wood's, Riemerschmid's, George Walton's or Stickley's furniture. Two important contemporary designers have examples of work in this section — Joe Columbo, a master of ingenuity who tragically died while he still had much to accomplish, and Dieter Rams who believes that objects should be self-effacing.

There is no shortage of designers whose work lends itself to re-creation — the drawings exist, or there are the pieces themselves to copy. Let us enjoy this furniture in our own homes — if we have the mind to — instead of having to go to museums, or to look at photographs. Nostalgia, after all, is not a vice.

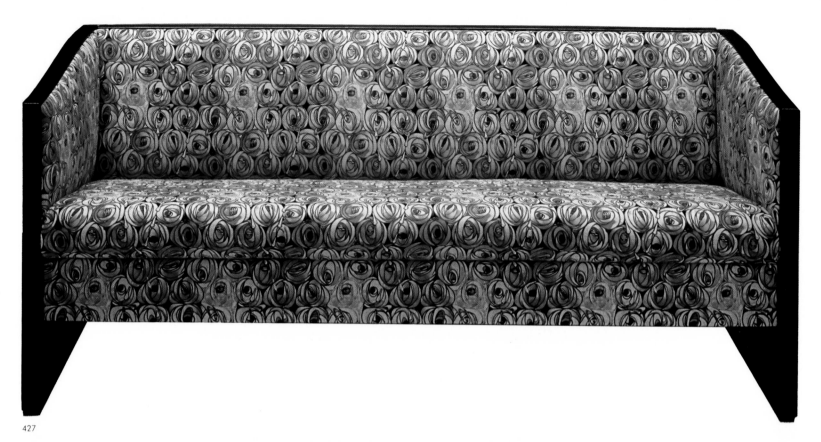

427

428

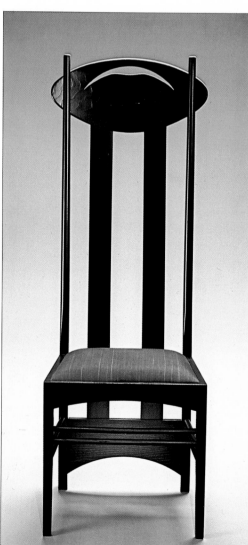

429

430

427 CHARLES RENNIE MACKINTOSH
Settee, *310 Argyle Set*
Stained walnut or ebonized ash frame. Polyurethane
foam and polyester padding. Upholstery in Mackintosh
fabric. Armchair also available. Designed in 1897.
H 70 cm (27 in). Seat H 41.5 cm (16 in). W 67 cm to 167 cm
(26 in to 65 in). D 67 cm (26 in)
Manufacturer: Cassina, Italy

428 CHARLES RENNIE MACKINTOSH
Side chair, *324 DS 3*
Ebonized ash frame inlaid with mother-of-pearl, sea grass
seat. Designed in 1918.
H 75 cm (29 in). Seat H 45 cm (17 in). W 49 cm (19 in).
D 45 cm (17 in)
Manufacturer: Cassina, Italy

429 CHARLES RENNIE MACKINTOSH
Chair, *302 Argyle*
Ebonized ash frame. Seat upholstered in
blue fabric. Designed in 1897.
H 136 cm (53 in). W 48 cm (18 in).
D 45.8 cm (17 in)
Manufacturer: Cassina, Italy

430 CHARLES RENNIE MACKINTOSH
Chair, *325 DS 4*
Ebonized ash frame with mother-of-pearl
inlaid. Sea grass seat. Designed in 1918.
H 75 cm (29 in). Seat H 45 cm (17 in).
W 52 cm (20 in).
D 45 cm (17 in)
Manufacturer: Cassina, Italy

431

432

431 CHARLES RENNIE MACKINTOSH
Table, *322 DS 1*
Ebonized ash frame, top folding on two
sides. Designed in 1918.
H 75 cm (29 in). W 125 cm (49 in). L 57 cm
to 177 cm (22 in to 69 in)
Manufacturer: Cassina, Italy

432 CHARLES RENNIE MACKINTOSH
Table, *304*
Ebonized ash or stained-walnut frame.
Veneered top with similar finish. Top has a
revolving central part with a diameter of
110 cm (43 in) that can be adjusted by
3 cm (1½ in) in height with a lever.
H 74 cm (29 in). D 190 cm (74 in)
Manufacturer: Cassina, Italy

433 CHARLES RENNIE MACKINTOSH
Ladderback chair, *292 Hill House 1*
Ebonized ash frame. Seat upholstered in
green or pink fabric. Designed in 1902.
H 141 cm (55 in). W 41 cm (16 in). D 39 cm
(15 in)
Manufacturer: Cassina, Italy

433

434 CHARLES RENNIE MACKINTOSH
Curved lattice back chair, *312 Willow 1*
Ebonized ash frame. Seat cushion
upholstered in green or beige fabric.
Designed in 1904.
H 119 cm (46 in). W 94 cm (37 in). D 41 cm
(16 in)
Manufacturer: Cassina, Italy

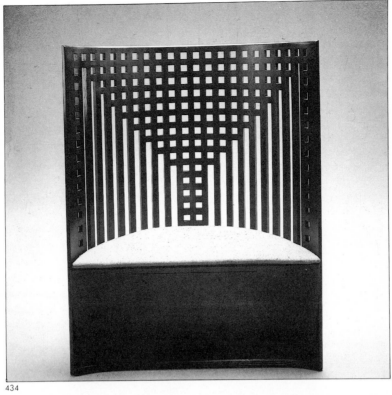

434

435 CHARLES RENNIE MACKINTOSH
Chair, *305 Ingram High*
High back, solid ash, ebony finish or
stained ash. Padding of the cushion is
polyurethane foam and polyester
padding. Upholstered in black/blue fabric.
Designed in 1900.
H 150.5 cm (59 in). Seat H 45 cm (17 in).
W 47 cm (18 in). D 44.5 cm (17 in)
Manufacturer: Cassina, Italy

436 CHARLES RENNIE MACKINTOSH
Chair, *306 Ingram Low*
Solid ash, ebony finish, or stained ash.
Padding of the cushion is polyurethane
foam and polyester padding. Upholstery
in exclusive fabric available in black/blue.
Designed in 1900.
H 106 cm (41 in). Seat H 45 cm (17 in).
W 47 cm (18 in). D 44.5 cm (17 in)
Manufacturer: Cassina, Italy

435

436

437

438

439

440

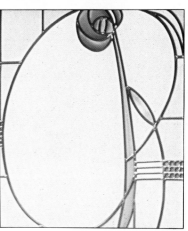

441

437 CHARLES RENNIE MACKINTOSH
Sideboard, *327 DS 5*
Ebonized ash frame. Enamelled-glass
mosaic decoration, bound with lead and
inlaid with mother-of-pearl. Designed in
1918.
H 151 cm (59 in). W 163 cm (64 in). D top
25 cm (9 in); base 57 cm (22 in)
Manufacturer: Cassina, Italy

438, 441 CHARLES RENNIE MACKINTOSH
Sideboard, *328 Sideboard 2*
Ebonized ash or stained ash. Enamelled-
glass mosaic decoration, bound with lead.
Doors with pink-glass square decorations.
Drawers with handles inlaid with mother-
of-pearl. Writing top which can be pulled
out. Designed in 1918.
H 160 cm (63 in). W 170 cm (66 in).
D 50 cm (19 in)
Manufacturer: Cassina, Italy

439 CHARLES RENNIE MACKINTOSH
Table, *323 DS 2*
Ebonized ash frame. Designed in 1918.
H 75 cm (29 in). 75 cm square (29 in)
Manufacturer: Cassina, Italy

440 CHARLES RENNIE MACKINTOSH
Side chair, *326 Willow 2*
Ebonized ash frame. Sea grass seat.
Designed in 1904.
H 104 cm (41 in). W 42 cm (16 in). D 39 cm
(15 in).
Manufacturer: Cassina, Italy

442

443

444

445

446

447

448

442 LUDWIG LOBMEYR
Glasses and decanter, *Tableset No 4*
Hand-blown clear crystal. In production since 1856.
Decanter H 30 cm (11 in)
Globe W 14 cm (5½ in)
Manufacturer: J. and L. Lobmeyr, Austria

443 JOSEF HOFFMANN
Glasses, *Tableset No 273, Hoffmann*
Hand-blown crystal, hand-cut base. Designed just before
Hoffmann's death in 1956 for Lobmeyr's participation at
the 1957 Triennale, Milan.
Beerglass H 22 cm (9 in). D 6.6 cm (2½ in)
Manufacturer: J. and L. Lobmeyr, Austria

444 OSWALD HAERDTL
Glasses and decanter, *Tableset No 257, The Commodore*
Hand-blown muslinglass. Designed for the 1951
Triennale, Milan, and in production ever since.
Decanter H 28.5 cm (11 in). D 10.2 cm (4 in)
Manufacturer: J. and L. Lobmeyr, Austria

445 JOSEF HOFFMANN, HANS RATH,
OSKAR STRNAD AND STEFAN RATH
Hand-blown muslinglass. From left to right:
Vase by Hoffmann designed in 1925
Vase by Strnad
Vase by Rath designed in 1930
Manufacturer: J. and L. Lobmeyr, Austria

446 ADOLF LOOS
Glasses and water pitcher, *Tableset No 248, Loos*
Hand-blown crystal with hand-cut base. Originally
designed for the Loos Bar in Vienna, the set has been in
production since 1931.
Water pitcher H 24 cm (9 in). Base D 9.7 cm (3½ in)
Manufacturer: J. and L. Lobmeyr, Austria

447 JOSEF HOFFMANN
Glasses and decanter, *Tableset No 238, The Patrician*
Thin hand-blown muslinglass. In production since 1920.
Decanter H 34 cm (13 in). W 9.8 cm (3½ in)
Manufacturer: J. and L. Lobmeyr, Austria

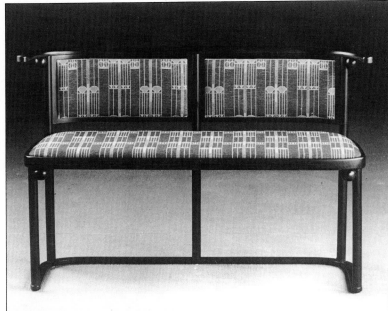

449

450

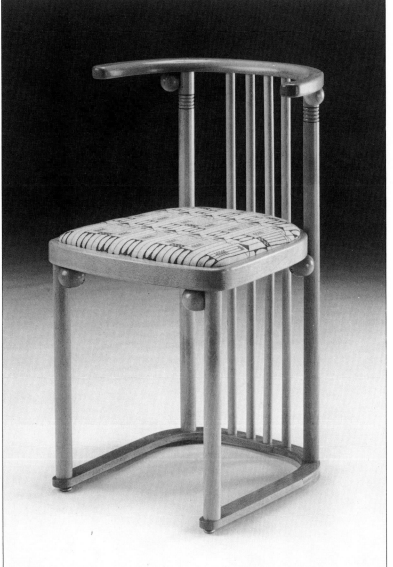

449 JOSEF HOFFMANN
Bench, *Fledermaus*
Bentwood elements. Used by Hoffmann for Cabaret Fledermaus. Upholstered seat. Spherical stiffening of the construction is characteristic. Wooden parts can be natural beech, stained mahogany, or varnished on request. Designed in 1909.
H 74 cm (29 in). D 46 cm (18 in). W 121 cm (47 in)
Manufacturer: Franz Wittmann, Austria

448 OSWALD HAERDTL
Set of glasses and decanter, *Tableset 240, The Ambassador*
Hand-blown muslinglass, very thin. In production since 1925 and in the permanent collection of New York's Museum of Modern Art.
Decanter H 28.7 cm (11 in)
Globe W 12.4 cm (5 in)
Manufacturer: J. and L. Lobmeyr, Austria

450 JOSEF HOFFMANN
Bench, *Fledermaus*
Construction as bench in illustration 449, but with upholstered back.
H 74 cm (29 in). D 46 cm (18 in). W 121 cm (47 in)
Manufacturer: Franz Wittmann, Austria

451 JOSEF HOFFMANN
Chair, *Fledermaus*
Construction as bench in illustration 449.
H 74 cm (29 in). D 46 cm (18 in). W approx. 50 cm (19 in)
Manufacturer: Franz Wittmann, Austria

451

452 JOSEF HOFFMANN
Armchair, *Cabinett*
Rectilinear wooden frame, stained dark;
textile covering by Kolo Moser. The chair
was part of Hoffmann's design for an
apartment; its frame is characteristic of his
chair designs at this time.
H 77 cm (30 in). D 68 cm (26 in). L 68 cm
(26 in)
Manufacturer: Franz Wittmann, Austria

452

453, 454 JOSEF HOFFMANN
Dining-room chair, *Armlöffel*
Made of limed ash, stained black with
loose seat cushion. In 1908 Hoffmann
designed variations of the chair for various
apartments. Characteristic are the armrests
shaped like spoons. A loose seat cushion
in leather is available.
H 96 cm (37 in). D 51 cm (20 in). L 66 cm
(26 in)
Manufacturer: Franz Wittmann, Austria

453

454

455 OTTO BLÜMEL
Chair, *Garmisch*
Frame of lacquered or natural ash.
Upholstered seat in
leather or fabric. Designed in 1911.
H 70 cm (27 in). Seat H 44 cm
Manufacturer: Aram Designs, UK

455

456 BRUNO PAUL
Table, *Washington*
Black granite base. Frame and top, gloss
lacquer finish in dark grey. Top
extendable. Designed in 1908.
H 72 cm (28 in). Top from 140 cm ×
190 cm (55 in × 74 in)
Manufacturer: Aram Designs, UK

456

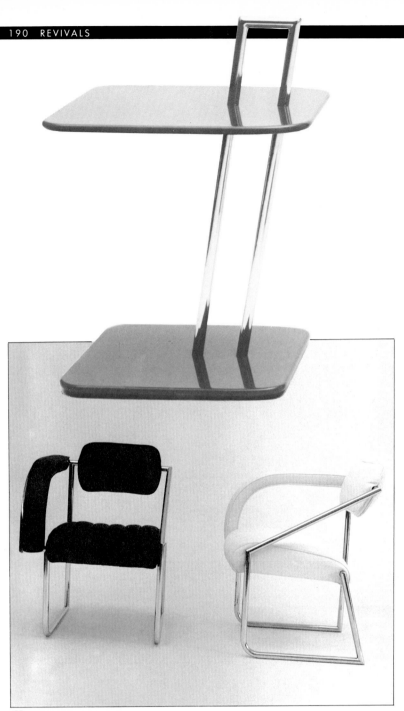

458 EILEEN GRAY
Chair, *Non Conformist*
Polished chromium-plated tubular steel
base. Fully upholstered seat, back and
armrest. Covered in aniline leather.
Designed in 1926.
H 78 cm (30 in). Seat H 45 cm (17 in)
Manufacturer: Aram Designs, UK

457

457 EILEEN GRAY
Occasional table
Polished chromium-plated tubular steel
base. Top gloss lacquer finish in black,
grey, red, white or ivory.
Round version: H 56 cm (22 in). D 40 cm
(15 in). Base D 36 cm (14 in)
Rectangular version: top H 56 cm (22 in).
36 cm × 40 cm (14 in × 15 in). Base 33 cm
× 36 cm (13¾ in × 14 in)
Manufacturer: Aram Designs, UK

458

459 EILEEN GRAY
Day Bed
Polished chromium-plated tubular steel
base. Support box and mattress covered
in leather or fabric.
H 61 cm (24 in). Seat H 33 cm (13 in).
L 190 cm (74 in). D 86 cm (33 in)
Manufacturer: Aram Designs, UK

459

460

461

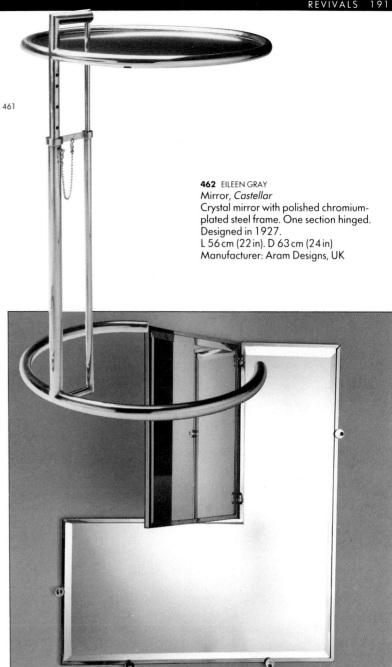

462 EILEEN GRAY
Mirror, *Castellar*
Crystal mirror with polished chromium-plated steel frame. One section hinged.
Designed in 1927.
L 56 cm (22 in). D 63 cm (24 in)
Manufacturer: Aram Designs, UK

462

460, 461 EILEEN GRAY
Adjustable table, *E 1027*
Polished chromium-plated tubular steel frame. Top polished plate glass clear or grey. Top adjustable to various heights. Designed in 1927. Part of the permanent collection of the Museum of Modern Art, New York.
H 64 cm to 90 cm (25 in to 33 in). D 51 cm (20 in)
Manufacturer: Aram Designs, UK

463 EILEEN GRAY
Tables, *Menton*
Polished chromium-plated tubular steel frame. Two heights. Pivoting top. Surface linoleum black/grey, beech edged. Designed in 1932.
High version: H 65 cm (25 in). L 126 cm (49 in). D 56 cm (21 in)
Low version: H 43 cm (16 in). L 126 cm (49 in). D 56 cm (21 in)
Manufacturer: Aram Designs, UK

463

464 EILEEN GRAY
Armchair, *Bibendum*
Polished chromium-plated tubular steel base. Fully upholstered seat, back and armrests, covered in aniline leather or fabric. Designed in 1929.
H 73 cm (28 in). Seat H 41 cm (16 in).
L 90 cm (35 in). D 83 cm (32 in)
Manufacturer: Aram Designs, UK

465 EILEEN GRAY
Sofa, *Lota*
Fully upholstered back and support and base on turned feet with four feather-filled loose cushions and seat mattress, back cushions with cross stitching, all covered in aniline leather or fabric. Two box units on castors detachable from sofa ends, finished in gloss polyurethane lacquer – front and back black, top and sides in contrasting colour. Designed in 1924. H 68 cm (26 in).
Seat H 42 cm (16 in). D 87 cm (34 in).
L 240 cm (94 in)
Manufacturer: Aram Designs, UK

464

465

466 EILEEN GRAY
Dressing table
Designed in 1932 for La Maison de
Castellar

466

467 EILEEN GRAY
Carpet, *Black Magic*
Designed in 1923 for the Salon des
Artistes et Décorateurs

467

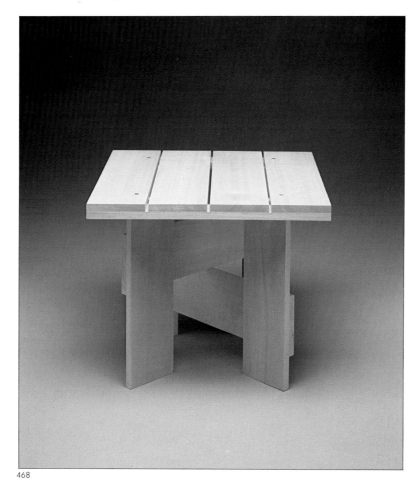

468

468 GERRIT T. RIETVELD
Low table, *Crate 2*
Solid unfinished beech. Designed in 1934.
H 46 cm (18 in). W 60 cm (23 in). L 60 cm (23 in)
Manufacturer: Cassina, Italy

469 GERRIT T. RIETVELD
Chair, *Zig-Zag*
Unfinished or finished elm. Designed in
1934.
H 74 cm (29 in). Seat H 43 cm (16 in).
W 37 cm (14 in). L 43 cm (16 in)
Manufacturer: Cassina, Italy

469

470 GERRIT T. RIETVELD
Table, *284 Crate 4*
Solid unfinished beechwood frame.
Unfinished beechwood top.
H 70 cm (27 in). W 76 cm (29 in). L 175 cm
(68 in)
Manufacturer: Cassina, Italy

470

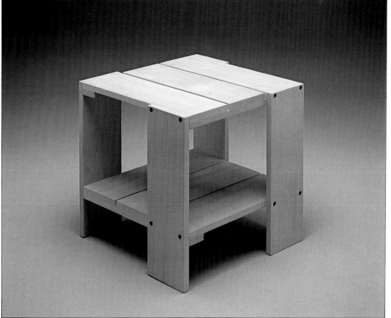

471 GERRIT T. RIETVELD
Low table, *Crate 6*
Solid unfinished beech. Designed in 1934.
H 45 cm (17 in). W 48 cm (18 in). L 48 cm
(18 in).
Manufacturer: Cassina, Italy

471

472

473

472, 473 GERRIT T. RIETVELD
Chair, *Red and Blue*
Beechwood frame, black and yellow
aniline finish. Seat, blue lacquer finish.
Back, red lacquer finish. Designed in
1918.
H 88 cm (34 in). Seat H 33 cm (12 in).
W 65.5 cm (26 in). L 83 cm (32 in)
Manufacturer: Cassina, Italy

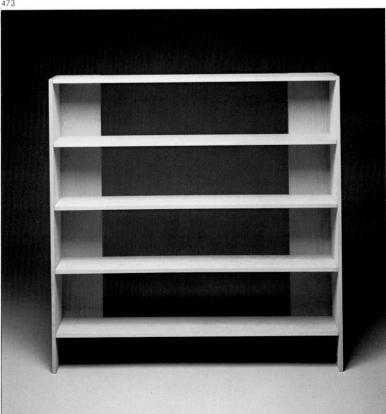

474

474 GERRIT T. RIETVELD
Bookcase, *Crate 3*
Unfinished beech. Designed in 1934.
H 124 cm (48 in). W 22 cm (8 in). L 127 cm
(50 in)
Manufacturer: Cassina, Italy

475

475 GERRIT T. RIETVELD
Table, *Schroeder 1*
In lacquered wood, available in red, white
and black. Designed in 1923.
H 60.5 cm (24 in). W 50 cm (19 in).
L 51.5 cm (20 in)
Manufacturer: Cassina, Italy

476

476 GERRIT T. RIETVELD
Chair, *Crate 1*
Solid, unfinished beechwood, available
with or without cushion upholstered in
special fabric. Designed in 1934.
H 62 cm (24 in). Seat H 28 cm (11 in).
W 56 cm (22 in). L 70 cm (27 in)
Manufacturer: Cassina, Italy

477

478

479

477–479 LE CORBUSIER, PIERRE JEANNERET AND CHARLOTTE
PERRIAND
Table, *LC6*
Matt black, light blue or bicoloured enamelled steel base.
Base has four supporting points with steel threaded shanks,
permitting height adjustment up to 5 cm (2 in). Glass,
natural or ebonized ash top. Designed 1925–9.
H 74 cm (29 in). W 85 cm (33 in). L 225 cm (88 in)
Manufacturer: Cassina, Italy

480

480 LE CORBUSIER, PIERRE JEANNERET AND
CHARLOTTE PERRIAND
Armchair and sofas, *LC3*
Polished chrome-plated or glossy basalt,
grey, light blue, green, bordeaux and
ochre, or matt-black enamel steel frame.
Loose cushions with polyurethane and
polyester padding. Leather and fabric
upholstery. Designed 1925–9.
H 62 cm (24 in). W 73 cm (28 in). L 99 cm
to 168 cm (39 in to 66 in).
Manufacturer: Cassina, Italy

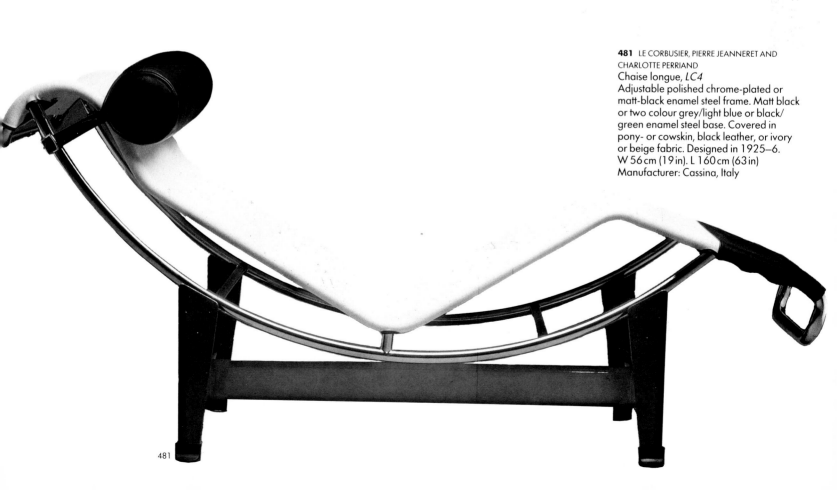

481

481 LE CORBUSIER, PIERRE JEANNERET AND
CHARLOTTE PERRIAND
Chaise longue, *LC4*
Adjustable polished chrome-plated or
matt-black enamel steel frame. Matt black
or two colour grey/light blue or black/
green enamel steel base. Covered in
pony- or cowskin, black leather, or ivory
or beige fabric. Designed in 1925–6.
W 56 cm (19 in). L 160 cm (63 in)
Manufacturer: Cassina, Italy

482 LE CORBUSIER, PIERRE JEANNERET AND
CHARLOTTE PERRIAND
Bathroom stool, *LC9*
Polished chrome-plated steel frame. Seat
with removable beige towelling. Designed
1925–9.
H 45 cm (17 in). W 36 cm (14 in). L 50 cm
(19 in)
Manufacturer: Cassina, Italy

483 LE CORBUSIER, PIERRE JEANNERET AND
CHARLOTTE PERRIAND
Armchair and sofa, *LC2*
Polished chrome-plated or glossy basalt,
grey, light blue, green, bordeaux and
ochre, or matt-black enamel steel frame.
Loose cushions with polyurethane and
polyester padding. Leather and fabric
upholstery. Designed 1925–9.
H 67 cm (26 in). W 70 cm (27 in). L 76 cm to
180 cm (29 in to 70 in)
Manufacturer: Cassina, Italy

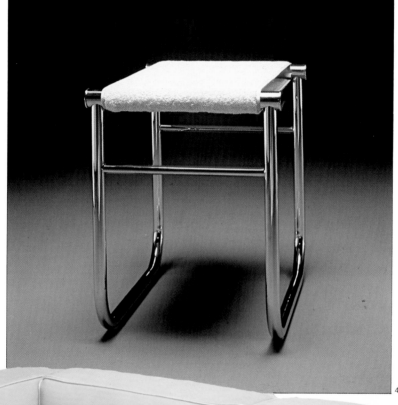

482

483

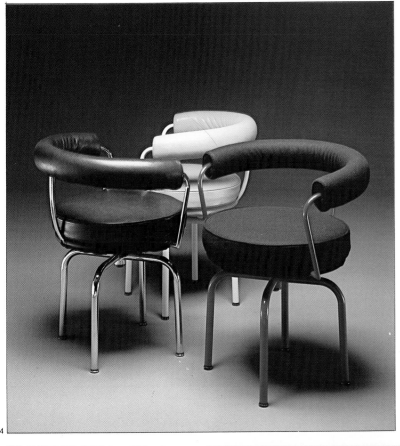

84

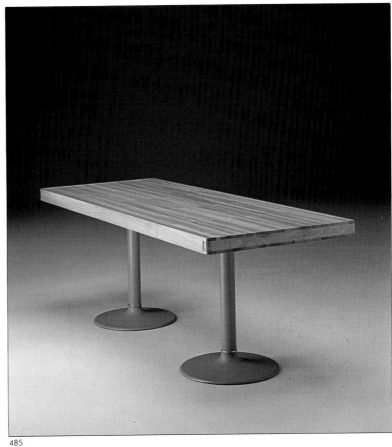

485

484 LE CORBUSIER, PIERRE JEANNERET AND
CHARLOTTE PERRIAND
Small revolving armchair, *LC7*
Polished chrome-plated or glossy basalt,
grey, light blue, green, bordeaux and
ochre, or matt-black enamel steel frame.
Two versions with four or five legs. Back
and seat cushion padded with
polyurethane, leather and fabric
upholstery. Designed 1925–9.
H 73 cm (28 in). Seat H 50 cm (19 in).
W 60 cm (35 in). D 58 cm (34 in)
Manufacturer: Cassina, Italy

485 LE CORBUSIER, PIERRE JEANNERET AND
CHARLOTTE PERRIAND
Table, *LC11-P*
Grey enamel cast-iron base with top in
walnut or fir-wood, natural finish.
Designed in 1934.
H 72 cm (28 in). W 80 cm (31 in). L 220 cm
(86 in)
Manufacturer: Cassina, Italy

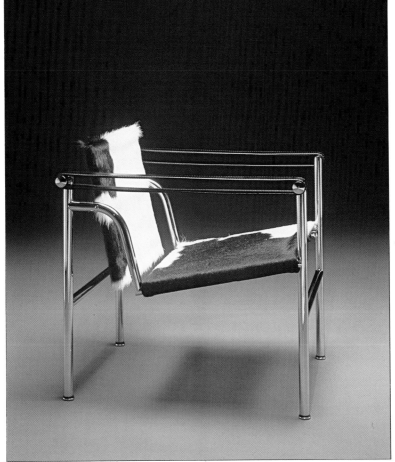

486

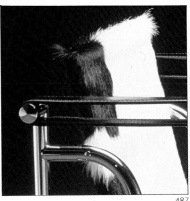

487

486, 487 LE CORBUSIER, PIERRE JEANNERET
AND CHARLOTTE PERRIAND
Sling chair, *LC1*
Polished chrome-plated or matt-black
enamel steel frame. Seat back: of pony-
or cowskin; Russian red leather, black
leather or beige fabric. Designed 1925–9.
H 64 cm (25 in). Seat H 40 cm (15 in).
W 60 cm (23 in). L 65 cm (25 in)
Manufacturer: Cassina, Italy

488

488 LE CORBUSIER, PIERRE JEANNERET AND
CHARLOTTE PERRIAND
Revolving stool, *LC8*
Polished chrome-plated or glossy basalt, grey, light blue,
green, bordeaux and ochre, or matt-black enamel steel
frame. Polyurethane padding. Leather and fabric
upholstery. Designed 1925–9.
H 50 cm (19 in). W 47 cm (18 in)
Manufacturer: Cassina, Italy

489 LE CORBUSIER, PIERRE JEANNERET AND
CHARLOTTE PERRIAND
Tables and low tables, *LC10–P*
Square and rectangular with polished-chrome steel legs
and steel frame enamelled in matt black or glossy basalt,
grey, light blue, green, bordeaux or ochre. Crystal tops.
Designed in 1928.
H 33 cm to 69.8 cm (13 in to 27 in). L 69.8 cm to 139.7 cm
(27 in to 54 in)
Manufacturer: Cassina, Italy

490 LE CORBUSIER, PIERRE JEANNERET AND
CHARLOTTE PERRIAND
Cabinets, *LC/Casiers Standard*
Ash-stained walnut or available in black,
blue, ochre, green, grey or bordeaux
finish with solid wood edges. Designed in
1925.
Modular units H 75 cm (29 in). W 37.5 to
112.5 cm (14 in to 44 in). D 37.5 cm to
75 cm (14 in to 29 in)
Manufacturer: Cassina, Italy

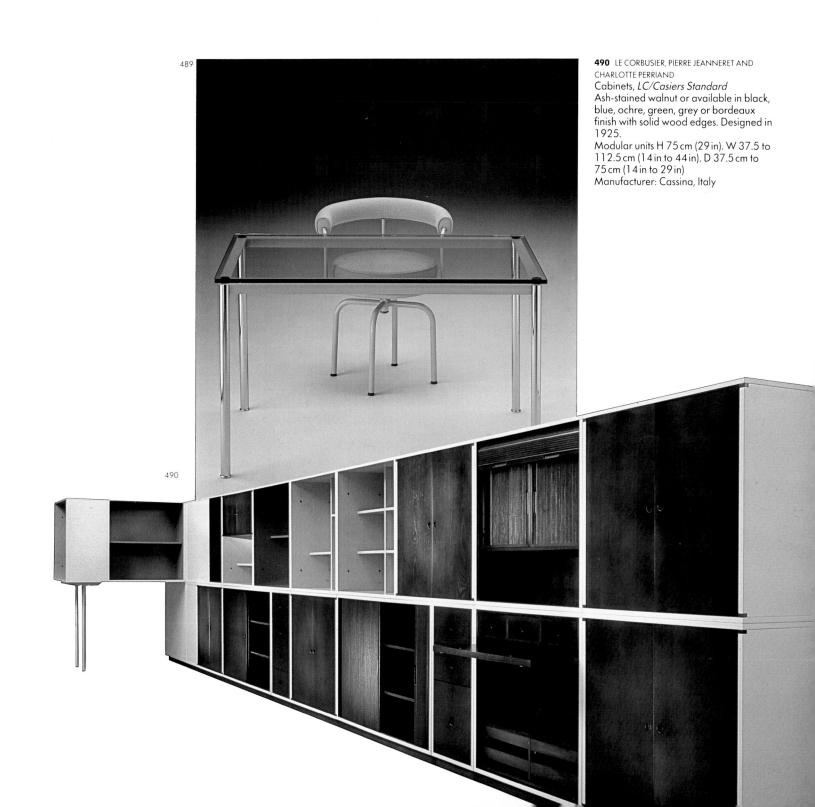

489

490

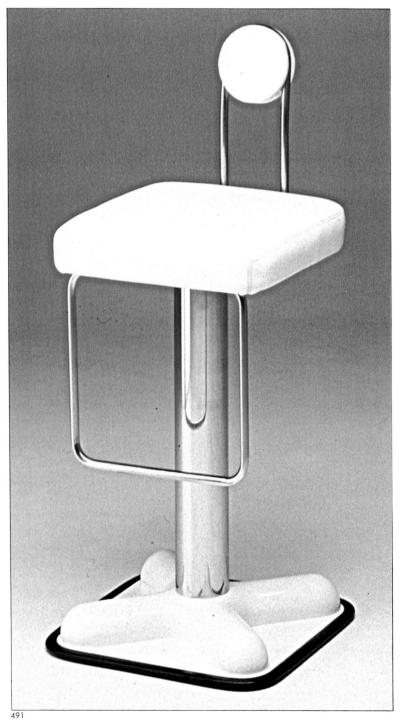

491

492

491 JOE COLOMBO
Bar stool, *Birillo*
Stem of stainless steel, fibreglass base, coloured white or black. Seat and back upholstered and covered with Vistram or leather. Produced in 1972, the stool has become a classic and was awarded the gold medal at its presentation in 1972 at the MIA international exhibition.
H 107 cm (42 in). Seat H 77 cm (30 in).
W 47 cm (18 in).
D 47 cm (18 in)
Manufacturer: Kartell, Italy

492 GIUSEPPE TERRAGNI
Chair, *Lariana*
Stainless steel structure. Seat and back of bent plywood, natural or black stained. Designed in 1936, it was made for the Casa del Fascio in Como and used in the Sant'Elia nursery school. It is part of the permanent collection of New York's Museum of Modern Art and London's Victoria and Albert Museum.
H 79 cm (31 in). Seat H 43 cm (16 in).
W 42 cm (16 in). D 56 cm (22 in)
Manufacturer: Zanotta, Italy

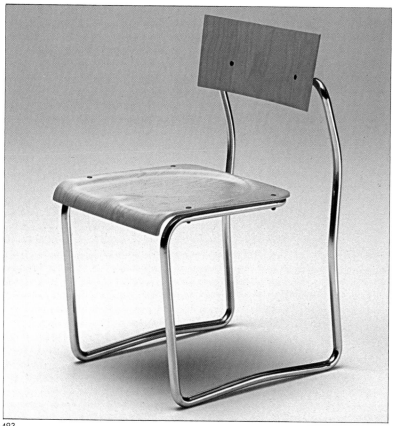

493

493 GIUSEPPE TERRAGNI
Chair, *Follia*
Solid wood, black lacquered. Back
supports of stainless steel. Designed by
Terragni between 1935 and 1936 for the
Casa del Fascio of Como, and not put into
production until 1972. Numbered and
signed, it is part of New York's Museum of
Modern Art's permanent collection.
H 80 cm (31 in). Seat H 38 cm (15 in).
W 50 cm (19 in). D 50 cm (19 in)
Manufacturer: Zanotta, Italy

494

494 GIUSEPPE TERRAGNI
Armchair, *Sant'Elia*
Frame of stainless steel, back and seat
upholstered and covered with leather.
Designed in 1936.
H 79 cm (31 in). Seat H 41 cm (16 in).
W 55 cm (21 in). D 68 cm (26 in)
Manufacturer: Zanotta, Italy

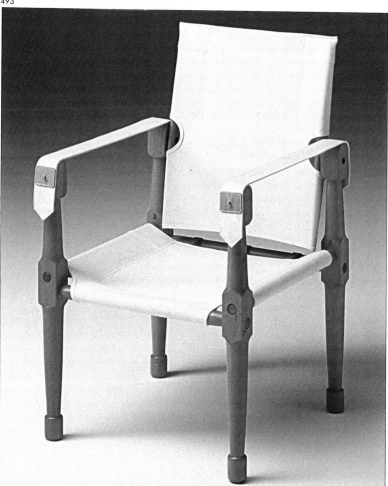

495

495 B. MARSTALLER
Demountable armchair with supple joints,
Morettina
Kiln-dried beech, natural colour.
Removable covering of Canapone or Tela
Strong. Tilts back. Designed in 1917.
H 88 cm (34 in). Seat H 37 cm (14 in).
W 56 cm (22 in). D 56 cm (22 in)
Manufacturer: Zanotta, Italy

496 ILMARI TAPIOVAARA
Stacking chair, *Tapiola*
Structure of fire-lacquered steel, black,
anthracite, pearl white or red rust. Seat
and back of beech plywood, natural or
black stained. Armrests of pressed ABS,
black. The chair has won six gold medals,
awarded on presentation at IX Triennale
of Milan, Helsinki, Chicago, Stockholm,
Paris and Buenos Aires. Designed in 1949.
H 76 cm (29 in). Seat H 46 cm (18 in).
W 54 cm (21 in). D 51 cm (20 in)
Manufacturer: Zanotta, Italy

497 MARCO ZANUSO
Chaise longue, *Maggiolina*
Frame of stainless steel, sling and armrests
of black or white cowhide. Cushions of
down in sections. Covered in leather,
coloured black or white. Designed in
1947, *Maggiolina* won the gold medal at
the 1948 Triennale in Milan.
Chaise longue H 82 cm (32 in). Seat
H 40 cm (15 in). W 71 cm (28 in).
D 102 cm (40 in)
Manufacturer: Zanotta, Italy

496

497

498

498 HANS CORAY
Stacking chair, *Landa*
Structure of fire-lacquered steel, black, anthracite, pearl white or red rust. Seat and back with or without holes, of bent beech plywood, natural or white lacquered. Designed in 1952. H 80 cm (31 in). Seat H 44 cm (17 in). W 48 cm (18 in). D 51 cm (20 in)
Manufacturer: Zanotta, Italy

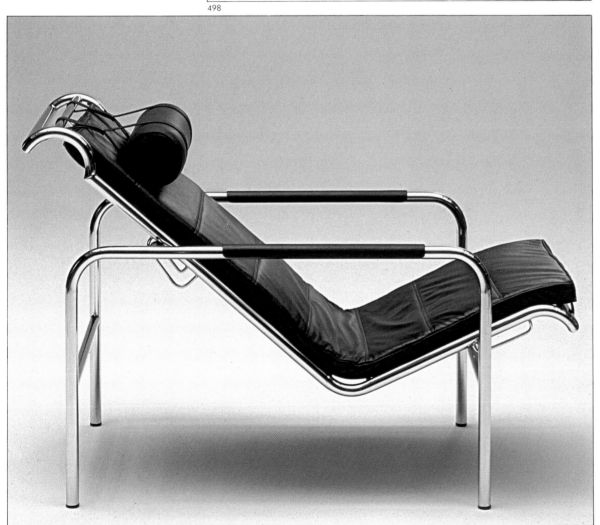

499

499, 500 GABRIELE MUCCHI
Chaise longue, *Genni*
Frame of chromium-plated steel or fire lacquered, colour pink-white. On steel springs. Cushion and headrest of polyurethane, removable. Covering of fabric or leather, removable. Designed in 1935.
H 76 cm (29 in). Seat H 41 cm (16 in). W 57 cm (22 in). D 109 cm (42 in)
Manufacturer: Zanotta, Italy

500

501 ALVAR AALTO
Trolley, *900*
Black or white tiled top, rattan basket.
H 56 cm (22 in). W 50 cm (19 in). L 90 cm
(35 in)
Manufacturer: Artek, Finland

501

502

502 ALVAR AALTO
Children's table, *4–905*
Top can be inlaid linoleum, white laminate
or ash or birch veneer. It has two semi-
circular leaves.
H 71 cm (28 in). W 120 cm to 220 cm
(47 in to 86 in)
Manufacturer: Artek, Finland

503

503 ALVAR AALTO
Reclining armchair, *41*
Seat lacquered black or white.
H 64 cm (25 in). Seat H 33 cm (13 in)
Manufacturer: Artek, Finland

504 ALVAR AALTO
Armchair, *46*
Covered with raffia, woollen fabric, PVC
Arelan, black, brown or natural leather.
H 75 cm (29 in). Seat H 43 cm (16 in).
L 65 cm (25 in). W 60 cm (23 in)
Manufacturer: Artek, Finland

504

505, 506   ALVAR AALTO
Armchair, *45*
Seat and back in linen webbing, natural rattan, natural
leather; or back in quilted canvas, vinyl, leather.
H 80 cm (31 in). Seat H 42 cm (16 in)
Manufacturer: Artek, Finland

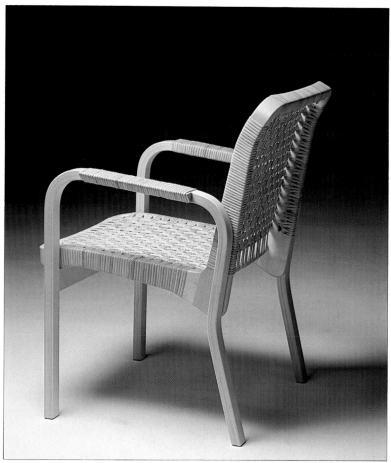

505

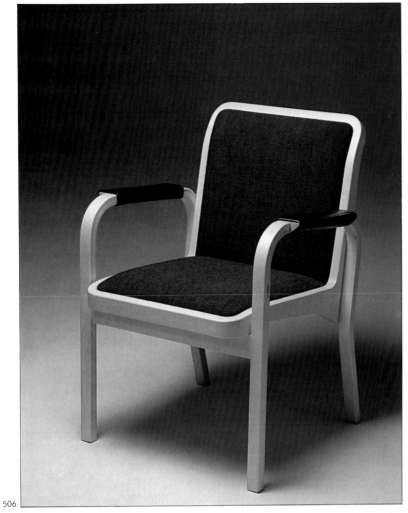

506

507

508

507 ALVAR AALTO
Cantilevered armchair, *402*
Upholstered and covered with woollen
fabric, raffia, linen canvas, black or brown
leather.
H 72.5 cm (28 in). Seat H 40 cm (15 in).
W 61 cm (24 in)
Manufacturer: Artek, Finland

508 ALVAR AALTO
Benches, *153A* and *153B*
Bent and laminated birch.
H 44 cm (17 in). W 40 cm (15 in).
L 72.5 cm or 112.5 cm (28 in or 44 in)
Manufacturer: Artek, Finland

509

509 ALVAR AALTO
Cantilevered armchair, *406*
Bent and laminated birch. Seat and back
in linen webbing, natural rattan, quilted
canvas, quilted PVC Arelan, quilted black
or brown leather, quilted natural leather.
H 84 cm (32 in). Seat H 36 cm (14 in).
W 60 cm (23 in). L 72 cm (28 in)
Manufacturer: Artek, Finland

510

510 ALVAR AALTO
Standard lamp, *A805*
Laminated birch.
H 174 cm (68 in). D 52 cm (20 in)
Manufacturer: Artek, Finland

511 RENZO FRAU
Armchair and sofa, *Vanity Fair*
Structure in naturally seasoned beech,
seat and backrest with biconical springs
on jute straps. Padding in vegetable and
rubber horsehair. Goose feather cushions.
Designed in 1930.
Armchair H 96 cm (37 in). D 91 cm (35 in).
L 94 cm (37 in)
Sofa H 99 cm (39 in). D 91 cm (35 in).
L 145 cm (57 in)
Manufacturer: Poltrona Frau, Italy

511

512

513

512, 513 DIETER RAMS
606 Universal Shelving System
One of his most famous designs for the home, it comprises shelving, bookcases and versatile containers. It was designed in 1960 for Vitsoe and has since become a classic. The uprights of extruded aluminium can be fixed to the floor and ceiling or to the walls. Shelves, containers and drawers are of wood and aluminium and colours are black and white. Sparely designed and precise, the system is characteristic of Rams' furniture designs for Vitsoe. Presented in 1984 as part of the De Padova Collection, Italy.

514 ROBERT MALLET-STEVENS
Sling back reclining chair
Designed in 1927.

514

515 ROBERT MALLET-STEVENS
Chair
Designed in 1930.

515

516 MICHEL DUFET
Chair
Metal frame and webbing.
Designed in 1930.

516

517

518

519

520

517 WILLIAM MORRIS
Wallpaper, *Willow Bough*
Hand-printed.
Manufacturer: Arthur Sanderson and
Sons, UK

518 WILLIAM MORRIS
Wallpaper, *Granville*
Hand-printed
Manufacturer: Arthur Sanderson and
Sons, UK

519 WILLIAM MORRIS
Wallpaper, *Blackberry*
Hand-printed
Manufacturer: Arthur Sanderson and
Sons, UK

520 WILLIAM MORRIS
Wallpaper, *Indian*
Hand-printed
Manufacturer: Arthur Sanderson and
Sons, UK

BIOGRAPHIES

SUPPLIERS

BIBLIOGRAPHY

BIOGRAPHIES

The figures following each entry refer to the illustrations in which the designer's work is represented.

ALVAR AALTO was born in Finland in 1898. He studied in Helsinki, and opened his own office in 1923. He founded the Artek firm in 1935, and was Professor at the Institute of Technology, Massachusetts from 1940 to 1949. His work has been widely exhibited and published. *(501–10)*

MARGARETA ABERG was born in Stockholm, Sweden in 1929. She studied interior architecture and furniture design at the Konstfack School in Stockholm, and in 1956 opened an architecture studio with her husband Rolf Aberg. She and her husband specialize in interior architecture, and have designed hotels, schools and hospitals. Most recently, they designed the Bracke Osterjard Hospital for handicapped children in Gothenburg, Sweden. *(131)*

HELEN ABSON was born in Melbourne, Australia in 1942. She graduated with a degree in architecture from Melbourne University in 1965 and for five years practised architecture. She established ZAB Design P/L in 1972. Since then she has designed all ZAB furnishing fabrics and is responsible for the printing and marketing of all ZAB designs. *(330–2)*

AD.SA is a design group working in France. *(16)*

ANNELI AIRIKKA-LAMMI was born in 1944 and attended Finland's University of Industrial Arts from 1963 to 1967. She was named Finland's textile artist of the year in 1982, and her textile designs have been represented in numerous exhibitions, including four one-man shows. *(333)*

EMILIO AMBASZ was born in Argentina in 1943 and studied architecture at Princeton University, where he obtained his Master's degree and later taught. He was Curator of Design at the Museum of Modern Art, New York, from 1970 to 1976, and co-founder of the Institute for Architecture and Urban Studies, New York. He has lectured and written widely and is currently President of the Architecture League. He has been commissioned to design buildings in Europe and the USA. He holds a number of industrial and mechanical design patents, and has received many prizes for his work, including the Compasso d'Oro in 1981. *(222–4, 239)*

CHRISTINA ANDERSSON was born in Sweden in 1948. She studied design and interior architecture in Copenhagen, receiving her diploma in 1971. She and her husband LARS ANDERSSON have their own design office in Sweden, where they specialize in furniture and boat design. *(59)*

LARS ANDERSSON was born in Sweden in 1946. He studied design and interior architecture in Copenhagen and practised different types of interior design after graduation. *See also* CHRISTINA ANDERSSON. *(59)*

HANS ANSEMS, born in 1951, is a Dutch designer. He has worked in the Netherlands, France and Italy. Currently he has his own design studio in Arnhem, the Netherlands, and is also a design teacher at the Academy of Arts, Arnhem. *(218)*

RON ARAD was born in 1951 in Israel. He studied architecture at the Architectural Association, London, graduating in 1979. After working for a firm of London architects, he founded the design company One-Off Ltd in 1981. He has exhibited in London, Milan and Tokyo. *(74)*

ARQUITECTONICA is an architectural and design firm based in Miami, Florida, USA. Since its establishment in 1977, the firm has won several design awards, including commendations from the American Institute of Architecture. An exhibition devoted to Arquitectonica, entitled 'Arquitectonica: Yesterday, Today, Tomorrow', has travelled throughout the USA. *See also* SPEAR. *(107)*

SVEIN ASBJØRNSEN, born in 1943, is a Norwegian designer. He graduated from the State College of Applied Art in 1967 and won a STI design scholarship in 1970. He is a NIL interior designer, and since 1970 has worked in partnership with JAN LADE. Their partnership, More Designteam, was awarded the Norwegian Design Prize in 1971 for its Ecco chair series. In 1976 it won the first prize in the Nordic Furniture Competition for the furniture programme 'People are Different'. Asbjørnsen and Lade also received the first prize in the 1981 Nordic Furniture Competition for the Split programme. *(138–9)*

SERGIO ASTI is an Italian architect who has designed the furnishings and interiors of several flats, shops and exhibitions. He has lectured and exhibited extensively, and has sat on a number of award juries since he completed his studies at the Milan Politecnico in 1953. *(198–200, 410)*

ANTONIA ASTORI was born in Milan in 1940. She studied industrial and visual design at the Lausanne Athenaeum, and began to work with Driade in 1968. She has dedicated a large part of her activity to the firm, helping to form its corporate image with her single pieces and series of furniture, the most significant of which bear her own name. *(147–8)*

GAE AULENTI was born near Udine in 1927 and studied architecture at the Milan Politecnico, graduating in 1954. From 1955 to 1961 she was a member of the influential Movement for Architectural Studies; and from 1960 of the Industrial Design Association. In 1964 she was awarded first prize for the arrangement of the Italian pavilion at the 13th Milan Triennale. Since 1967 she has designed interiors and exhibitions for Olivetti, has had numerous one-man shows and participated in exhibitions in Italy, America and Japan. She is active on the editorial boards of several architectural magazines, and since 1974 has been a member of the executive committee of Lotus International. Her office in Milan deals with architecture, industrial design and, since 1975, with stage design. During the mid-1970s Aulenti began her collaboration with the theatre director, Ronconi, working with him in his Laboratory for Theatrical Projects at Prato. She has designed furniture for Poltronova and Knoll, lighting for Francesconi, Martinelli, Artemide and Stilnovo, and villas and gardens for private clients in Tuscany. *(417, 420)*

GIJS BAKKER was born in Holland in 1942. He graduated in jewellery design in Amsterdam in 1962 and has designed and exhibited ever since. He has taught widely, and has written extensively. *(143)*

DENIS BALLAND is French. He studied business and marketing and for the last 10 years has been responsible for design at Neyrati-Peyronie and Fermob. He is in charge of design for Fermob's Chiche, Camille and Kis lines. *(4)*

MARCO BALZAROTTI was born in Italy in 1951. He studied under Professor Carlo Scarpa at the Architecture Institute of Venice, graduating in 1977. Since then he has researched the best use of modern materials such as thermo-plastics. In 1982 he founded Como Numeri. He collaborates with MASSIMO FUSCO and ROBERTO GANGEMI. *(95, 97)*

WENDY BARBER studied in Sussex, England and at the Slade, London, between 1960 and 1965. She has designed textiles and produced tapestries, and in 1981 formed a partnership with JOHN HINCHCLIFFE to design and produce textiles and ceramics. In 1983 she began to work to commission. She has published, and has exhibited together with Hinchcliffe. *(276)*

JHANE BARNES lives in New York City. An internationally recognized clothing designer for both men and women, she was the first woman to receive a Coty Award for menswear designs. Her multi-coloured, richly textured fabrics for apparel have been transposed to fabrics for Knoll International. *(303)*

RAMON BIGAS BAUCELLS was born in Barcelona, Spain, and holds a degree in technology from Barcelona University. He and PEP SANT have formed a design company called Associated Designers. They have designed halogen lamps for the firm Augusti of Barcelona and are working on several projects for Luxo Italiana and Luxo America. *(196)*

MARTINE BEDIN was born in Bordeaux, France in 1957. She studied architecture in Paris, and in 1978 was awarded an Italian scholarship and worked at the Superstudio in Florence. She has been working for ETTORE SOTTSASS since 1980, designing lamps and furniture for Memphis since 1981; and has been a freelance industrial designer since 1982. She also teaches design at the École Camondo, Paris. *(191, 221)*

MARIO BELLINI was born in Milan, Italy in 1935 and graduated in architecture in 1959. He works in architecture and industrial design for firms such as Artemide, B&B Italia, Cassina and Rosenthal. Since 1965 he has been a consultant with Olivetti. He has won several awards including the Compasso d'Oro in 1962, 1964, 1970, 1979 and 1981. His works are included in the collection of the Museum of Modern Art, New York. *(399)*

GIANDOMENICO BELOTTI was born in Italy in 1922. He studied sculpture with Marino Marini in Monza before attending the Brera Academy's Secondary School of Fine Arts in Milan, the School of Architecture at Milan University, and Venice University. He has worked for both private companies and public institutions in the fields of urban planning and industrial design. In 1979 he began to·work with Alias, for whom he created the *Odessa* chair (called the *Spaghetti Chair* when it was first presented in New York), and the other furniture items that make up the Belotti Collection. *(56)*

WARD BENNET is a New York designer who has made a name for himself in both fine and applied art. He has worked in interior design, textiles, sculpture, jewellery and furniture. Recently he created more than 100 designs in office furniture for Brickel. He has studied with Brancusi, Harold Hoffman and Louise Nevelson, and his work has been exhibited in the Whitney Museum and the Museum of Modern Art, New York. *(169)*

FRANCO ALBERTO BERG was born in 1948 and studied at the University of Art (HBK) in Brunswick, West Germany, receiving his Master's degree from HBK in 1978. In 1979 he founded the Berg Design Studio for product

development in Brunswick, which has since moved to Hanover. Berg has worked on a wide range of consumer and investment goods. *(209, 212)*

BERNT (Bernt Petersen) was born in Denmark in 1937. He graduated in 1960 and worked with Hans J. Wegner until 1963, when he opened his own studio. He has worked mainly with furniture, and has undertaken several important commissions, including the Olympic Games in Munich, 1972. He has been widely exhibited, has taught, and has received several prizes. *(96)*

OTTO BLÜMEL was born in Augsburg in 1881 and died in 1973. He studied architecture in Munich and later painting. He taught and wrote widely, and was director of museums and colleges. *(455)*

CINI BOERI is an Italian designer who graduated from the Milan Politecnico in 1950. She collaborated with MARCO ZANUSO until 1963 when she applied herself to civil and interior architecture and industrial design, specializing in houses with minimal areas. She has lectured and written widely and has taken part in several competition juries. She has herself received many awards for her work. *(418–19)*

JONAS BOHLIN is a Swedish designer living in Stockholm. He was born in 1953 and studied at the High School of Arts, Crafts and Design in Stockholm from 1976 to 1981. He concentrates on interior architecture, stage craft and furniture design. His work is represented in the National Museum of Art, Stockholm, and the Rohsska Museum of Artcrafts, Gothenburg. *(20)*

PEP BONET was born in Barcelona, Spain in 1941. He graduated from the School of Architecture, Barcelona in 1965. Together with Cristián Cirici, OSCAR TUSQUETS and Lluís Clotet he founded the firm of Studio Per in 1965. They turned their attention after 1972 to the production of furniture and building components. He taught at the School of Architecture, Barcelona between 1975 and 1978, and in the Washington School of Architecture, St Louis, Missouri in 1981. *(43)*

KAREL BOONZAAIJER was born in the Netherlands in 1948. He attended the Academy of Modern Art in Utrecht, and for 10 years worked as a designer for Pastoe, a modern furniture manufacturer. In 1979 he went into partnership with PIERRE MAZAIRAC. They have their own design studio specializing in product development and interior architecture. *(19)*

IVANA BORTOLOTTI is an Italian designer who has worked for B&B Italia. She was a fourth-year student under Roberto Lucci and Paolo Orlandini at the European Institute of Design, Milan. *(68–9)*

MARILI BRANDÃO is a designer who has worked for B&B Italia. She was a fourth-year student under Roberto Lucci and Paolo Orlandini at the European Institute of Design, Milan. *(76)*

PAULINE BURBIDGE was born in Dorset, England in 1950. She studied at Yeovil Technical College, the London College of Fashion, and St Martin's School of Art, London. In 1972 she began designing clothes for a small London company, working in partnership from 1973 to 1976, at which time she started making patchwork quilts. She now

teaches and works to commission. Her work has been exhibited and awarded, and she has also published. *(362–5)*

REMO BUTI was born in Florence, Italy in 1938. He studied architecture at Florence University and now has a studio in Florence where he designs lamps, ceramics, jewellery and furniture. He also paints and is a professor at Florence University. *(208, 211, 229, 232)*

SARAH CAMPBELL has worked with her sister SUSAN COLLIER since 1968. She first licensed a range of dress fabrics to Soieries Nouveautés in 1975; Susan began working on the project in 1977. Associates joined them in 1977 and 1978 to form Collier Campbell Ltd in 1979. She and her sister received the 1984 Design Council Award. *(347–52)*

RONALD CARTER is a well-known English furniture designer. After graduating in interior design at Birmingham College of Art in 1949, he studied furniture design at the Royal College of Art, London, and was awarded a first-class diploma and silver medal for work of special distinction. From 1952 to 1953 he was a staff designer with Corning Glass Works in New York, and in 1954 he started a freelance design practice in Birmingham and London. He was a partner in the firm Design Partners from 1960 to 1968, and a partner in Carter Freeman Associates from 1968 to 1974, when he started a private design consultancy practice. In 1980 he was named design director of Peter Miles Furniture Ltd, whose clients include the British Museum, St John's College, Cambridge, and the British Council. From 1956 to 1974 he served as a tutor at the Royal College of Art in the School of Furniture Design. He was named as fellow of the college in 1966 and an honorary fellow in 1974. That same year he was also appointed Royal Designer for Industry by the Royal Society of Arts. *(33)*

ASHLEY CARTWRIGHT is a British furniture designer and maker. He attended Kingston College of Art from 1967 to 1970 and later studied at the Royal College of Art, London. For several years he worked with JOHN MAKEPEACE and in 1976 set up his own workshop. He has exhibited in Britain, Japan and on the Continent. *(184)*

STEFANO CASCIANI was born in Rome in 1955. After studying architecture in Rome, he worked as an industrial designer for the Istituto Superiore di Disegno Industriale. From 1979 he collaborated with *Domus*, and he has published in *Modo* and *Raum*. He participated in the Venice Biennale of 1980 and in the 1981 Milan Triennale. Since 1980 he has been a consultant to Zanotta, and he has taught architecture in Milan and Florence. He lives and works in Rome and Milan. *(207)*

ACHILLE CASTIGLIONI was born in Milan, Italy in 1918. He began designing with his brothers Livio and Pier Giacomo Castiglioni. Today he is internationally known for his furnishings and lighting, and for his mass-produced objects in the field of radio-telecommunications. In addition to working as a designer, he is an architect and university lecturer. He has received seven Compasso d'Oro awards; six of his pieces are in the Museum of Modern Art, New York. *(1, 295–6, 409)*

JOHN CEDERQUIST was born in 1946, and has worked for the USA Formica Corporation. *(151)*

CENTROKAPPA is a design group within Kartell, directed by ANNA CASTELLI FERRIERI. *(67)*

BIOGRAPHIES

PAUL CHIASSON was born in 1955 and works in New York. He received his Master's degree from Yale University in 1981 and runs the PDCC Studio, specializing in highly crafted interior design. *(165–6)*

ANTONIO CITTERIO was born in Italy in 1950. He studied at the Milan Politecnico, and has been involved in industrial design since 1967. He founded a studio in 1972 with PAOLO NAVA, and in 1973 they began permanent collaboration with B&B Italia. They have worked for a number of other major firms, and in 1979 were selected for the Compasso d'Oro. *(6)*

SUSAN COLLIER works with her sister SARAH CAMPBELL, with whom she has been heading design teams since 1968. She became design and colour consultant to Liberty of London Prints in 1971. *(347–52)*

JOE COLOMBO was born in Milan in 1930 and died in 1971. He studied at the Milan Politecnico and participated in numerous exhibitions and award juries. He received many prizes for his work, which is exhibited in the Museum of Modern Art, New York; Stedelijk Museum, Amsterdam; CCI, Louvre, Paris; the Victoria and Albert Museum, London: and the Werkbund, Germany. Many publications discuss or are entirely devoted to his work. *(491)*

HANS CORAY was born in Zurich, Switzerland in 1906. He attended Zurich University and became a figurative artist, though he has also worked as a designer. For the past few years, he has dedicated himself to painting and graphics. *(498)*

ANTOINETTE DE BOER grew up in Hamburg and Berlin. After studying at the High School for Visual Arts, she attended the College of Pictorial Arts, Hamburg, where she studied under Professor Margret Hildebrand. She subsequently became his postgraduate student-assistant. Since 1963 she has been a designer with Stuttgarter Gardinenfabrik GmbH. She is head of the company's design studios and since 1973 has had her own line there of 'de Boer design'. She has received awards from the Philadelphia Museum of Art; the Deutsches Museum and Die Neue Sammlung, Munich; and the Gwerbemuseum and Museum für Gestaltung, Basel; and has also won the Biennale Ljubljana and the Roscoe Award, New York. *(304–7)*

PAOLO DEGANELLO was born in Este, Italy in 1940. He studied in Florence and from 1963 to 1974 he worked as a town planner for the Florence municipality. In 1966 he founded, with Andrea Branzi, Gilberio Corretti and Massimo Morozzi, the then avant-garde group, Studio Archizoom. In 1975, with Corretti, Franco Gatti and Roberto Querci, he founded the Collettivo Tecnici Progettisti. He has taught widely, including at Florence University and the Architectural Association, London, and has published several books and articles. He has designed products for Marcatré, Driade and Cassina and has taken part in many international exhibitions and competitions. *(55)*

LILLIAN DELEVORYAS is an American now living in England. She was educated at the Pratt Institute and Cooper Union in New York City and studied woodblock printing and calligraphy in Tokyo and Kyoto. She received the Louis Comfort Tiffany Award in 1965 and has won several grants from the South West Arts and Crafts Council for her work in design and fibre art. She has a workshop in Gloucestershire, England, and has been the subject of several one-man shows in America and England, including two shows at the Robert Schoelkopf Gallery, New York. *(361)*

MICHELE DE LUCCHI was born in Ferrara, Italy in 1951. He studied first in Padua and then at Florence University, where he founded the Gruppo Cavat, which produced avant-garde and radical architecture projects, films, texts and happenings. He obtained his degree in architecture from Florence University in 1975 and subsequently became assistant professor to Adolfo Natalini at the Faculty of Architecture there, as well as at the International Art University of Florence. In 1978 he left teaching and moved to Milan, where he began a close collaboration with ETTORE SOTTSASS. He worked and designed for Alchimia, Milan, until the establishment of the international group Memphis in 1981. For Memphis he designed and carried out some of its best-known products. In 1979 he became a consultant for Olivetti Synthesis in Massa and in 1984 for Olivetti SpA in Ivrea. Under the supervision of Sottsass he designed Olivetti's *Icarus* office furniture. At the same time, with Sottsass Associati, he designed both the interior decoration and the image of more than 50 Fiorucci shops in Italy and abroad. A series of his household appliances for Zirmi was shown at the Milan Triennale of 1979, while at the Triennale of 1983 he exhibited a prefabricated holiday house in plastic material. Currently he is designing for a wide range of important furniture manufacturers; among others, Acerbis, Artemide, Vistosi, RB Rossana and Fontana Arte. *(108, 113–15, 118, 121)*

PIERO DE MARTINI was born in Milan in 1939. He graduated in architecture in 1964 and has since concentrated on home design, particularly its industrial aspects. He is now engaged in design research for Cassina, which has produced several of his designs for furniture. *(10–11)*

JONATHAN DE PAS was born in Italy in the 1930s. He studied in Milan, and in the mid-1960s, with PAOLO LOMAZZI and DONATO D'URBINO, he set up a studio specializing in architecture and interior design. The three of them have exhibited widely since 1970 and have received many awards. Their work is in several major museums. *(41–2, 94)*

MENNO DIEPERINK, born in 1949, is a Dutch industrial designer. He graduated from the Royal Academy at The Hague and is in partnership with MICHEL KRECHTING. Some of their products are initiated and produced by themselves; most are executed on commission. Among those who have commissioned works are Philips, General Motors and the Dutch Government. *(217, 237)*

ALAIN DOMINGO was born in France in 1952. He completed his architectural studies in 1979 and founded the design group NEMO together with FRANÇOIS SCALI in 1982. They have exhibited in Europe, America and Japan, and their works have received several prizes. *(127–9, 192)*

PETER DRAENERT was born in Germany in 1937. He studied philosophy, history of art and literature in Tübingen, and has manufactured modern furniture since 1968. He is one of the few hardware specialists among furniture producers. *(100–1)*

JEAN CLAUDE DUBOYS was born in Limoges, France in 1938. He studied at the National School for Decorative Arts, obtaining his diploma in 1962. His line of chairs and tables, which goes under the label *Via,* has been exhibited at the Scandinavian furniture fair, Copenhagen in 1981; the International Furniture Salon, Cologne in 1982; the

International Furniture Salon, Milan in 1982; the International Salon of the Society of Decorative Artists, Paris in 1983; and the Exhibition of French Regions, Tokyo in 1984. *(3)*

SYLVAIN DUBUISSON, born in 1946, is a French designer. He studied at Tournai in Belgium, and now works as a freelance designer. *(193)*

MICHEL DUFET was born in France in 1888. Architect, decorator and writer on art, he is one of the promoters of the Modern functional style. He introduced Cubism into interior decoration, but is widely known as a creator of unique and luxurious pieces. In 1947 he married the daughter of the sculptor Antoine Bourdelle and became curator of the latter's museum in 1972. *(516)*

DONATO D'URBINO was born in Italy in the 1930s. *See also* JONATHAN DE PAS and PAOLO LOMAZZI. *(41–2, 94)*

HANS EBBING was born in the Netherlands in 1954 and studied at the Academy of Arts, Arnhem. In 1978 he founded and collaborated with the Vormgeversassociatie Ebbing/Haas/ Schindel, and in 1980 Designum and Skizo. In 1983 he founded Ebbing Haas Industrial Concepts with TON HAAS. Their work has been widely discussed and published, has been produced by a number of firms, and received the German 'Gute Form' prize in 1983. *(120, 214–15, 230)*

CLARK ELLEFSON was born in 1949. He and JIM LEWIS were awarded first prize in the professional category by the USA Formica Corporation for their *Temple Chair*, and Best Conceptual Design Award at the New York and Chicago 'Surface and Ornament' exhibition in 1983. Lewis and Clark is a small cabinetmaker firm in Columbus, South Carolina. *(160, 163)*

VUOKKO ESKOLIN-NURMESNIEMI is a Finnish designer who trained in ceramics but has expanded into other fields. She founded Vuokko Oy in 1964 and directs the design and co-ordination of textiles and clothing. She has received many prizes, and her works appear in the collections of the Victoria and Albert Museum, London, and of the Metropolitan Museum of Art, New York, among others. She collaborates with her husband, ANTTI NURMESNIEMI. *(374)*

BRIAN FAUCHEUX was born in 1954. He is an associate architect at Turchi, Cusick, Drew Associates, Inc., in Metairie, Louisiana. He was awarded a prize by the USA Formica Corporation for his *Table draped with a tablecloth*. *(161)*

ANNA CASTELLI FERRIERI began her career as a town planner and became involved in architecture in the early 1950s. For 15 years she worked with Ignazio Gardella on various public-housing and furniture projects. She began to work with Kartell in the mid-1960s and is now its art director. Centrocappa is the in-house design group of the company. *(66)*

CARLO FORCOLINI was born in Como, Italy in 1947. He studied at the Institute of Graphic Arts, the Secondary School of Fine Arts, Brera, and the Academy of Fine Arts at Brera, Milan. From 1970 to 1974 he designed for the Amar Collection, and in 1976 he began working with VICO MAGISTRETTI. In 1978 he moved to London, and a year

later he helped to found Alias SRL, which began production of the *Broomstick Collection* designed by Magistretti and of the *Spaghetti Chair* designed by GIANDOMENICO BELOTTI. In 1980 he founded Alias UK, for distribution of Alias products under their own brand name in the UK, and three years later he founded Artemide GB, a subsidiary of Artemide SpA, Italy. He became managing director of the entire Alias company in 1983. *(111, 119)*

JOEL FOURNIER was born in 1954. He graduated from l'École Boulle in 1974 and has a BTS in Interior Architecture and Model Building. He has worked for various design firms, but since 1982 has been working freelance. *(170)*

ALBERTO FRASER was born in Glasgow in 1945, moved first to America and then to Milan, where he now lives and works. He studied at the Rhode Island School of Design and received several awards. He has designed for a number of Italian and American firms, including Wang Computer Laboratories, Artemide, Stilnova and Arflex. *(202–04)*

RENZO FRAU was born in Sardinia in 1880. After his military service, he moved to Turin in the early years of the century where he worked as a joiner to the Italian royal household. In 1912 he founded the Poltrona Frau company, and in 1919 he made the famous Poltrona Frau armchair. In 1926 he received a warrant as a supplier to the royal household and in the 1930s he was very active as an interior designer to the aristocracy. *(511)*

PELLE FRENNING was born in 1943 in Sweden. He studied industrial design at Gothenburg University and worked for several interior architecture firms, among them Folke Sundberg and Lund Valentin, before joining White Architects in Gotenborg. In 1982, *Forum Närmiljö*, the magazine for interior architects in Sweden, awarded him first prize for his work on the Swedish Metalworkers Union headquarters. His design for lamps for the elderly won a first prize from the Swedish Lighting Association in 1980. He also designs furniture, and he has participated in several exhibitions. *(132)*

MASSIMO FUSCO was born in Italy in 1945. He graduated in architecture from Florence University in 1973 and opened an architectural office that same year. He has been widely published and has received many architecture and design awards. He has collaborated with MARCO BALZAROTTI and ROBERTO GANGEMI for Numeri SRL. *(95, 97)*

JØRGEN GAMMELGAARD is Danish. He graduated from the School of Arts and Crafts and Industrial Design in 1962 and was a visiting student at the Royal Academy in Copenhagen from 1962 to 1964. He was a consultant to the UN and UNESCO in Samoa, Sudan and Ceylon from 1965 to 1968, and served as a consultant to the Technological Institute of Copenhagen from 1971 to 1973. He has been a lecturer at the School of Arts and Crafts and Industrial Design, and since 1973 has had his own design practice. He won the Danish Furniture Design Award in 1971 and has been a designer for Schiang Production since 1982.

NIELS GAMMELGAARD was born in Denmark in 1944. He joined the staff of the Royal Academy of Fine Arts, School of Industrial Design, Copenhagen in 1970, having founded Box 25, Architects, with four other architects in 1969. In 1978 he founded Pelikan Design with LARS MATHIESEN, and he continues to teach at the Royal Academy, and at

the School of Architecture, Århus. He has won numerous prizes in Scandinavia and Japan. *(57–8, 72)*

ROBERTO GANGEMI was born in Italy in 1947 and studied architecture at Florence University, graduating in 1973. He has worked as an interior designer and architect for public and private building, and began to collaborate with Numeri SRL in 1979. He has co-operated with MARCO BALZAROTTI and MASSIMO FUSCO. *(95, 97)*

BRUNO GECCHELIN is an Italian architect, born in Milan in 1939. He studied architecture at the Milan Politecnico and began his professional career in 1962, since when he has worked with many major companies. *(194, 235)*

FRANK D. GEHRY is a principal of the firm Frank D. Gehry and Associates in Los Angeles, California. He has won many awards and is a Fellow of the American Institute of Architects. His furniture and designs have been widely published and exhibited at the Museum of Modern Art, New York, and at the Louvre, Paris. *(154–5)*

ENRICO GERLI is an Italian architect and designer. He graduated from the Milan Politecnico in 1977 with a degree in architecture, and since then has worked as a freelance architect and designer. Most of his design work has been commissions for Tecno and Robots. *(26)*

KEITH GIBBONS was born in London in 1946 and attended the Royal College of Art there. In 1972 he started his own workshop, and in 1974 opened a shop selling one-off and small-production furniture. In 1983 he formed a new company, Products, to manufacture his own designs. *(105–6)*

NATALIE GIBSON is a British textile designer. She studied painting at the Chelsea School of Art, London from 1956 to 1958, and printed textile design at the Royal College of Art, London from 1958 to 1961. She has designed fabrics for a wide range of shops, including Heals and Habitat in the UK and Fieldcrest and Connaissance in the USA, but now works primarily with dress fabrics. She has designed fabrics for Mantero, Bini and Stehli in Italy, and has designed for Cacharel, Chloe, Galleries Lafayette and Mafia in France. Liberty's of London, Caroline Charles and Stirling Cooper carry her work in the UK. Her fabrics have been featured in fashion magazines as well as in the major British newspapers. Her work has been included in numerous exhibitions and she is a senior lecturer at St Martins School of Art, London. *(355–60)*

ERNESTO GISMONDI is an Italian designer who has worked for Artemide. *(240)*

MICHAEL GRAVES was born in the USA in 1934. He is Schrimer Professor of Architecture at Princeton University, and is architect of the Newark Museum and of the Whitney Museum. He has received many awards for his architectural works, and has been widely exhibited. His paintings and murals are in several major museums. *(393)*

EILEEN GRAY was born in Ireland in 1879 and died in 1976. She trained in the Slade School, London, and moved to Paris in 1907. She made wood and lacquer furniture in her own atelier there from about 1920. She then took up architecture, and with Jean Badovici designed the famous villa E 1027 at Roquebrune. She was a member of the UAM along with René Herbst, Pierre Chareau, Jean

Prouvé, ROBERT MALLET-STEVENS, LE CORBUSIER and others. *(457–67)*

BRUNO GREGORI was born in Milan, Italy in 1954 and studied at the Academia di Brera there. He works with ALESSANDRO MENDINI and his work has been included in several exhibitions. *(122–6)*

VITTORIO GREGOTTI was born in Italy in 1927. Between 1953 and 1968 he collaborated with Ludovico Meneghetti and Giotto Stoppino, and in 1974 founded Gregotti Associates, an architectural firm. He has taught at universities all over the world, has edited journals, and has written a number of books. His work has been widely exhibited. *(415–16)*

MARTIN GRIERSON studied furniture and interior design at Central School of Arts and Crafts, London, receiving his degree in 1953. Since 1960 he has been a freelance designer, and his work has won numerous awards in national and international furniture competitions, including the Arflex/Domus competition in 1959. In 1975 he opened his own workshop in London, where he manufactures his own designs, mostly to commission. He is a part-time lecturer at Central School of Art and Design. *(185–6)*

HANS GUNNARSSON was born in 1945 in Sweden. He studied at the industrial design school in Gothenburg and later worked as a freelance interior designer, designing hotels, restaurants, exhibitions and museums. In 1982 he joined the firm of White Architects. *(130)*

CHARLES GWATHMEY was born in the USA in 1938. He received his Master's degree from Yale in 1962, where he won a scholarship for 'the outstanding graduating student in architecture'. Since 1964 he has taught architectural design at Yale, Princeton, Columbia and Harvard and has served on numerous design-award juries. After only four years of private practice, in 1970, he was awarded a prize for making 'a significant contribution to architecture as an art'. In 1981 he became a fellow in the American Institute of Architects. *(81, 277–8, 367)*

GWATHMEY SIEGEL & ASSOCIATES ARCHITECTS is a well-known New York architectural firm that has won over 45 design awards. In 1982 the American Institute of Architects (AIA) awarded its highest honour to Gwathmey Siegel & Associates Architects: the 1982 Architectural Firm Award. In 1983 the New York AIA celebrated CHARLES GWATHMEY and ROBERT SIEGEL with the Gold Medal. *(81, 277–8)*

H-DESIGN is a textile design group working for Mira-X. The collaborators are Trix and Robert Haussmann and Alfredo Hablützel. *(324–5)*

TON HAAS was born in the Netherlands in 1954. He studied at the Academy of Arts, Arnhem and the Kingston Polytechnic, London. In 1979 he joined and helped to run the Vormgeversassociatie Ebbing/Haas/Schindel. *See also* HANS EBBING. *(120)*

OSWALD HAERDTL was an Austrian designer and architect who died in 1962. He is best known for his design work, much of which was done for LOBMEYR and includes drinking sets, gift items, candlesticks and crystal lighting. He also designed furniture and other products for the home. *(444, 448)*

TINA HAHN is a German designer who grew up in Wuppertal. She studied at the Meisterschule für Mode, where she qualified in theatrical costumery, and at the Hochschule für Bildende Kunste, both in Hamburg, and qualified as a textile designer. She has worked since 1975 as a freelance designer of fabrics, carpets and wallpapers, and as an assistant wardrobe designer. *(308–9)*

ANNAGRETE HALLING-KOCH was born in Copenhagen in 1947. She studied at the Art Handcraft School, Copenhagen, training as a ceramicist, and now works at the Bing & Gröndahl porcelain factory, where she decorates and designs porcelain. She also designs textiles, and her work has been exhibited in Copenhagen and Minneapolis, USA. *(353–4)*

CHRIS HIEMSTRA was born in Voorburg, the Netherlands in 1942. He studied industrial design at the Rietveld Academy, Amsterdam, and the Royal Academy of Art, The Hague. Since 1970 he has been a designer for Lumiance. *(236)*

JOHN HINCHCLIFFE was born in Sussex, England in 1949. He studied textile design between 1967 and 1973, and has taught, lectured and written since that time. He has received awards, has also broadcast, and examples of his work appear in several collections. He collaborates with WENDY BARBER. *(276)*

MONICA HJELM was born in Sweden in 1945 and attended the high school of Arts, Crafts and Design, Gothenburg from 1965 to 1969. Since 1969 she has worked as a designer for Mark Pelle Vävare AB and is now responsible for the product development of curtain and cotton fabrics. She has designed curtains, mast woven and printed cotton fabrics, plaids in wool and furnishing fabrics. *(315–16, 318–19)*

LABBAR HOAGLAND worked for 35 years with Tiffany's in New York and collaborates with ALFONSO SOTO SORIA and PEDRO LEITES. *(402–3, 404–5)*

MARC VAN HOE was born in Zulte, Belgium in 1945, and studied at the Royal Academy of Fine Arts, Kortrijk. Since 1975 he has been a freelance designer and technical researcher in the field of industrial textiles and tapestry. He is a teacher at the Royal Academy of Fine Arts, Kortrijk and a Docent at the Academie voor Beeldende Vorming in Tilburg, the Netherlands. He has had exhibitions of his work in Belgium, France, Switzerland, Poland, Hungary and England. *(327)*

JOSEF HOFFMANN died in 1956. He was one of the most brilliant interior designers and architects Austria had in this century. Together with Koloman Moser he founded the Wiener Werkstätte. For LOBMEYR, he designed numerous drinking sets, flowerbowls and fancy glasses in clear, cut enamel-painted crystal. His work as an architect includes the Palais Stoclet in Brussels. Major works were shown at the Werkbund exhibition in Cologne, Germany in 1914. *(443, 445, 447, 449–54)*

HANS HOLLEIN was born in Vienna, Austria in 1934. Since 1967 he has taught at the Academy of Art, Dusseldorf, and since 1976 at the College of Applied Arts, Vienna. He has exhibited widely and has been commissioned to design a large number of buildings. *(29, 32, 394)*

ANDREW HOLMES was born in Britain in 1947. He studied at the Architectural Association, London, and has had his work exhibited in Britain and in Eastern Europe. He has received several prizes. *(225–6)*

ISAO HOSOE was born in Tokyo, Japan in 1942. He studied in Tokyo until 1967, and collaborated with Alberto Rosselli until 1974 in Milan. In 1981 he founded the Design Research Centre in Milan. He has received major prizes and has exhibited and written widely. *(73, 201)*

JOHAN HULDT was born in Stockholm, Sweden in 1942. He graduated from the Swedish State School of Arts and Design in 1968, and in the same year founded and became managing director of Innovator Design AB. From 1974 to 1976 he served as director of the Swedish Furniture Research Institute, and in 1983 was named chairman of the National Association of Swedish Interior Architects. His work is represented in the Swedish National Museum, Stockholm; the Museum of Modern Art, New York; the Museum of Art, São Paolo; and the Museum of Modern Art, Rio de Janeiro. *(35)*

FUJIWO ISHIMOTO was born in Ehime, Japan in 1941. He studied graphic design at Tokyo National University of Art and worked for Ichida Co from 1964 to 1970. In 1970 he moved to Finland and became a designer for Decembre Oy. In 1974 he joined Marimekko Oy, where he continues to work as a designer of interior textiles. His fabrics have been exhibited in Scandinavia, Central Europe, Japan and the USA. *(328–9)*

JOUKO JARVISALO was born in 1950 in Varkaus, Finland. He has worked both as an interior architect and as a freelance designer. Since 1983 he has worked in an interior-design office, designing home and office furniture for Artek, Asko, Arsel, Laukaan Puu and Inno. *(14)*

PIERRE JEANNERET collaborated with LE CORBUSIER. *(477–90)*

CHARLES A. JENCKS was born in Baltimore, Maryland, in the USA in 1939. He teaches at the Architectural Association, London, and California University, Los Angeles. He is widely known for his writings on architecture. His architecture and furniture have been most influential. *(140–3, 398)*

MENNO JETTEN was born in the Netherlands in 1952. He studied architecture at the Technical University, Delft, before going on for further training at the Gerrit Rietveld Academy, Amsterdam. In 1978 he began to work on prototypes and small-batch production. He continues to make furniture and has taken on several projects as a set designer. *(45–6)*

ANTONIN JIRAN, born in Indonesia in 1951 of Czechoslovakian parents, is a Dutch designer living in Amsterdam. He studied city planning before becoming an industrial and product designer. *(210)*

EVA JIRICNA was born in Czechoslovakia in 1939. She trained as an architect in Prague, before moving to London in 1968. She worked for a firm of architects for several years and in 1980 began designing interiors for Joseph Ettedgui. She has designed several shops in London for him, as well as the Caprice Restaurant. *(181)*

WENDY JONES is a British textile designer. She studied at the Hornsey College of Art and the Royal College of Art, London, qualifying in 1971, and is now a freelance designer who also works on one-off and limited productions. She teaches and works to commission. *(312, 317)*

JORGEN KASTHOLM was born in Roskilde, Denmark, in 1932. He studied at the School of Technology, and served as an assistant to Professor Arne Jacobsen from 1954 to 1958. He opened his own office in Copenhagen in 1960 and moved to West Germany 12 years later. He has his own studio in Dusseldorf, and since 1975 has been a professor at Wuppertal University. His work has been exhibited in the Louvre, Paris, the Museo de Arte, Portugal, the Ringling Museum, USA, and the Royal Albert Hall, London. His furniture has won several awards, including the Illum Award, Ringling Award, Bundes Award (German National Award) at the Design Centre Essen, Design Centre Stuttgart, and the Design Centre Munich. *(25)*

SACHA KETOFF was born in France in 1949. He studied at the Academia di Brera in Milan, Italy and returned to Paris in 1971 to study architecture. He began working with sculpture around the same time and held his first one-man show in 1975 at the Galerie Space. He has had many exhibitions since then. In addition to designing furniture, he has designed books and film sets and has published widely. His furniture is represented in the permanent collection of the Museum of Modern Art, Hamburg, and the Museum of Decorative Arts, Paris. *(190, 514)*

PERRY A. KING was born in London in 1938 and studied at the School of Industrial Design, Birmingham. He later moved to Italy to work as a consultant to Olivetti, designing among other things the Valentine typewriter in collaboration with ETTORE SOTTSASS. He started to work with SANTIAGO MIRANDA on a project called Unlimited Horizon, an exploration of the elements that make and divide private and public spaces. At the same time they began working on typeface design for Olivetti, and one of their dot matrix founts was adopted by the European Computer Manufacturers Association. For the last 10 years he and Miranda have worked together from their office in Milan, where they are active in the fields of industrial design, furniture and interior design and graphics. Their graphic work includes posters and catalogues for Olivetti and corporate-image programmes for a number of firms. Together with G. Arnaldi they have designed light fittings for Arteluce/Flos and at present are working on office furniture, the design of power tools for Black and Decker, and a design programme for the identification and control elements of the new Olivetti machines. Their work has received several awards and has been exhibited in Italy and abroad. *(242–52)*

RODNEY KINSMAN was born in Britain in 1943. He studied at the Central School of Art and received the NDD and Central School Diploma in Furniture Design. In 1966 he formed OMK Design Ltd, a design group offering consultancy to furniture manufacturers. It began a limited production of its own designs in 1967. The recipient of numerous awards, Kinsman has had his work widely published and exhibited. *(24, 174)*

TOSHYUKI KITA is a Japanese designer who in the late 1960s worked in Milan, developing interior products in cooperation with Italian companies. He has received many awards, and some of his designs have been included in the collection of the Museum of Modern Art, New York. *(86)*

HARRI KORHONEN was born in Helsinki in 1946. He designs furniture and lamps, and his work has been included in the Museum of Crafts and Arts, Helsinki. He is the owner of Inno-tuote Oy, which he started in 1977. *(133, 135)*

MICHEL KRECHTING, born in 1953, is a Dutch industrial designer and a graduate of the Academy of Industrial Design, Eindhoven. *See also* MENNO DIEPERINK. *(217, 237)*

JOHANNES KUHNEN was born in Essen, West Germany in 1952. He trained as a goldsmith and designer in Dusseldorf and worked in jewellery design before starting his own workshop with Hellen Aitken-Kuhnen. He is currently a lecturer in the gold and silversmithing workshop at the Canberra School of Art, Australia. *(400)*

YRJO KUKKAPURO was born in Ywipuri, Finland in 1933. He is the furniture designer for Avarte Oy, and from 1974 to 1980 was a professor at the University of Industrial Arts, Helsinki. From 1978 to 1980 he was rector of the university. Examples of his work are in the permanent collection of the Victoria and Albert Museum, London and the Museum of Modern Art, New York. His awards include the Design Award of the Republic of Finland, 1970; the Artek Prize, 1982; and the Pro Finlandia Award, 1983. In 1984, the Institute of Business Designers in the USA awarded him the IBD award for his design of the *Experiment* chair. *(134)*

KISHO KUROKAWA was born in Japan in 1938 and received his PhD in architecture from Tokyo University in 1964. Recent major works include the Roppongi Prince Hotel, Tokyo (1984); Wacoal Kojimachi Building, Tokyo (1984); Japanese Studies Centre, Bangkok; Japanese-German Culture Centre, West Berlin; National Bunraku Theatre, Osaka (1983); Saitama Prefectural Museum of Modern Art (1982). Kurokawa has had his works exhibited in London, Paris, New York, Dublin, Rome, Florence, Milan, Moscow, Budapest and Sofia. Recent books include *Architecture of the Street* (1983); *A Cross Selection of Japan* (1983) and *Thesis on Architecture* (1982). *(79, 87)*

MASAYUKI KUROKAWA was born in Nagoya, Japan, in 1937. He graduated from the Department of Architecture at the Nagoya Institute of Technology in 1961 and completed his training in the Graduate School of Architecture at Waseda University in 1967. That same year he established Masayuki Kurokawa Architect and Associates. He has been accorded numerous prizes for his work. In 1970 he won first prize in the International Design Competition for a mass-production house; in 1973 he won first prize in the Competition for Interior Vertical Element of House; and in 1976 he won the annual prize of the Japan Interior Designers' Association for a series of interior elements. He has won six IF prizes for his designs of tables and lighting fixtures. *(253–62, 376–81)*

JAN LADE, born in 1944, graduated from the College of Applied Art, Copenhagen in 1969 and is a NIL interior designer. *See also* SVEIN ASBJØRNSEN. *(138–9)*

GERD LANGE was born in Wuppertal, Germany in 1931. He received his diploma from the High School for Design and Art, Main in 1956, and practised interior, exhibition and industrial design from 1957 to 1961. Since 1961 he has had his own studio in industrial design in Kapsweyer, where he specializes in the production of furniture, mainly to contract. *(17–18)*

UGO LA PIETRA graduated from the Faculty of Architecture of the Milan Politecnico. Since 1964 he has been a design consultant to various furnishings manufacturers, and in 1984 became art director of the Busnelli Industrial Group. He teaches industrial design at Palermo University and the State Institute of Art, Monza, and is an editor of *Domus*. He won the Compasso d'Oro design competition in 1979. *(51–4)*

TOVE KINDT LARSEN was born in Copenhagen, Denmark in 1906. She trained as an architect at the Royal Academy, Copenhagen and for several years worked for the well-known Danish architect Tude Svrss. After the Second World War, she and her husband, Edward Kindt Larsen, opened a studio together, designing furniture, silver and glasses, and their furniture was widely exhibited and received many prizes. For the last 25 years she has worked with textiles and has been awarded many prizes for her work. *(310)*

JACK LENOR LARSEN is an American textile designer known throughout the world. He was born in Seattle, Washington in 1927 and studied at Washington University and the Cranbrook Academy of Art. In 1953 he founded Jack Lenor Larsen Inc. His work has been included in the permanent collections of the Metropolitan Museum and the Museum of Modern Art, New York, the Victoria and Albert Museum, London, the Stedelijk Museum, Amsterdam, and in many other museums. He has had innumerable exhibitions, and in 1981 was the subject of a 30-year retrospective at the Louvre, Paris. *(311, 313)*

ANN LARSSON-KJELIN was born in Sweden in 1953. In 1974 she received a degree from the Textile Institute, and since 1977 has been associated with the Swedish firm of Marks Pelle Vävare AB. She has designed upholstery fabrics, bedspreads and cotton fabrics, and has worked in conjunction with interior architects on such projects as the Swedish Parliament, the Government Building in Stockholm, the City Express (the Swedish public railway), and the jet-cat ferries in Hong Kong. *(314)*

GIULIO LAZZOTTI was born in Pietrasanta, Italy in 1943. He has a diploma in architecture from Florence University, where he specialized in construction engineering. He has designed for a number of companies, including Artipresent, Bernini, Camp, Casigliani, Gaiac, Mageia and Up & Up. His works are in the Museum of Modern Art, New York, and in Chicago, and he has won several design prizes. *(82)*

YONEL LEBOVICI was born in 1937. He has his own design office, where he designs a wide range of products: furniture, lights, glass, and gift items for such famous names as Jansen, Cardin, Club Méditerranée and Lancel. *(180)*

LE CORBUSIER was born in 1887 and died in 1965. He worked under Peter Behrens in Berlin, and with Mies van de Rohe and Walter Gropius. Arguably the most famous twentieth-century architect, he wrote prolifically. *(477–90)*

PEDRO LEITES is a Mexican designer who collaborates with LABBAR HOAGLAND and ALFONSO SOTA SORIA. *(402–5)*

JIM LEWIS was born in 1941. *See also* CLARK ELLEFSON *(160, 163)*

LUDWIG LOBMEYR, an Austrian designer, and owner of the firm with the same name, died in 1917. Starting in 1855, he designed roughly 100 different drinking sets in clear, cut engraved and enamel-painted crystal. He also designed gift items and special pieces for major exhibitions, particularly world exhibitions. He designed mirrors and light fixtures in bronze and crystal and designed the first electrified chandelier in 1883. He was a great collector of nineteenth-century fine art. *(442)*

TOM LOESER was born in Boston, USA, in 1956. He graduated from Boston University in 1982. *(179)*

PAOLO LOMAZZI was born in Italy in the 1930s. *See also* JONATHAN DE PAS and DONATO D'URBINO. *(41–2, 94)*

ADOLF LOOS was an Austrian designer, born in Brno, Moravia, in 1870, who died in 1933. He was one of Vienna's most revolutionary architects of this century, designing both in Europe and the USA. He is well known for his essays on the architect's responsibility. *(446)*

ROBERTO LUCCI was born in Milan, Italy in 1942. He studied at the Institute of Design, Chicago and the Design School, Venice. For several years he worked for the architect and designer MARCO ZANUSO. In 1970 he and PAOLO ORLANDINI began working independently, and they have designed for a number of different companies, including Artemide (lamps and chairs), Antonelli, ArcLinea, Brionvega (TV sets), Candy-Kelvinator (refrigerators), Magis (furniture) and Velca (office furniture). He teaches at the European Institute of Design, Milan and has lectured in universities in Australia and the USA. *(7–9)*

CHARLES RENNIE MACKINTOSH was born in Glasgow in 1868 and died in London in 1928. He established an international reputation in the late 1890s through the publication of illustrations of his work in the *Studio*. His reputation was further enhanced by a portfolio of his competition designs for the House of an Art Lover (*Haus eines Kunstfreundes*) which was issued by Alexander Koch of Darmstadt in 1902. His Glasgow School of Art (1897–1909), which was little publicized at the time, is now considered to be one of the most brilliant of proto-Modern Movement buildings. Mackintosh was a prolific designer of furniture, textiles and graphics. He was also an accomplished watercolour artist. *(427–41)*

LINDA MACNEIL was born in Boston, Massachusetts in 1954. She studied jewellery and metalsmithing at the BFA School of Design, Rhode Island and later taught and was Guest Artist at a number of institutions. Her work has been widely produced, exhibited and written about, and has been purchased by several museums and collections. *(293)*

MARIANO FORTUNY Y MADRAZO was born in Grenada, Spain in 1871. In his youth he divided his time between Paris, where he was at school, and Venice, where his mother lived after the death of his father. He later moved permanently to Venice, to the Orfei Palace, now the Fortuny museum. Called 'the magician of Venice', he was a painter, engraver, sculptor, interior decorator, photographer, lighting and furniture designer, and theatrical-set and costume designer. In addition, with the collaboration of his wife Henriette, he designed and printed the famous Fortuny fabrics that were sold throughout the world. *(514)*

VICO MAGISTRETTI was born in Milan, Italy in 1920. He took a degree in architecture in 1945 and subsequently joined his father's studio. Until 1960 he was mainly concerned with architecture, town planning and the interior layout of buildings. He started designing furniture and household articles for his buildings in about 1960, and from then on began collaborating with the companies who realized his designs. He has participated in nearly all the Triennali since 1948, and in 1960 joined the National Academy of S. Luca. He was awarded the Medaglia d'Oro at the 9th Triennale in 1951, the Gran Premio at the 15th in 1954 and the Compasso d'Oro in 1967 and 1979. He has designed furniture lamps and other household objects for Artemide, Cassina, B&B Italia, Conran, Knoll International and many other firms. Twelve of his pieces are in the permanent collection of the Museum of Modern Art, New York. (5, 60, 189, 195)

ERIK MAGNUSSEN was born in Copenhagen in 1940 and trained as a potter. Later he also turned his attention to plastics and furniture, particularly school furniture, producing as well utensils and lamps. In 1983 he was chosen as Danish Designer of the Year. He has taught at the Royal Academy of Fine Arts, Copenhagen, has received numerous prizes, and designs furniture for several companies. (406–7)

JOHN MAKEPEACE was born in 1939. He was educated at Denstone College in Staffordshire, England, and trained as a cabinet-maker with Keith Cooper. Since 1961, he has been designing and making furniture. In 1964 he established workshops at Farnborough Barn, Banbury, and in 1976 moved to Parnham House in Dorset, where he founded the School for Craftsmen in Wood. Most of his work is in private hands, but exceptions include the Oxford Centre for Management Studies; Toynbee Hall; Keble College, Oxford; Reed International; and the Royal Society of Arts. His work has been collected by several museums: the Victoria and Albert, London; Birmingham City Art Gallery; the Fitzwilliam Museum, Cambridge and the Museum of Crafts, Frankfurt. (182–3)

ROBERT MALLET-STEVENS was born in Paris in 1886 and died in 1945. He was the first of the avant-garde architects to work with Jean Prouvé and his eclectic use of modern materials demonstrated their aesthetic as well as practical value. Among his best-known works are the Vicomte de Noailles' villa at Hyères and the houses in the street that bears his name in Paris. He created numerous film décors and wrote many articles on architecture. A professor at l'École Speciale d'Architecture, he organized in 1924 an exhibition that combined the works of the De Stijl movement with the designs of Pierre Chareau and Francis Jourdain. (514–15)

ALAIN MARCOT is a French interior architect. He studied at the École des Arts Décoratifs in Nice and received his diploma from the École Nationale Supérieure des Arts Décoratifs in Paris. He was a course assistant there for many years and was also Vice-President of the school. He has worked freelance since 1977 and is an associate in Cabinet Concepteurs Associés. He has won several prizes, including the Formica prize in 1966 and the Prix Révélations CREAC UNIFA in 1969. (173)

WENDY MARUYAMA was born in California in 1952. She graduated in 1975 from the San Diego State University, California. She is on the faculty of the Appalachian Center of Crafts. (177)

NOTI MASSARI was born in Venice, Italy. She collaborates with RENATO TOSO, with whom she studied architecture until 1967 and whom she married in 1968. She worked first in the family glass factory – Toso of Murano – and has since moved into furnishings, ceramics and textiles. Their works are on display in the Museum of Modern Art, New York; and in the Louvre and Pompidou Centre, Paris. (323)

LARS MATHIESEN was born in Denmark in 1950. Following his architectural studies he was employed by Box 25, Architects, and by Vast-Kyst Stugan. In 1978 he founded Pelikan Design with NIELS GAMMELGAARD. He has won several prizes for his work and teaches at the Royal Academy of Fine Arts, Copenhagen. (57–8)

INGO MAURER was born in West Germany in 1932. After training as a typographer and graphic artist in Germany and Switzerland, he emigrated to the USA in 1960. He moved back to Europe in 1963 and started his own design firm, Ingo Maurer GmbH, in 1966. His work has been collected by museums in Israel and Japan, by the Museum of Modern Art, New York, and by the Neue Sammlung, Munich. (216, 231)

PIERRE MAZAIRAC was born in the Netherlands in 1943 and studied at the Academy of Modern Art, Utrecht. He worked as a designer for Pastoe, a manufacturer of modern furniture, before setting up his own design studio with KAREL BOONZAAIJER in 1979. (19)

LUCIE MCCANN is British and received her BA degree from Kingston Polytechnic, where she studied three-dimensional design. In 1984 she won House & Garden and Deloret's Young Designer of the Year award for furniture. She is currently working for John Stefanidis in London. (187)

RORY MCCARTHY was born in New York in 1948. He is a Registered Architect and has exhibited at the American Craft Museum, New York. He has published in the Industrial Design Magazine and received a prize in the Progressive Architecture Magazine Furniture Design Competition in 1984. (172)

MARGARET MCCURRY is an American who has collaborated with STANLEY TIGERMAN. (273–4)

JOHN MCNAUGHTON was born in Winchester, Indiana, in 1948. He is Professor of Art at Indiana State University, and has exhibited at the Indianapolis Museum of Art. (168)

RICHARD MEIER was born in the USA in 1934. He worked in various architectural partnerships, including Owings and Merrill, and Marcel Breuer and Associates, before founding Richard Meier and Partners Architects in New York in 1963. He has taught at the Cooper Union, New York; Yale and Harvard universities; and has designed housing, hospitals, museums, schools and university buildings. (263–5, 300–2, 385–7)

DAVID MELLOR is British and originally trained as a silversmith. A Royal Designer for Industry, he has won numerous design awards for his cutlery. His work is in many international collections, including the Victoria and Albert Museum, London; the Worshipful Company of Goldsmiths; the Museum of Modern Art, New York; and the Philadelphia Museum of Art. Broom Hall, an historic building in Sheffield, has recently been restored by him and converted into purpose-designed workshops, where all design and development on David Mellor cutlery is carried out. He has a number of retail shops specializing in kitchenware and tableware and recently received the Duke of Edinburgh's RSA Presidential Award for Design Management. (411)

ALESSANDRO MENDINI was born in Milan, Italy in 1931. He was a partner of Nizzoli Associates until 1970, and a founder member of Global Tools. He then edited Casabella and Modo and, since 1979, Domus. He has collaborated with a number of companies, has written widely, and received the Compasso d'Oro prize in 1979. (122–6, 382–3)

DAVIDE MERCATALI was born in Milan, Italy in 1948. After receiving a degree in architecture in 1973, he worked as an illustrator and graphic designer for advertising agencies, publishing houses and his own clientele. His first forays into industrial design were decorations for materials and tiles. Then in 1978 he and PAOLO PEDRIZETTI designed I Balocchi, a collection of coloured taps and bathroom accessories produced by Fantini. Since then he and Pedrizetti, with whom he formed a design partnership, Associated Studio, in 1982, have branched out into a number of different areas, designing household goods, electrical appliances, interior decoration, lighting fixtures, accessories and building components and tools. They have twice won the Compasso d'Oro. (207, 408, 422–5)

PHILIPPE MICHEL is a French designer who studied in Paris and now works freelance. (220)

MINALE, TATTERSFIELD AND PARTNERS is a firm of international design consultants working in the field of graphic design, corporate identity, packaging, architectural graphics, interior design, and furniture and product design. It is the design consultant for Cubic Metre Furniture Ltd, and has also undertaken major product/furniture projects for such companies as Zanotta Furniture and Aqualisa Showers. (15, 99, 136–7)

SANTIAGO MIRANDA was born in Seville, Spain in 1947 and studied at the School of Applied Arts, Seville. He then moved to Italy. See also PERRY KING. (242–52)

MARTA MOIA was born in Argentina and studied fine art and theatre design in Buenos Aires. She trained as a textile designer at the Chelsea School of Art, London, and sold fabric designs before starting to work on one-off commissions, painting directly on fabric. In 1984 her work was included in the 'Maker Designers Today' exhibition at the Camden Arts Centre, London. She continues to paint furnishing fabrics to commission, and she also produces a range of hand-printed fabrics that are available by metre. She recently designed a collection for Toulemonde-Bochart at Divertimenti, London. (334)

CHARLES MOORE is partner in the Connecticut architectural firm of Moore, Grover, Harper, and in the Californian firm of Moore, Ruble, Yudell. He is principal architect of the Urban Innovations Group and head of the architecture programme at the University of California, Los Angeles. He has won more than 40 architectural awards. His work spans three decades and has been seminal in the growth of Post-Modernism. (158–9)

CARLO MORETTI was born in Murano, Italy in 1934. Several generations of his family had worked in the glass industry there – his great-grandfather, Vincenzo Moretti, founded a 'Murrina' glass and bead factory at the end of the

BIOGRAPHIES

eighteenth century – and after a brief period during which he read law at Padua University, Moretti also began working with glass. In 1958 he opened a small furnace for decorative glass where he made engraved glassware, coloured liqueur glasses and opaline goblets. In 1973 he began to create more refined objects, most of them in Murano crystal. He designed first the hexagonal glasses with gold borders and then the more famous octagonal ones; both have been shown at the Museum of Modern Art, New York. (297–8)

ULF MORITZ was born in Poland in 1939. He was employed by a variety of textile firms from 1960 to 1969, and from 1969 to 1972 worked on a textile programme for Gamma Holdings, Helmond. He has produced numerous commissions and has collaborated with several companies. Since 1971, he has directed the textile design department at the Academy of Industrial Design, Eindhoven. He also designs shops and exhibition rooms for fabrics, and has had his work exhibited. (368–73)

WILLIAM MORRIS was born in Walthamstow, London in 1834, and died in Kelmscott House, Hammersmith, London in 1896. He was originally intended for a career in the Church. However, after graduating from Oxford he articled himself to George Edmund Street – a leading Gothic Revival architect. After a few months he abandoned architecture in favour of painting, but did not pursue this for long. The experience he gained in building and furnishing the Red House for his young bride Jane Burden (1859), which had been designed by his friend Philip Webb, encouraged him to set up a co-operative of designers which included Burne-Jones, Webb, Rossetti and Ford Madox Brown. The 'Firm' – Morris, Marshall, Faulkner and Co. – started trading in 1867. Morris took entire control of the enterprise in 1875. He designed wallpapers, tapestries, carpets, the backgrounds of stained-glass windows, and was an expert craftsman in many fields. He was also a poet, translator, writer of romances and a political activist. It is this latter activity which has particularly engaged the attention of recent historians. (517–20)

NICK MOUNT was born in Australia in 1952 and studied at the South Australian School of Art and Gippsland Institute of Advanced Education. His work has been included in numerous exhibitions in Australia and abroad and is represented in the National Gallery, South Australia; the National Gallery, Victoria; the Queensland Art Gallery; the National Gallery, Canberra; and in various private collections in Australia, the USA and Europe. He has received two Crafts Board grants to study glass in the USA and in 1983 was the recipient of the Stuart Devlin Award and the Sterling Craft Award for glass. (299)

GABRIELE MUCCHI was born in Turin, Italy in 1899. By training an engineer, he later became one of the most important figures in the Corrente and Realist movements. In 1934 he designed the house on the Via Marcora, one of the first examples of Rationalist architecture in Milan. In 1935 he designed an important series of metal furniture. He participated in the 5th, 6th, 7th and 8th Milan Triennale and for several years taught at the Academia in East Berlin and Greisswald University. In later life he has devoted himself to painting. In 1983 he was the subject of exhibitions at the Museum of Modern Art in Berlin, the Pushkin Museum in Moscow and the Society of Actual Arts in Brema. (499–500)

PAOLO NAVA was born in Italy in 1943 and studied at the Milan Politecnico and in Florence. He worked for various design studios in England. See also ANTONIO CITTERIO. (6)

NEMO is a design group founded in 1982 by ALAIN DOMINGO and FRANÇOIS SCALI. (127–9, 192)

FRANS VAN NIEUWENBORG was born in Venlo, the Netherlands in 1941. He studied at the Academy of Industrial Design, Eindhoven before setting up a design partnership with MARTIJN WEGMAN. Their works have been collected by the Stedelijk Museum, Amsterdam; the Museum of Modern Art, New York; the University Museum, Mexico City; and by the Dutch cities of Leiden and Arnhem. (197)

ANTTI NURMESNIEMI is a Finnish designer who trained in interior design and began work in the 1950s. After five years in an architectural office he started Studio Nurmesniemi in 1956. He has taught and been exhibited widely and has received many awards. He collaborates with his wife, VUOKKO ESKOLIN-NURMESNIEMI, and is responsible for the furniture and lighting design of Vuokko Oy. (374)

GIOVANNI OFFREDI was born in Milan in 1927. He has designed for Bazzani, Ultravox, GM Arredamenti, Bando Line, ITT and Saporiti Proposals, among others. He took part in the 1959 Formica-Domus competition in Milan, the 1964 to 1968 Marionao Biennal Exhibitions and the 1968 exhibition in Trieste. His work has been shown in the Museum of Modern Art, New York, and the Victoria and Albert Museum, London, and was selected for the 1981 Compasso d'Oro. (213)

PAOLO ORLANDINI was born in Italy in 1941 and took a degree in architecture at the Milan Politecnico. He worked several years for the architect and designer MARCO ZANUSO before establishing himself as an independent designer in 1970. He is a teacher at the European Institute of Design, Milan. See also ROBERTO LUCCI. (7–9)

DAVID PALTERER was born in Haifa, Israel in 1949. He graduated from Florence University, where he was an assistant to Professor Adolfo Natalini, and teaches product design at Syracuse University in addition to working as an architect and designer. His works have been shown at the Milan Triennale, the Dokumenta Urbana in Kassel, and the Museum of Art and Design, Hamburg. He lives in Florence. (392)

VERNER PANTON was born in Denmark in 1926. He completed his studies at the Royal Academy of Fine Arts, Copenhagen in 1955, and worked in several European countries before moving to Basel, Switzerland, in 1963. Since 1969 he has worked exclusively for Mira-X. He has received many awards for his designs and architecture. (326)

NATHALIE DU PASQUIER was born in France in 1957. She moved to Italy in 1979 and shortly after came in contact with the Memphis group. She began working with textiles and later moved on to furniture and graphics as well. She is a freelance designer who lives and works in Milan. She often collaborates with GEORGE SOWDEN. (103–4, 112, 335–46)

BRUNO PAUL was born in 1874 and died in 1968. He joined the Munich Academy in 1894. In 1907 he was a founder-member of the Deutscher Werkbund. He taught and designed widely and was regarded as the leading German architect of his day. (456)

PIERRE PAULIN was born in France in 1927. He studied at the École Camondo and for 30 years has worked as a furniture and interior designer. Examples of his work can be seen in the Victoria and Albert Museum, London, and in the Museum of Modern Art and Metropolitan Museum, New York. Recently his furniture has been on exhibition at the Museum of Decorative Arts and the Pompidou Centre, Paris. In addition to his work in furniture and interior design, he designs products for the Calor Company. He is a partner in the design group ADSA which he founded in 1975. *(16)*

CHRISSIE PEARCEY-COBBOLD, born in 1948, graduated from the Chelsea School of Art, London in 1969, and trained and worked as a professional photographer. She lives in southwest France where she collects and experiments with traditional regional tiles. She now collaborates with architects in designing bathrooms and kitchens. *(266, 268–9, 270–1)*

PAOLO PEDRIZZETTI studied architecture at the Milan Politecnico, graduating in 1973. He worked in building design and building-site management until 1978, when he turned to product design. Pedrizzetti is also a journalist and collaborates with various Italian and foreign newspapers and magazines. *See also* DAVIDE MERCATALI. *(207, 408, 422–5)*

CHARLOTTE PERRIAND collaborated with LE CORBUSIER. *(477–90)*

GIANCARLO PIRETTI was born in Bologna, Italy in 1940. He studied and later taught design for several years at the State Institute of Art, Bologna, while working for Anonima Castelli. He holds a number of industrial and mechanical patents, and his works appear in permanent collections in the USA, Austria, Czechoslovakia and Yugoslavia. Several of his prizes have been shared with EMILIO AMBASZ, with whom he collaborates. *(239)*

PAOLO PIVA was born in Italy in 1950. He attended the International University of the Arts, Venice and studied at the Faculty of Architecture, Venice under Carlo Scarpa. In 1975, while working for the Institute of History and Architecture, Venice, he organized a major exhibition on Vienna during the socialist period. This exhibition gave birth to a similar one in Rome in 1980 called 'Red Vienna'. In 1980 he was invited to design the Kuwait Embassy in Qatar. He has worked for a wide variety of companies in Europe and the USA and has designed the interior displays of several clothing-shop chains. *(28, 34)*

FERDINAND ALEXANDER PORSCHE is a grandson of the inventor of the Volkswagen and son of the founder of the firm of sports car manufacturers which bears his name. Porsche began by continuing the family tradition, but later moved into the wider world of industrial design. He studied at the Waldorf school, Stuttgart, Germany, and later at the School of Design, Ulm. In 1972 he founded Porsche Design in Stuttgart, which later moved to Zell am See Austria. *(61–2)*

PAOLO PORTOGHESI was born in Rome in 1931, and since 1980 has taught in Rome University. He has designed numerous buildings and urban plans, and has published widely. He is editor of *Controspazio*, and has directed the architecture sector of the Venice Biennale since 1979. In 1983 he was appointed chairman of the Venice Biennale. *(395)*

GIANCARLO POZZI was born in Turin, Italy in 1924. He received his PhD in architecture from the Milan Politecnico in 1953, and before establishing his own studio worked in that of Ponti, Fornaroli, Rosselli from 1950 to 1954. Italian companies he has designed for include Arlfex, Cassina, Omfa, Safin, Tecno, Zanotta, Flexarmide, Kervit, Fiat and Lancia. He has collaborated frequently with ACHILLE CASTIGLIONI and Enzo Mari and he has written for such magazines as *Casa Bella, Domus* and *Stile Industria*. In 1973 he won the silver medal at the Milan Triennale with Castiglioni and Ernesto Zerdi. Their design of a hospital bed for Onsa brought them a Compasso d'Oro in 1979. He has been a member of ADI (the Association of Industrial Design) since 1956 and served as president between 1977 and 1980. *(1)*

RÉGIS PROTIÈRE was born in Algeria in 1948, and studied at the École Nationale Supérieure des Arts Décoratifs. He has lived and worked in Paris since 1969. In 1970 he began to design stores and exhibitions in Paris, and in 1979 founded a design and interior-design firm. His work includes a wide range of public, commercial and private interiors. *(75)*

FREIA PROWE was born in Germany and now lives in Switzerland. She studied textiles and their history and now designs home textiles for both German and Swiss firms. She has been invited by the German Development Aid programme to advise on handloom weaving in Indonesia. She also teaches textile history in Zurich. *(320–1)*

ANDRÉE PUTMAN was born and educated in Paris. She studied music with Poulenc and for a time worked as a journalist covering design. In 1978 she founded Écart, which reproduces furniture and textiles by such famous designers as Eileen Gray, Robert Mallet-Stevens, Fortuny, Gaudi and Herbst. She is also the founder of Écart International, and designs for it a wide range of products, including fabrics, tableware, stationery and cutlery. *(412)*

FRANCO RAGGI was born in Milan in 1945 and graduated in architecture from the Milan Politecnico in 1969. He has edited a number of journals and organized several major design exhibitions. He has written extensively and his work has been widely published. He has collaborated with a number of major companies. *(49–50)*

PIER GUISEPPE RAMELLA was born in Italy in 1934. He graduated in architecture from the Milan Politecnico in 1960, and from 1961 to 1968 worked as a university assistant for the courses of town planning in the Faculty of Architecture in Venice and then Milan. For many years he devoted himself exclusively to architecture, designing major residential and industrial complexes in Milan and elsewhere. Since 1981 he has again turned to design and now creates lamps for Arteluce. *(219)*

DIETER RAMS was born in Germany in 1932. He was apprenticed as a joiner and then studied architecture and design at the Werk-Kunstschule, Wiesbaden. After working for the architectural firm of Otto Apel, he was appointed chief designer for Braun AG, many of whose products, by 1959, were on display at the Museum of Modern Art, New York. *(512–13)*

HANS H. RATH, who died in 1968, owned, together with his father STEFAN RATH, the Viennese firm of Lobmeyr following LUDWIG LOBMEYR'S death. The two of them guided the firm through the difficulties of the 1930 depression and the Second World War and found time for design work in addition to their management responsibilities. *(445)*

STEFAN RATH, who died in 1960, was an Austrian designer who became the owner of Lobmeyr after LUDWIG LOBMEYR'S death. *See also* HANS H. RATH. *(445)*

GABRIELE REGONDI was born in Milan, Italy in 1948. He graduated in 1969 and received his Master's degree in architecture at the Milan Politecnico. He teaches planning, furniture and design at the Experimental Institute of Art, Monza. His designs have been produced by such firms as Rosenthal, Flexform and Rimadesio. *(98)*

GERRIT T. RIETVELD was born in the Netherlands in 1888 and died in 1964. He was an apprentice cabinetmaker to his father between 1899 and 1906; was a jewellery-design draughtsman until 1911; and an independent cabinetmaker until 1919, when he opened his own architectural office. He was a member of De Stijl until 1931. *(468–76)*

GASTONE RINALDI was born in Padua, Italy in 1920. He has designed metal chairs and furniture since the 1950s and has been awarded several prizes for his work. He won the 1954 Compasso d'Oro and received a mention at the 1955 Compasso d'Oro. He was awarded a silver medal at the 11th Milan Triennale, and his *Aurora* and *Dafne* chairs won mentions at the 1980 and 1981 Compasso d'Oro. His work has been collected by the Amsterdam and Philadelphia museums. Rinaldi lives and works in Padua, where he is director of Thema SPA. *(12–13)*

WENDY ROBIN was born in London in 1943. She studied at the City and Guilds School of Art, London, receiving a Diploma in Drawing and Printing, and later received her Master's degree in painting from the Royal College of Art, London. She has produced murals, book illustrations and stage sets and since 1983 has been in partnership with ALAN STANTON. Her work has been widely exhibited. She has taught in Newcastle and London. *(149–50)*

ALDO ROSSI was born in Milan, Italy in 1931. In 1971 he started working with Gianni Braghieria. Since 1975 he has held the Chair of Architecture Composition in Venice University. He has taught at the Federal Polytechnic of Zurich, and has collaborated with the principal American universities since 1976. In 1983 he was named director of the architecture sector of the Venice Biennale. He has designed many buildings for which he has received prizes. *(384, 389)*

MITCH RYERSON was born in the USA in 1955 and received a BAA from the Boston University Program in Artisanry. He has published in the *New York Times* design section, *Progressive Architecture* and *Boston Magazine*. *(178)*

CLAUDIO SALOCCHI was born in Italy in 1934. He studied at the Milan Politecnico and has run his own architecture and interior design office in Milan since 1965. He has lectured at Lissoni, has designed showrooms and interiors in major Italian cities, and has exhibited at several furniture exhibitions. *(39–40)*

ALBERTO SALVATI was born in Milan, Italy in 1935. He took a degree in architecture in 1960, and from 1961 to 1964 was assistant at the Faculty of Engineering at Milan

BIOGRAPHIES

Politecnico. He was also an assistant at the Faculty of Architecture there from 1962 to 1963. In conjunction with Viale Umbria, he designed the *Miamina* armchair, selected for the Compasso d'Oro, for Saporiti Italia. He has collaborated with AMBROGIO TRESOLDI. *(71, 83, 85, 375)*

PEP SANT was born in Barcelona and studied physics at the University of Madrid. *See also* RAMON BIGAS BAUCELLS. *(196)*

RICHARD SAPPER was born in Munich, West Germany in 1932. He studied philosophy, anatomy, graphic art, engineering and graduated in economics. His early design experience was gained at Daimler-Benz. His main interests are concentrated on high-technology products such as microprocessors and conveyance systems. He has received many awards: five Compasso d'Oro, three gold medals of the BIO of Lubiana, the German award 'Die gute Form' and the SMAU award. Many of his works can be found in the Museum of Modern Art, New York. *(44, 388)*

TIMO SARPANEVA was born in Helsinki, Finland in 1926. He studied in Helsinki and has worked and taught since 1950, exhibiting widely and receiving numerous prizes. He became a professor in 1976. His works are included in a large number of major collections, including the Museum of Modern Art and the Metropolitan Museum of Art, New York: and the Victoria and Albert Museum, London. *(413–14)*

ALESSIO SARRI was born in Italy in 1954. He trained at the Ceramic Academy, Florence and since 1978 has been designing ceramics in conjunction with MATTEO THUN. He has his own company near Florence where he produces top-quality pottery, and his work has won several prizes in Italian ceramic fairs. He and Thun have exhibited widely in Italy and Germany as well as in Paris, New York and London. *(292)*

FRANÇOIS SCALI was born in France in 1951. He received his Master's degree in economics in 1974, and graduated in architecture in 1979. He and ALAIN DOMINGO founded the design group NEMO in 1982, since which time they have exhibited together in Europe, America and Japan. Their works have received several awards. *(127–9, 192)*

AFRA SCARPA was born in Montebelluna, Italy in 1937, and graduated from the Architectural Institute, Venice. She and TOBIA SCARPA have worked together for more than 25 years. In 1958 they began working in glass with Venini at Murano. They created the *Bastiano* divan and *Vanessa* metal bed for Gavina, and for Cassina they designed the *Soriana* armchair, which won the Compasso d'Oro award in 1970, and the *925* armchair, which is on permanent display at the Museum of Modern Art, New York. The *Torcello* system, designed for Stildomus, and the *Morna* bed are among their other famous creations. They are responsible for the image of the Benetton shops in Europe and America, and they occasionally work as architects as well as designers. Examples of their architectural work include the restoration of the Fragiacomo family house in Trieste, the Lorenzin family house at Abano Terme, and the Benetton woollen factory and house at Ponsano. Their pieces can be seen in major museums all over the world, and many have been chosen for various international design exhibitions. *(84)*

TOBIA SCARPA was born in 1935 in Venice, Italy. After a brief time working in the glass industry, he launched a highly successful design collaboration. *See also* AFRA SCARPA. *(84, 234)*

MART Z. VAN SCHIJNDEL was born in Hengelo, the Netherlands, in 1943. He has worked as a carpenter, building engineer, interior architect, product designer, architect, teacher and university lecturer. Since 1969 he has run an architectural office in Utrecht. His interior designs and products for interiors have been used in the railway station, museum and Chamber of Commerce in Utrecht, and in offices, houses, shops, factories, restaurants and cultural and educational centres. His glass vase, *Delta*, won the Arango prize. *(233)*

ROBERT SIEGEL was born in 1939 in New York City. He graduated in architecture at Pratt Institute in 1962, and received his Master's degree from Harvard University in 1963. Prior to the formation of GWATHMEY SIEGEL & ASSOCIATES ARCHITECTS, he was an associate with Edward L. Barnes and Associates, Architects, in New York City. In 1979 he was elected vice-president of the New York Chapter of the American Institute of Architects. *(81, 277–8)*

ASAHARA SIGHEAKI was born in Tokyo in 1948. He lived in Italy between 1967 and 1971, and opened a design and furnishing studio in Tokyo in 1973. He now divides his time between Japan and Italy. He has worked for a number of companies in each country, and is also interested in conceptual sculpture. *(227)*

DANILO SILVESTRIN was born in 1942 in Bolzano, Italy. He studied architecture at the Milan Politecnico from 1961 to 1963 before continuing his education at the Academy of Fine Arts, Florence. After two years he moved to New York for a year, then took a course in sculpture at the Folkwang School, Essen, West Germany. In 1968 he returned to architectural studies at the Academy of Arts, Dusseldorf and began working as a freelance designer and interior designer. Since 1971 he has lived and worked in Munich. *(21, 23)*

SITE An architectural practice founded by JAMES WINE and ALISON SKY. *(176)*

ALISON SKY is an American designer, born in 1946. In 1970 she and JAMES WINE founded the architectural practice SITE (Sculpture In The Environment). *(176)*

JOHN SMITH was born in Britain in 1948 and studied at the School of Art, Chesterfield and College of Art and Technology, High Wycombe. Since emigrating to Australia in 1970 he has worked as a furniture designer and maker, and has been awarded design prizes in Japan, Poland and Australia. In addition to designing and producing furniture and wood products he is a senior lecturer at the School of Art, University of Tasmania, and is the coordinator of its 'Design in Wood' course. *(90–2)*

PETER GLYNN SMITH was born in 1932 and educated in England, studying fine art at Stoke on Trent College of Art, and design at the Bartlett School of Architecture, University College, London. In 1964 he established the Glynn Smith Associates Design Studio in London. He has worked on a wide range of interior design projects, including hotels, restaurants, airports and offices. *(175)*

PENNY SMITH lives in Tasmania, Australia where she teaches ceramics in addition to developing domestic tableware in her own studio. Her work has been exhibited both nationally and internationally and is represented in collections around the world. *(285–91)*

JOHNNY SØRENSEN was born in Denmark in 1944. He graduated with a diploma in crafts and design in 1966, and opened an office together with RUD THYGESEN in the same year. Together they have been awarded many prizes and have been the subject of exhibitions. Examples of their work have been purchased by the Danish State of Art Foundation. *(36)*

ALFONSO SOTO SORIA is a Mexican anthropologist who collaborates with LABBAR HOAGLAND and PEDRO LEITES. *(402—5)*

ETTORE SOTTSASS JR was born in Austria in 1917. He studied at the Milan Politecnico, and opened an office there in 1947. Since 1957 he has worked for Olivetti, but is also active in fields as various as ceramics, jewellery, decorations, lithographs and drawings. He has taught and exhibited widely. In 1980 he established Sottsass Associati with some other architects, and has designed many pieces of furniture that are part of the Memphis collection. *(109)*

GEORGE SOWDEN was born in England in 1942. He studied architecture at the Gloucestershire College of Art from 1960 to 1968, and in 1970 moved to Milan to work as a consultant to Olivetti. He has participated in all the Memphis exhibitions as well as other exhibitions in Milan, Switzerland and Denmark. He often collaborates with NATHALIE DU PASQUIER. *(103—4, 335—46)*

LAURINDA SPEAR was born in Rochester, Minnesota, USA in 1951. She graduated from Brown University in 1972 and received her MA in architecture from Columbia University in 1975. In 1977 she and her husband, Bernardo Fort-Brescia, founded Arquitectonica in conjunction with three other architects; the firm has won several Progressive Architecture Design Awards, and awards from the American Institute of Architecture. In 1985 Spear and Fort-Brescia founded Arquitectonica Products, for which they design furniture, fabrics and ceramics. Spear's work has been included in several exhibitions, and an exhibition devoted to Arquitectonica and entitled 'Arquitectonica: Yesterday, Today, Tomorrow' has travelled throughout the USA. In 1978 Laurinda Spear won a fellowship to the American Academy, Rome. *(272)*

ELS STAAL was born in the Netherlands in 1959. He studied product design at the Academy of Art, Arnhem between 1977 and 1982, and has worked as a freelance designer, except for 1983 to 1984, when he was guest-designer at the Concepts Design Studio in Amsterdam. *(70)*

JAY STANGER was born in Boston, USA, in 1956. He graduated from Boston University in 1982. *(162)*

ALAN STANTON was born in 1944. He studied at the Architectural Association, London, and received his Master's degree in Architecture and Urban Design from California University, Los Angeles, in 1969. He has worked on projects in France, Britain, Germany and Japan, has taught in Britain and America, and has received prizes for his work, which has also been widely exhibited. He and WENDY ROBIN have worked together since 1983. *(149—50)*

ROBERT A.M. STERN was born in New York in 1939. He studied at Columbia and at Yale universities, and became a partner in the firm John S. Hagmann, architects and planners, in 1969. He also worked as a designer in Richard Meier's New York office, and as a consultant to Philip Johnson for a television documentary on New York. He teaches at Columbia, and has held office in a number of professional bodies, and been a member of several architectural and pedagogical committees. *(275, 366, 390)*

MICHAEL STEWART was born in Toronto, Canada, in 1940. He studied fine art at Ontario College of Art from 1959 to 1963 and in 1966 spent a year studying design in Finland. In 1968 he formed an industrial design partnership with Keith Muller, but since 1973 he has worked primarily as a freelance interior designer and a furniture designer for Ambiant Systems Ltd. *(88—9)*

ELISABETH STRÄSSLE was born in Switzerland in 1942. Following a teaching degree, she studied art at Krefeld, Sindelfingen and Stuttgart, and became a freelance textile designer in Zurich in 1969. In 1974 she moved to Paris, and in 1977 to New York where she is a painter. In 1982 she turned again to textile design, producing a collection for Mira-X. *(322)*

OSKAR STRNAD was a Viennese stage and interior decorator who designed sets and gift items for LOBMEYR. *(445)*

TAKASHI SUDO was born in Tokyo in 1953. He studied graphic design and photography in Japan before moving to England in 1977. In 1978 he and Charles Crittall set up a design partnership, 'Oval 31 Design', concentrating largely on the design and production of fine furniture. *(47)*

KAZUHIDE TAKAHAMA was born in Nobeoka, Japan in 1930. He graduated from the Faculty of Architecture at Tokyo in 1953 and has lived in Bologna, Italy since 1963 where he is an established designer. He has designed furniture for Simon International, B&B Italia and Gavina. *(238)*

ILMARI TAPIOVAARA was born in Finland in 1914. He trained in Helsinki and worked with LE CORBUSIER in Paris. He ran an office with Annikki Tapiovaara from 1950, collaborating with major companies and teaching widely. *(496)*

RITA TASKINEN was born in Helsinki, Finland in 1949. She attended the University of Applied Arts, Helsinki from 1977 to 1982. Since 1979 she has been a freelance designer, working in furniture and interior design, exhibition design and graphic design. In addition to her work as a designer, Taskinen has worked as a journalist and has written extensively about the design field. *(93)*

GIUSEPPE TERRAGNI was born in Italy in 1904 and died in 1942. He was one of the most important figures of the early Modern Movement in Italy, though his work covers a period of only thirteen years, from his graduation in Milan in 1926 to the time of his call-up for the army in 1939. He was responsible for some of the most significant buildings produced during this period and was a member of the Gruppo Sette along with Figini, Frette, Larco, Librera, Pollini and Rava. *(492—4)*

MATTEO THUN was born in Austria in 1952 and graduated from Florence University. He was a founding member of the Memphis design group and established his own design company in Milan in 1984. His work has been shown in Berlin, Hanover, Dusseldorf, Vienna, Los Angeles and at the 1983 Milan Triennale. He is a professor of product design and ceramics at the Academy of Arts, Vienna. *(30, 294)*

RUD THYGESEN was born in Denmark in 1932, and opened an office together with JOHNNY SØRENSEN in 1966. *(36)*

STANLEY TIGERMAN was born in 1930. He is a controversial American architect who studied at the Yale School of Architecture, and is now a principal in Tigerman, Fugman, McCurry, in Chicago. He organized the 'Chicago Seven' and curated their shows. His designs have been exhibited internationally, including the Museum of Modern Art, New York. He has published widely and has been awarded numerous prizes. *(152—3, 273—4, 397)*

PETER TING was born in Hong Kong in 1959. He studied ceramics in Surrey, Wales and Staffordshire in the UK, and his work has been exhibited widely. *(281—4)*

RENATO TOSO was born in Venice. *See also* NOTI MASSARI. *(323)*

AMBROGIO TRESOLDI was born in Italy in 1933. He took a degree in architecture in 1960 and from 1961 to 1964 was assistant at the Faculty of Architecture of the Milan Politecnico. His and ALBERTO SALVATI'S design of the *Miamina* armchair was selected for the Compasso d'Oro. *(375)*

JUDITH TRIM is a British potter who studied at the Academy of Art, Bath from 1961 to 1964. She teaches ceramics in London and has lectured in London, Bath and Belfast. She has exhibited since 1980, published widely and has works included in several collections. *(279—80)*

OSCAR TUSQUETS was born in Barcelona in 1941. He attended the Higher Technical School of Architecture, Barcelona and in 1964 he established Studio PER with Lluis Clotet, with whom he collaborated on nearly all of his projects until 1984. He has been a guest professor and lecturer at universities in Germany, France and the USA, and his work has been exhibited in many parts of Europe and in the USA. He has received many awards, both for his work as an architect and as a designer. *(63—5, 291)*

ALAN TYE studied as an architect, but has practised product design for 20 years. His firm, Alan Tye Design, is one of Britain's leading design practices and has received 23 design awards. Over ten million Alan Tye Design products have been sold worldwide. *(426)*

CARLO A. URBINATI-RICCI was born in Italy in 1955. He studied architecture at Rome University and now works in partnership with ALESSANDRO VECCHIATO designing lamps for Foscarini. *(205—6)*

ALESSANDRO VECCHIATO was born in Italy in 1959. He studied architecture in Venice. *See also* CARLO A. URBINATI-RICCI. *(205—6)*

ROBERT VENTURI, born in 1925, is an American architect whose works have won international recognition. He has been the subject of innumerable exhibitions, awards and special publications. He was educated at Princeton University, where he received both his AB and MFA, and at the American Academy, Rome. He was a Rome Prize Fellow from 1954 to 1956. He holds several honorary

BIOGRAPHIES

doctorates from American universities, and in 1983 was the recipient of the Louis Sullivan Award and Prize of the International Union of Bricklayers and Allied Craftsmen. That same year Virginia University honoured him with the Thomas Jefferson Memorial Foundation Medal. He is a partner in the architectural firm Venturi, Rauch and Scott Brown, and is the author of several books on architecture. *(27, 144–6, 156–7, 396)*

DAVID VICKERY was born in 1943 and educated in London. He joined Conran Associates in 1973, for whom he worked on a wide variety of interior schemes, including designs for Habitat, Intercontinental Hotels, and the Milton Keynes Development Corporation. He left Conran Associates in 1976 to work for Dale Keller and Associates, designing hotels for the Mariott Corporation. He subsequently worked for Fitch and Co. and Wrenn and Co. before rejoining Conran in 1980. He was recently appointed Associate Director of Conran Associates. *(171)*

LELLA AND MASSIMO VIGNELLI are a husband-and-wife team. They studied in Venice, Italy, and in 1960 established the Massimo and Lella Vignelli Office of Design and Architecture in Milan, working with graphics, products, furniture and interiors. In 1965 they founded Unimark International Corporation, and, in 1971, Vignelli Associates, with an office in New York and liaison offices in Paris and Milan. They provide designs for a wide range of major companies, and have received awards and honorary doctorates for their work. *(80)*

BURKHARD VOGTHERR was born in 1942 and works in Karden-Holzen in West Germany. He graduated in industrial design at the Technical Institute of Kassel and Wuppertal, and was apprenticed for three years. In 1970 he began to work as a freelance designer, having received in 1969 a government award for 'Gute Form'. *(48)*

VUOKKO *see* VUOKKO ESKOLIN-NURMESNIEMI and ANTTI NURMESNIEMI. *(374)*

MARTIJN WEGMAN was born in 1955 in The Hague, the Netherlands, and studied at the Gerrit Rietveld Academy, Amsterdam. *See also* FRANS VAN NIEUWENBORG. *(197)*

DANIEL WEIL was born in Buenos Aires in 1953. He studied architecture at Buenos Aires University and did an MA in industrial design at the Royal College of Art, London. He lives in London, but the reputation he has earned for his work in product design is international. He has exhibited in London, Milan, Venice, Hanover, San Francisco, Philadelphia and Dallas. His work is in the permanent collection of the Museum of Modern Art, New York. *(116–17)*

VOLKER WEINERT was born in 1943 in Wilster, West Germany. He studied at the School of Arts and Crafts, Flensburg; the High School for Visual Arts, Hamburg; and the High School for Fine Art, Berlin; obtaining diplomas as an industrial designer. He has worked as a freelance designer for Karl Kittert, Schwabisch Gmund, Nanna Ditzel, and Herbert Lindinger. He is an assistant at the High School of Fine Art, Berlin, the Institute of Industrial Design. *(228)*

LYNNE WILSON was born in England in 1952. She entered the Royal College of Art, London in 1976 and in 1978 was awarded the Sanderson Scholarship for a study tour in south-east Asia, where she undertook research into the decorative arts. In 1979 she received her Master's degree from the Royal College of Art. Since then she has worked as a freelance designer in Italy. *(37–8)*

JAMES WINE is an American designer born in 1932. In 1970 he founded the design practice SITE (Sculpture In The Environment) together with ALISON SKY. He is chairman of the Parsons School of Design in New York. *(176)*

DIETER WITTE was born in Germany in 1937. He studied in Hanover from 1957 to 1961, and worked in a design group until he opened his own office in 1966 together with his designer wife, Heidi Witte. In 1977 he began to work permanently with Osram. *(241)*

DAVID WOLTON was born in Britain in 1938. He studied brewing science at the Herriot Watt University, Edinburgh, and later attended the London School of Economics. He is now a hop merchant and publisher, who for 20 years has experimented with designs for furniture. These are shortly to go into production. *(77–8)*

LESLIE JOHN WRIGHT was born in Australia in 1951. He has taught and run a design and photography business. He studied craft and design from 1982 to 1984, and has since had several exhibitions of his work. *(2)*

RICK WRIGLEY was born in 1955 in Arlington, Virginia, USA. He graduated in 1981 with a BFA from New York in technology. His exhibitions include one at the Cooper Hewitt Museum in 1982. His work has so far focused on large corporate commissions. *(167)*

KAZUMASA YAMASHITA was born in Tokyo in 1937. He was on the staff of Niken Sekkei Planners, Architects and Engineers from 1959 to 1964 and from 1966 to 1969. From 1969 to 1978 he taught at the Institute of Art and Design, Tokyo; in 1980 he was visiting professor at the Technical College, Nova Scotia, Canada; and in 1983, lecturer at the Institute of Technology, Tokyo. In 1977 he received the most prestigious award for architecture in Japan. He works as a designer as well as an architect. *(401)*

MARCO ZANINI was born in Italy in 1954. He studied architecture at the University of Florence, graduating in 1978. Since 1978 he has been a designer with Sottsass Associates in Milan. *(110)*

MARCO ZANUSO was born in Milan in 1916 and graduated in architecture at the Milan Politecnico in 1939. He subsequently became first a lecturer, then professor of architecture at the Politecnico, and was a member of the CIAM (International Congresses of Modern Architecture). He was editor-in-chief of *Casabella* from 1947 to 1949, then served as the editor under Ernesto Rogers. Since 1945 he has been practising as an architect, designer and town planner. He has won prizes at all the Milan Triennales; and in 1956 he received the Compasso d'Oro for the sewing-machine designed for Borletti. In 1962 he won the same prize for the Doney Brion Vega television set. He has acted as a consultant to Olivetti for many years and he lives and works in Milan. His principal works include the *Ladi* armchair for Arflex, the *Lambda* chair for Gavina and the Auso-Siemens *Grillo* (Cricket) telephone. For Olivetti he has designed a number of factories in Brazil, Argentina and Italy. *(421, 497)*

SUPPLIERS

ACERBIS Via Brusaporto, 31-Seriate, Bergamo, Italy.
Main Retailers USA: Memphis Milano, 150 E. 58 Street, New York, N.Y. 10155. UK: Artemide G.B. Ltd, 17/19 Neal Street, London WC2H 9PU. France: Roger Von Barry, 18 Rue Laffitte, Paris 75009.

A. AHLSTROM OY 14500 Iittala, Finland.

ALESSI SPA Via Priv. Alessi 6, 28023 Crusinallo (NO), Italy.
Main Retailers USA: D.F. Sanders & Co., 386 West Broadway, New York, N.Y. 10012. UK: Conran Shop, 77–9 Fulham Road, London SW3. Paris: Au Printemps SA, 64 Boulevard Haussman, Paris 75451.
The Netherlands: Binnenhuis, Huidenstraat 3–5, 1016 Amsterdam. Japan: Italia Shoji Co. Ltd, 7th Kojimachi Bldg, 5 4-chome, Kojimachi, Chiyoda-Ku.

ALIAS SRL Via Ottorino Respighi 2, 20122 Milan, Italy.
Main Retailers USA: ICF Co. Furnishing, 305 E. 63 Street, New York, N.Y. 10021. London: Alias UK, 17–19 Neal Street, London WC2. Paris: Roget Von Barry, 18 Rue Laffitte, 75009 Paris. Amsterdam: Kreymborg, Minervallin 63, 1077 NR Amsterdam N11. Tokyo: Casatec Ltd, French Bank Bldg, 1/1/2 Akasaka, Minoto Ku, Tokyo 107.

G.&S. ALLGOOD LTD 297 Euston Road, London NW1 3AQ, UK.

ALUMINOR C.D. 15 La Roseyre, 06390 Contes, France.

AMBIANT SYSTEMS LTD 76 Richmond Street East, Toronto, Canada.

ARAM DESIGNS LTD 3 Kean Street, London WC2, UK.

ARFLEX SPA Via Monte Rosa 27, Limbiate (Milan), Italy

ARTEK OY AB Keskuskatu 3, 00100 Helsinki 10.

ARTELUCE Via Moretto 58, Brescia, Italy.
Main Retailers USA: Atelier International, 595 Madison Avenue, New York. UK: Floss Ltd, Heath Hall, Heath, Wakefield, W. Yorkshire WF1 5SL. France: Floss Sarl., 23 Rue de Bourgogne, Paris 73007. Switzerland: Floss Sa., 36 Place de Bourg de Four, Geneva 1204.

ARTEMIDE Via Brughiera, 20010 Pregna Milanese, Milan, Italy.

ARTHUR SANDERSON AND SONS 53 Berners Street, London W1, UK.

ATTITUDE Rue Arsène d'Arsonval, Le Ponteix, 87220 Feytiat, France.
Main Retailers UK: Liberty, Regent Street, London W1R 6AH. France: Galerie Philippe Parent, 48 Rue Dauphine, Paris 75006. The Netherlands: Metz & Co., Keizersgracht 455, 1017 dk Amsterdam.

AVARTE OY Kalevankatu 16, SF-00100 Helsinki.
Main Retailers USA: Beylerian Ltd, 305 E. 63 Street, New York, N.Y. 10021. Agent in UK: Bristol International, Euroway Industrial Park, Swindon SN5 8YW.

B&B ITALIA SPA Strada Provinciale, Novedrate, Italy.

BERG LICHT & OBJEKT GMBH D-3400 Isernhagen 1, Am Walde 2, W. Germany.
Main Retailers W. Germany: Loeser, PO Box 3000, Oster Str., Hanover. Agent in Japan: Jamagiwa Trading Co. Ltd, 3124 Sotokanda, Tokyo 101.

G.B. BERNINI SPA Via Fiume 17, Milan, Italy.

BIEFFEPLAST SPA PO Box 406, 1–35100 Padua, Italy.

GABRIEL BOLIGTEXTILER A/S Hjulmagervaj 55, 9000 Aalborg, Denmark.

BUDGEREE GLASS 20 William Street, Norwood, Adelaide, South Australia.

PAULINE BURBIDGE 4 Haddon Road, West Bridgford, Nottingham N42 6EQ, UK.

BUSNELLI EDIZIONI SPA Via Kennedy 34, 20020 Misinto, Italy.
Main Retailers Agent in USA: Limn, 457 Pacific Avenue, San Francisco, Ca. Agent in France: Reminiscence, 6 Boulevard de Guillaume, Antibes. Agent in Norway: Italian House, Skilledebca 205, Oslo.

CAPPELLINI International Interiors snc, di Cappellini Enrico & Co., 22060 Carugo, Italy.

CASAS Milagro 40, 08028 Barcelona, Spain.
Main Retailers Agent in USA: ICF, 305 E. 63 Street, New York, N.Y. 10021. Agent in UK: Bristol International, Euroway Industrial Park, Swindon, SN5. Agent in France: Oggi Design, 151 Avenue de Maine, Paris 75017. Agent in Belgium: Vosen Quatro, Centre Lesquat, Jodoigna B5900.

CASIGLIANI Via Cannizzaro 5, 56010 Ospedaletto, Pisa, Italy.
Main Retailers USA: Roche Bobois, Suite 819, 183 Madison Avenue, New York, N.Y. 10016. UK: Maples, Waring & Gillow, 145 Tottenham Court Road, London W1P 9LL. France: Stephen Simon, 14 Rue de Châteaudo, 94200 Ivry, Paris.

CASSINA SPA 20036 Meda, Milan, Italy.
Main Retailers USA: Atelier International, 595 Madison Avenue, New York. UK: Environment, Heath Hall, Heath, Wakefield, W. Yorks. WF1 5SL. France: Cassina, 168 Rue du Faubourg St Honoré, Paris. The Netherlands: Mobica, Middenweg 31, M.B. Ijsselstein. Spain: Mobil Plast SL, Corso Milagro 40, Barcelona 28.

CIATTI SPA 500100 Badia A. Settimo, Florence, Italy.
Main Retailers UK: Idea for Living, 5 Kensington High Street, London W8.

COLBOC-DUBOIS 11 Rue Servandoni, Paris 75006, France.

JOHN COLES The Old Gospel Hall, Standford Hill, Standford, nr Bordon, Hants, UK.

SUPPLIERS

COLLECTION KALLEMO AB PO Box 605, 331 01 Varnamo, Sweden.

COLLIER CAMPBELL LTD 41 Old Town, London SW4 0JL, UK.

CORTINA VOF 1ᵉ Helmerstraat 106, Amsterdam.
Main Retailers USA: Appenzeller, Madison Avenue, New York. France: Modernismes, 16 Rue Franklin, Paris 75016. The Netherlands: Metz & Co., Keizersgracht 455, Amsterdam.

COSE CASA Industrie Cassalinghi Mori spa. 25066 Lumezzane, Pieve (BS), Italy.

CUBIC METRE FURNITURE LTD 17–18 Great Sutton Street, London EC1, UK.
Main Retailers UK: Cubic Metre Furniture, 6–10 Clerkenwell Road, London EC1. Sweden: Widen Sales Promotion, PO Box 39020, 40075 Gothenberg.

DAICHI CO., LTD 3–24–14 Toyo, Koto-Ku, Tokyo, Japan.

BRUNO DANESE SNC Piaza San Fedele 2, Milan 20121, Italy.

DE PADOVA SRL Corso Venezia 14, 20121 Milan, Italy.

DESIGN IN THE ROUND 502 Nelson Road, Mt Nelson, Hobart, Tasmania, Australia 7007.

DESIGNUM PO Box 10, 6998 26 Laag-Keppel, Netherlands.
Main Retailers The Netherlands: Jager Interiors, Vrijheidslaan 100, Amsterdam 1078 PS.

DISEÑO & DISEÑO 9 de Julio 1037, 5500 Mendoza, Argentina.

DIVERTIMENTI 86 Westbourne Grove, London W2, UK.

DOMUS SPA 25070 Lavenons, BS, Italy.
Main Retailers USA: Mediterranean Export Inc., 3401 N.W. 7 Street, Miami, Fla. UK: James Lewis Ltd, Builders Hardware, 257 Hospital Street, Birmingham B19 2YF. W. Germany: Hahne-Domus GmbH, 20 Zur Helle, 5860 Iserlohn, Droschede.

DRAENERT STUDIOS GMBH Steigwiesen 3, 7997 Immenstaad/Bodensee, W. Germany.
Main Retailers Agent in USA: Modern Bauhaus, Suite 104, The Marketplace, 2400 Market Street, Philadelphia, Pa. 19103. Agent in UK: Ramchester Furnishings, 63 Buckingham Gate, London SW1. Agent in France: Alter Ego, 10 Rue de Caligny, Paris 75012.

ERCO LIGHTING LTD PO Box 2460, Lüdenscheid, W. Germany.

FERMOB BP 48, 71102 Châlon-sur-Saône, France.
Main Retailers Agent in UK: King Easton, Garden Centre, The Green, Station Road, London N21. France: Opportune, 5 Rue Saint Opportune, Paris 75001.

FLOS SPA Via Moretto 58, Brescia, Italy.
Main Retailers Agent in UK: Floss Ltd, Heath Hall, Heath, Wakefield, W. Yorks. WF1 5SL. Agent in France: Floss Sarl, 23 Rue de Bourgogne, Paris 75007.

FORM PROGRAM AB PO Box 151, 199 01 Enköping, Sweden.

FORMICA CORPORATION USA: 1501 Broadway, New York, N.Y. 10036. Italy: Via le Majno 34, Milan 20129. UK: 21 The Green, Richmond, Surrey TW9 1PJ.

FOSCARINI SPA Fondamenta Manin 1, 30121 Murano, Italy.
Main Retailers UK: Harrods Ltd, Knightsbridge, London SW1. France: Duo Sur Canapé, 36 Rue Etienne Marcel, Paris 75002. W. Germany: Alta Linea, Sandhof 6, 4040 Neuss 21 Nord.

FURNITURE OF THE 20TH CENTURY INC 227 W. 17 Street, New York, N.Y. 10011.

FUSITAL SPA Via Gavazzi 16, 22035 Canzo (Co), Italy.

FUSO GOMU LTD 5–15–9 Minami-Aoyama, Minato-Ku, Tokyo 107.

G. GERVASONI SPA 33050 Pavia di Udine, Italy.

MARTIN GRIERSON Workspace, 10 Barley Mow Passage, London W4 4PH, UK.

HAG AS PO Box 7159, Homansbyen, Oslo 3.
Main Retailers Agent in USA: Hag USA Inc., The Merchandise Mart Plaza, PO Box 4109, Chicago, Ill. 60654. Agent in UK: The Back Store, 324A King Street, London W6. Agent in the Netherlands: Safinex BV, 2 Bessemerstraat, 3316 GB Dordrecht.

HALLING KOCH DESIGN CENTER PO Box 2152, Loensboda, Sweden S28070.

CARL HANSEN & SON A/S Kochsgade 97, 5000 Odense C, Denmark.
Main Retailers Denmark: Salesco, Bella Center, 2300 Copenhagen. The Netherlands: Morin, Julianalaan 195, HV14 32 Aalsmeer.

FRITZ HANSENS A/S DK-34500 Allerød, Denmark.

HINCHCLIFFE & BARBER Charlton Cottage, Charlton Marshall, Blandford, Dorset DT11 9NG, UK.
Main Retailers UK: Designers' Guild, 277 King's Road, London SW3. France: Jansen, 9 Rue Royale, Paris 75008.

HIROMORI Akasaka, 1614 Minato Ku, Tokyo 107.

ICF 305 E. 63 Street, New York, N.Y. 10021.

IKEA OF SWEDEN S-343 00, Almhult, Sweden.
Main Retailers W. Germany: Ikea, Isernhagenerstrasse 14, G3006 Burgwedel.

INNO-TUOTE OY Pietarinkatu 9, 00140 Helsinki, Finland.
Main Retailers Agent in USA: Polyr Design, 2112 Hystyd, Chicago, Ill. 60614. Agent in Italy: Fin Form, Viale Montesanto, 4 Milan. Agent in Japan: Okakyu Department Store, 1–3 Nyshy, Shynguku, Tokyo.

MENNO JETTEN J. de Bekastraat 24, 3514 VM Utrecht, Netherlands.

WENDY JONES 2 Brook Cottages, Brook Lane, Plaxtol, Kent TN15 0RF, UK.
Main Retailers UK: Designers' Guild, 277 King's Road, London SW3.

KARTELL Via Delle I, 20082 Noviglio (Milan), Italy.

KNOLL INTERNATIONAL 655 Madison Avenue, New York, N.Y. 10021.

KOSUGA & CO. 15–4, Higashi-Nihonbashi 2-chome, Chuo-ka, Tokyo.

JOHANNES KUHNEN Hedglea Cottage, Michelago 2620, New South Wales, Australia.

KUROKAWA INC. 5–15–9 Minami-Aoyama, Minato-Ku, Tokyo.

LAMM SPA 43017 S. Secondo, Parmense PR, Italy.
Main Retailers UK: J.T. Contract, 29 Store Street, London WC1. The Netherlands: J. Molenar, PO Box 56 2100, Heemstede. Austria: Centroform, Lasserstr. 10, Salzburg, Switzerland: Pasetta, Marktgasse 6, Rapperswil.

LEVESTA Apartado 154, Granollers, Barcelona, Spain.

LITA 5 Rue de l'Allée Verte, 41600 Lamotte-Beuvron, France.

J. & L. LOBMEYR Kaerntner Strasse 26, A-1015 Vienna, Austria.

LUMIANCE BV Transvaalstraat 10, 2021 RL Haarlem, Netherlands.
Main Retailers USA: Basic Concepts, 141 Linzer Avenue, Garfield, N.J. 07026. UK: Linolite, Lumiance, Malmesbury, Wilts. SN17 0BN. France: Lumiance, 4 Rue Sadicarnot, Bagnolet 93170. The Netherlands: Byenkorf, Damrak 90, 1012 LP Amsterdam.

LUXO ITALIANA Via Rocca 3, 24030 Presezzo, Bergamo, Italy.
Main Retailers Agent in USA: Luxo Lamp Corp., Monument Park, PO Box 951, Port Chester, N.Y. 10573. Agent in France: Lumiance, 4 Rue Sadicarnot, Bagnolet 93170. Agent in Germany: Luxo Leuchten GmbH, Fedelstrasse 18 b-22, Postfach 521, D-3200 Hildesheim. Agent in Canada: Luxo Lamp Ltd, 30 Place Sicard, Ste Therese, Quebec J7E 4J9. Agent in Spain: Ulsan International SA, Gran Via de Las Cortes, Barcelona 4. Agent in Japan: Otake & Co. Ltd, Higashi Ginza Bldg 18–4, 8-chome, Chuo-Ku, Tokyo 104.

JOHN MAKEPEACE LTD Parnham House, Beaminster, Dorset, UK.

LUCIANO MARCATO SRL Via Pacinotti 30, Cinisello Poalsano (Milan), Italy.
Main Retailers Agent in USA: Clarence House, 111 Eighth Avenue, Room 801, New York, N.Y. 10011. UK: Pallu & Lake Furnishings Ltd, 18 Newman Street, London W1.

MARCATRÉ SPA Via Sant Andrea 3, I-20020 Misinto, Milan, Italy.

MARIMEKKO OY Puusepankatu 4, SF-00810, Helsinki 81.
Main Retailers USA: Marimekko, 7 W. 56 Street, New York, N.Y. 10019. UK: Reflex IDC Ltd, 53 Blandford Street, London W1H 3AS. France: Opportune, 5 Rue Saint Opportune, Paris 75001.

MARKS PELLE VÄVARE AB S-51105 Kinna, Sweden.
Main Retailers Agent in UK: House of Sweden, 4425 Hampstead Road, London NW1. Agent in France: Tischa France, 45 Rue de Grenelle, Paris 75007. Agent in the Netherlands: Hans Hazevoet, Interior Stauffen, Kamerlign Oonesstrhaat 73, 20014 Haarlem.

MARTECH Geertestraat 2 bis, Utrecht, Netherlands.
Main Retailers The Netherlands: Hans Appenzeller, 125 Grimburgwal, 10126A Amsterdam.

MATSUSHITA ELECTRIC WORKS, LTD 1048 Kadoma, Kadoma-Shi, Osaka, Japan.

INGO MAURER GMBH Kaiserstrasse 47, 8 Munich 40, W. Germany.
Main Retailers USA: Museum of Modern Art, 53 Street, New York. UK: The London Lighting Co. Ltd, 135 Fulham Road, London SW3. France: Au Printemps SA, 21 Rue Auber, Paris. Italy: De Padova srl, Corso Venezia 14, Milan. Japan: Murata Interior Design Inc., PO Box 5400, Tokyo.

MEC ENGINEERING Harston Yard, Abbey Road, Bush Hill Park, Enfield, Middlesex, UK.

MÉGALIT Z.E. du Braoil, B.P. 55, 183000 Saint-Florent-sur-Cher, France.

DAVID MELLOR 1 Park Lane, Sheffield S10 2DU, UK.
Main Retailers USA: Henri Bendel, 10 W. 57 Street, New York, N.Y. 10019. UK: David Mellor, 4 Sloane Square, London SW1. Agent in the Netherlands: P. Andriessen, Molenkampf Straat 6, 4157 GN Enspije. Italy: Seambe SRL, Via Marchesi de Taddei 10, 20146 Milan.

MEMPHIS SRL Via Breda, 1-20010 Pregnana, Milan, Italy.
Main Retailers Agent in UK: Artemide GB, 17–19 Neal Street, London WC1 2HG. Agent in France: Artemide, 157–9 Rue du Faubourg St Honoré, Paris 75008. Agent in W. Germany: Agentur Brombauer, Eckstrasse 51, 2800 Bremen 33.

METAFORM BV Stephensonstraat 5, 384 GAK Harderwyk, Netherlands.
Main Retailers UK: Heal & Son Ltd, 196 Tottenham Court

Road, London W1A 1BJ. France: Company Marketing International, 4 Rue du Sergent Hoff, Paris 75017. The Netherlands: Metz & Co., Keizersgracht 455, Amsterdam 1017 DK.

METAL PLASTICA LUCCHESE SPA 55060 Monsagrati, Lucca, Italy.

MIL DESIGNS 9 Pylle Hill, Bristol B53 4T2, UK.
Main Retailers UK: Pointers Design Gallery, 20 Upper Maudlin Street, Bristol BS2 8DJ.

PETER MILES FURNITURE LTD Millers Green, Wirksworth, Derbyshire, UK.
Main Retailers UK: Heal & Son Ltd, 196 Tottenham Court Road, London W1.

MIRA-X SA Ch-5034 Suhr, Switzerland.
Main Retailers USA: MIRA-X International Furnishings Inc., 246 E. 58 Street, New York, N.Y. 10022. Agent in UK: Philip Edwards Ltd, Saint Michael's House, Bell Close, Mickleham, Dorking, Surrey RH5 6EE. France: MIRA-X France, 24 Rue Letellier, Paris 65015. Japan: Liebermann Waelchli & Co. Ltd, PO 243, Tokyo 160.

MOBILIA ITALIA SRL Via Lazzaroni, 4, 20124 Milan, Italy.

MARTA MOIA 20 Tregunter Road, London SW10 9LM, UK.

VETRERIA CARLO MORETTI SRL Fdm. Manin 3/13, Murano (Venice), Italy.
Main Retailers UK: Thomas Goods, 19 South Audley Street, London W1.

M.W. UNITED 19 Dacre Street, London SW1H 0DJ, UK.

NIEUWENBORD & WEGMAN Plantsoen 99-C, 2311 KL Leiden, Netherlands.

NUMERI SRL Via Olginati 3, Florence, Italy.

VUOKKO AND ANTTI NURMESNIEMI Studio Nurmesniemi Oy, Merikatu 1, 00140 Helsinki 14.

MAGNUS OLESEN A/S Tonderingvej 10, Durup, 7870 Roslev, Denmark.
Main Retailers Agent in UK: Friends of Scandia, Dalton Park, Amesbury, Wilts. Agent in France: MD Enterprises, 17 Rue du Moulin, Bonneuil-sur-Marne 94380.

OLIVARI SRL 28021 Borgomanero, Italy.
Main Retailers UK: Sigma Ward Ltd, 240 Station Road, Edgware, Middlesex HA8 7AU. France: RDC, Rue Jean Giraudoux, Paris 75116. W. Germany: Georg Stemeseder, Eichendorfstrasse 28, Freilassing 8228.

O-LUCE ITALIA SPA Via Conservatorio 22, 20122 Milan, Italy.

ONE-OFF 56 Neal Street, London WC2, UK.

OSRAM GMBH Hellabrunner Strasse 1, Berlin, W. Germany.

PALLUCCO SRL Via Salaria 1265, Rome, Italy.

CHRISSIE PEARCEY-COBBOLD Moulin de Quatre Carée, 47150 Monflanquin, France.

MICHEL PHILIPPE 19 Rue Raspail, 93270 Sevran, France.

POLTRONA FRAU SPA S.S.77 Km. 74,5, Tolentino, Italy.
Main Retailers UK: Class International, 31 Sloane Street, London SW1. France: Poltrona Frau Fr., 242 bis Boulevard St Germain, Paris 75007.

POLTRONOVA 51037 Montale, Pistoia, Italy.

SWID POWELL 55 E. 57 Street, 5th Floor, New York, N.Y. 10022.

PRODUCTS 4–6 Northington Street, London WC1, UK.
Main Retailers USA: Hothouse, 345 West Broadway, New York, N.Y. 10013. UK: Strangeways, 19 The Market, Covent Garden, London WC2. France: Axis, 18 Rue Guénégaud, Paris 75006.

PROFILIGHT Gr. Egtenrayseweg 76, Venlo, Netherlands.
Main Retailers USA: Lighting Gallery, 1162 Second Avenue, New York, N.Y. 10021. France: Contra Courant, 12 Rue des Halles, Paris. The Netherlands: Eikelenboom, Archanada 5B, Amsterdam 10013 BE.

PROFORMA Hietalahdenkatu 4, 00180 Helsinki, Finland.

THE MAX PROTECH GALLERY 37W. 57 Street, New York, N.Y.

QUARTETT GMBH Knochenhauerstrasse 30, D-3000 Hanover, W. Germany.

RAAK LICHT Lakenbleken Straat, 52 Halsmeer, Amsterdam, Netherlands.
Main Retailers UK: Lighting Design Service, 5 Kenninghall Road, Edmonton, London N18 2PE. France: Raak Eclairage Architectural, 153 Rue Legendre, Paris 75017. The Netherlands: Raak Lighting Architecture, Lakenbleken Straat, 52 Halsmeer, Amsterdam.

RIMADESIO SPA Via Tagliabue, 91, 20033 Desio, Milan, Italy.
Main Retailers USA: Rapport, 435 North Brea, Los Angeles, Ca. 90032. France: Duo sur Canapé, 36 Rue Etienne Marcel, Paris 75002. W. Germany: Thomas Herendorf, Fasanen Strasse 61, 1000 Berlin.

ROBOTS SPA Via Galvani 7, 20082 Binasco, Milan, Italy.
Main Retailers UK: Oscar Woollens Interior International, 421 Finchley Road, London NW3. Italy: Robot, Viale Caldara 34, Milan.

DETLEF ROSEN Ackerstrasse 82, 4000 Dusseldorf, W. Germany.

ROSENTHAL EINRICHTUNG Wittelsbacherstrasse 43, 8672 Selb, W. Germany.
Main Retailers USA: Rosenthal USA Ltd, 411 E. 76 Street, New York, N.Y. 10021. UK: Aram Designs Ltd, 3 Kean Street, London WC2. France: Norr Distribution Saal, Cit Tour de Montparnasse, Paris 1002. The Netherlands: Sunn Home Bee, 10 Peethavenstraat, N1077 Amsterdam.

RB ROSSANA Via Maglio del Lotto, 24-24100 Bergamo, Italy.

ROSSI & ARCANDI Monticello C. Otto, Venice, Italy.

SACEA SAS Via Ronchi 43, Legnano (MI) 20025, Italy.

SAPORITI ITALIA Via Gallarate 23, Milan, Italy.
Main Retailers USA: Campaniello Imports, 20025 E. 57 Street, New York. UK: Contract Interior International, 45A Topsfield Parade, Tottenham Lane, London N8. France: Perspectives, 92 Rue de Rennes, Paris. Italy: Saporiti, Via Monte Napoleone 27E, Milan.

SCHIANG PRODUCTION Sjolundsparken 14, DK-3510 Hellebaek, Denmark.

SEKTOR 3 Fluggestrasse 22, 3000 Hanover 1, W. Germany.
Main Retailers W. Germany: Deplana, Knesebeckstrasse, Berlin 12.

SIÈCLE PARIS 84 Rue Grande, 77570 Bougligny, France

SIRRAH SPA Via Molino Rosso 8, 40026 Imola, Italy.

SKIPPER Via S. Spirito 14, Milan, Italy.

SKIZO PO Box 536, 6800 AM Arnhem, Netherlands.
Main Retailers Agent in France: Martin Bronckhorst, Aspects in Dutch Design, 17 Rue de Buce, Paris 75006. The Netherlands: Metz, Keizersgracht 455, 1017 DK Amsterdam.

SOCIÉTÉ JACQUES PARISOT 70800 St Loup-sur-Semouse, France.

ELS STAAL 1ᵉ Helmerstraat 106, 1054 EG Amsterdam, Netherlands.

STAMP 10760 Nurieux, France.
Main Retailers USA: CLS, 133 W. 19 Street, New York, N.Y. 10011. Agent in UK: Garden Arp, 1 Mansfield Park Industrial Estate, Guildford Road, Cranleigh, Surrey. France: Samaritaine, 1 Rue Monnaie, Paris 75001. Japan: Asahi Grant, Maison Mita 1103, 2820 Mita, Minato Ku, Tokyo.

A/S STELTON G1. Vartov Vej 1, DK-2900 Hellerup, Denmark.
Main Retailers USA: Royal Copenhagen Porcelain Co., 225 Fifth Avenue, New York, N.Y. 10010. UK: Royal Copenhagen Porcelain Co., 15 New Bond Street, London W1. France: La Boutique Danoise, 42 Avenue de Friedland, Paris 75008. The Netherlands: AVN, Kerkstraat 27, Almkerk 4286.

STILNOVO SPA Via Borromini 12, 20020 Lainate (Milan), Italy.

STUTTGARTER GARDINENFABRIK GMBH D-7033 Herrenberg, Schiebmauer I, W. Germany.
Main Retailers USA: Modern Bauhaus Interiors, The Market Place, 2400 Market Street, Philadelphia, Pa. Agent in UK: Corve River Ltd, Old Rectory, Apton, Craven Arms, Salop. SY7 982. Agent in France: Bisson Bruneel,

160 Rue Vendôme, Lyons 69003. Agent in Japan: Actus Corp., 2–1–13 Shibuya-Ku, Tokyo.

SUNAR/HAUSSERMAN 18 Marshall Street, Norwalk, Conn., USA.

SWEDFUN PO Box 2502, 40317 Gothenburg, Sweden.

TAMPELLA HABIT SF 33180 Tampere 18, Finland.

TANE ORFEBRES Edgar Allan Poe 68, Polanco 11560, Mexico City.
Main Retailers Mexico: Tane Orfebres, Amberes 70, Sona Rosa, Mexico City.

TARGETTI SANKEY SPA Via Pratese 164, 50100 Florence, Italy.

TENDO CO. LTD 810 Oaza-Midarekawa, Tendo, Yamagata Prefecture, Japan.

TER MOLST INTERNATIONAL Molstenstraat 44, Obst-Rozebeke 8780, Belgium.

THEMA SPA Via 4 Novembre 18, 35010 Limena (PD), Italy.
Main Retailers UK: Practical Styling, 16–18 St Giles High Street, London WC2.

GEBR. THONET GMBH PO Box 15 20, 3558 Frankenberg, W. Germany.
Main Retailers Agent in UK: Aram Designs Ltd, 3 Kean Street, Covent Garden, London WC2. Agent in France: Claude Cenet, PO Box 823, 80 Avenue de la Plaine, Annecy, France 74016. Agent in the Netherlands: Bitter Culemborg BV, Berkeboom 8, 4100 AE Culemborg.

PETER TING 71a Poyle Road, Tongham, Farnham, Surrey, UK.

JUDITH TRIM 186 New North Road, London N17 BJ, UK.
Main Retailers UK: Anatol Orient, 28 Shelton Street,

London WC2. USA: Westminster Gallery, 132A Newbury Street, Boston, Mass. 02116.

VEMO INDUSTRI AB 286 00 Orelljunga, Sweden.

TIM WELLS 1 Banbury Road, Brackley, Northants, UK.

FRANZ WITTMANN KG A-3492, Etsdorf am Kamp, Austria.
Main Retailers USA: Stendig Inc., 410 E. 62 Street, New York, N.Y. 10021. UK: MW United, 19 Dacre Street, London SW1. France: First Time, 17 Rue Mazarine, Paris 75006. The Netherlands: Fellini, Willemseparkweg 10, 1011 NL Amsterdam.

DAVID WOLTON 34 Belsize Lane, London NW3, UK.

WORKSPACE 10 Barley Mow Passage, London W4 4PH, UK.
Main Retailers Agent in USA: Charles Nesbit Fine Art Inc., The Studio, 4001 N.E. Second Avenue, Miami, Fla. 33137:

LESLIE JOHN WRIGHT c/o Crafts Council of Western Australia, PO Box D178, Perth 6001, W. Australia.

YAMAGIWA CORP 4-1-Sotokanda, Chiyoda-Ku, Tokyo, Japan.

ZAB DESIGN P/L 12 Wilson Street, South Yarra 3141, Australia.

ZABRO SRL Atelier Alchimia, V.F. Ili Gabba, Milan 5, Italy.
Main Retailers Italy: Museo Alchimia, Foro Bonaparte 55, Milan.

ZANOTTA SPA Via Vittorio Veneto 57, Milan, Italy.

ZOEFTIG & CO., LTD Kings Hill Industrial Estate, Bude, Cornwall EX23 8QN, UK.

ABITARE, 'From September 15 to 23, 1981', *Abitare* (Italy), no. 201 (Jan./Feb. 1982), pp. 16–69.
(Milan Furniture Fair describing the work of 138 designers including Memphis)

ABITARE, 'Furniture for 1984: Videosalone', *Abitare* (Italy), no. 221 (Jan./Feb. 1984), pp. 38–115, 126–8.
(Visual review of the 1984 Salone de Mobile, Milan)

ABITARE, 'Many Shades of Grey', *Abitare* (Italy), no. 208 (Oct. 1982), pp. 28–31.
(Furniture by Cassina, room design by Valerio Morpurgo)

AARTSEN, M., 'Holland: Products for the World', *Design*, no. 411 (Mar. 1983), p. 64.

OFFICINA ALESSI, *Tea and Coffee Piazza: 11 Servizi da tè e caffè disegnati da . . . Michael Graves, Hans Hollein, Charles Jencks, Richard Meier, Alessandro Mendini, Paolo Portoghesi, Aldo Rossi, Stanley Tigerman, Oscar Tusquets, Robert Venturi, Kazumasa Yamashita*, Crusinallo, 1983.

ANDERSON, S., 'Modern Architecture and Industry: Peter Behrens, the AEG, and Industrial Design', *Oppositions*, no. 21 (Summer 1980), pp. 78–93.

ARATO, R., 'Canadian Designers Push Themselves From Branch Plant to World Markets', *Industrial Design*, vol. XXIX (July/Aug. 1982), pp. 31–3.

L'ARCHITECTURE D'AUJOURD'HUI, 'Dossier: politique industrielle et architecture: le cas Olivetti', no. 188 (Dec. 1976), pp. 1–104.

ARCHITECTURAL RECORD, 'Product Reports 1984: Furnishings', *Architectural Record*, vol. CLXXI (Dec. 1983), pp. 71–80.

ARTNEWS, 'When Artists Make Furniture, Is It Furniture or Is It Art?', *Artnews* (USA), vol. LXXX, pt. 2 (Feb. 1981), pp. 93–8.

BANHAM, REYNER, (Penny Sparke ed.), *Design by Choice*, London, 1981.

BAYLEY, STEPHEN, 'Are You Sitting Comfortably', *Crafts*, no. 50 (May/June 1981), pp. 17–21.
(Discussion on the 'Handmade Chair Vintage 1981')

BAYLEY, STEPHEN, 'Body Tools', *Crafts*, no. 45 (July/Aug. 1980), pp. 26–9.
(Chairs by Erik de Graaf)

BAYLEY, STEPHEN, *The Good Design Guide: 100 Best Ever Products*, London, 1985.

BAYLEY, STEPHEN, *In Good Shape*, London, 1979.

BAYLEY, STEPHEN AND WOUHUYSEN, JAMES, *Robots*, London, 1984.

BAYLEY, STEPHEN, *Sony Design: An Exhibition at the Boilerhouse at the Victoria and Albert Museum*, London, 1982.

BAYLEY, STEPHEN, *Memphis in London*, Boilerhouse Project, 1982.

BAYLEY, STEPHEN, *Taste: An Exhibition About Values in Design*, London, Boilerhouse Project, Victoria and Albert Museum, 1983.

BAYLEY, STEPHEN, 'T.V. Design: East Meets West at Bucharest', *Design*, no. 364 (April 1979), pp. 48–9.
(Roumanian design of a portable television set using Western 'good design' concepts)

BAYNES, K., 'Young Blood', *Art & Artists*, no. 210 (Mar. 1984), pp. 13–15.
(An exhibition on Industrial design at the Barbican Centre Art Gallery, London)

BERTONI, DANIELE, *L'oggetto lampada, forma e funzione: storia degli apparecchi d'illuminazione a luce elettrica*, Milan, 1981.
(Achille Castiglione)

BEST, A., 'Design Review: Chairs', *Architectural Review*, UK, vol. CLXV, no. 165 (April 1979), pp. 240–2.

BEST, A., 'Design Review: Martin Grierson: Cabinetmaker', *Architectural Review*, vol. CLXIII, no. 974 (April 1978), pp. 229–31.

BLAKSTAD, MICHAEL, *The Risk Business: Industry and the Designers*, London, 1979.

BLUMENBERG, HANS C., *Meister der perfekten Form. Die Aufgabe des Industrie-Designers*, Dusseldorf, 1969.

BOILERHOUSE PROJECT, *Design at Kingston: An Exhibition of Work by Students from the School of Three Dimensional Design Kingston Polytechnic: Furniture, Product, Interior Design*, held at the Boilerhouse Project, Victoria and Albert Museum, 4–11 July, 1984, London, 1984.

BOILERHOUSE PROJECT, *Kenneth Grange at the Boilerhouse*, 1983, London, 1983.

BOSSON, P., 'Furniture with a Future?', *Connoisseur*, vol. CCIX, no. 836 (Jan. 1982), pp. 42–5.
(Memphis as a manufacturer of experimental furniture)

BRANZI, A., 'Il design secondo Vittorio Gregotti', *Domus*, no. 636 (Feb. 1983), pp. 52–3.

BULOW, L., 'Scandinaviska Möbelmassan' (The Scandinavian Furniture Fair), *Form* (Sweden), vol. LXXVII, no. 606 (1981), pp. 26–7 (summary in English).
(Includes Jan Eskelius's stackable chair, *High Tech*)

BUSCH, A. (ed.), 'Annual Design Review', *Industrial Design*, vol. XXX (Sept./Oct. 1983), pp. 7–104.

BIBLIOGRAPHY

CARTER, C. L., 'Industrial Design: On Its Characteristics and Relationships to the Visual Fine Arts', *Leonardo*, vol. XIV, pt. 4 (Autumn 1981), pp. 283–9.

CASTRO, FEDERICA DI, (ed.), *Sottsass Scrapbook*, Milan, 1976.

CENTRE GEORGES POMPIDOU, (ed.), *L'Objet Industriel*, Centre du Création Industrielle, Paris, 1980.

CHADWICK, A.-M., 'John Makepeace at Work', *Connoisseur*, vol. CCVII, no. 833 (July 1981), pp. 219–21.

CHAZELLE, C., 'Pierre Cardin lance le meuble oeuvre d'art', *Galerie des Arts*, no. 188 (Feb. 1979), pp. 74–5.

CLARK, A., 'Keen Competition for UK Knives', *Design*, no. 406 (Oct. 1982), pp. 47–50.

CORDWELL, J. M., *The Visual Arts: Plastic and Graphic*, The Hague, 1979.

CRAFTS COUNCIL, *Makers: An Illustrated Guide to the Work of More Than 350 Artist-Craftsmen*, London, 1980.

DANISH DESIGN COUNCIL, *Design: The Problem Comes First (Design: d'abord le problème)*, Copenhagen, 1983. (Published to accompany an exhibition, parallel English and French texts)

DESIGN, 'Bathrooms', *Design*, no. 411 (Mar. 1983), pp. 30–41.

DESIGN, 'B.T. Goes Cordless', *Design*, no. 140 (Feb. 1983), pp. 48–9. (Industrial design)

DESIGN, 'Great Ideas by Young U.K. Designers', *Design*, no. 411 (Mar. 1983), p. 5.

DESIGN, 'Programmable Products', *Design*, no. 414 (June 1983), pp. 30–9.

DESIGN, 'Technology: Use It, Don't Lose It', *Design*, no. 413 (May 1983), p. 54. ('Tomorrow's Technology Today', London, Design Centre Exhibition)

DESIGN CENTRE, STUTTGART, *Industrial Design im Werkzeugmaschinenbau, Herausforderung für Entwicklung Konstruktion, Management und Vertrieb*, Stuttgart.

DESIGN CENTRE, STUTTGART, *Textildesign 1934–1984 am Beispiel Stuttgarter Gardinen*, Eine Ausstellung des Design Center, Stuttgart von 3 bis 31 Mai, Stuttgart, 1984.

DOBLIN, JAY, *One Hundred Great Product Designs*, New York, 1970.

DOMUS, *Il design Italiano degli anni '50*, Milan, 1980. (Achille Castiglione)

DOMUS, 'Installation as Research', *Domus*, no. 606 (May 1980), pp. 42–5. (Achille Castiglione)

DOMUS, 'Telefono ad angolazione differenziata', *Domus*, no. 617 (May 1981), p. 44. (Achille Castiglione)

DORFLES, GILLO, *Introduction à l'Industrial Design*, Paris, 1974.

ELLINGSON, D.G., 'Designer's Choice: A Special Issue', *Industrial Design*, (Annual Review 1982), pp. 6–96.

FINNISH FOREIGN TRADE ASSOCIATION, *Design in Finland*, Helsinki, 1981.

FORM, 'Desing på storföretagen' (Design in Big Industries), *Form* (Sweden), vol. LXXVIII, no. 616 (1982), pp. 34–7. (Investigates the role of the industrial designer in major industries such as Saab and Electrolux)

FOSSATI, P., 'L'ergonomique lyrique', *L'Architecture d'Aujourd'hui*, no. 188 (Dec. 1976), pp. 72–4. (Olivetti Corporation)

FRATELLI, ENZO, *Design e civiltà della macchina*, Rome, 1969.

FREY, GILBERT, *Das moderne Sitzmöbel von 1850 bis heute*, Teufen, 1970.

GAUDIN, THIERRY, *Comment naissent les produits industriels*, Paris, 1974.

GLOAG, JOHN, 'English Furniture in the Later Twentieth Century', *Connoisseur*, vol. CC, no. 806 (April 1979), pp. 248–9.

GRASSI, ALFONSO, *Atlante de design Italiano 1940/1980*, Milan, 1980. (Achille, Livio, Pier Castiglioni)

GREEN, L.W., 'Product Design in a Contract Design Context', *Interior Design*, vol. LIV (May 1983), pp. 268–71.

GREENWOOD, D.P., *Modern Design in Plastics*, London, 1983.

GREGOTTI, VITTORIO, *Il disegno del prodotto industriale: Italia 1860–1980*, Milan, 1982.

GRESLERI, GIULIANO, *Josef Hoffmann*, Bologna, 1981.

HAMILTON, NICOLA, *Design and Industry: The Effects of Industrialisation and Technical Change on Design*, London, 1980.

HAMILTON, NICOLA, (ed.), *Svensk Form: A Conference About Swedish Design*, London, 1981.

HARPERS AND QUEEN, 'Milan's Post-Modern Masters', *Harpers and Queen*, (May 1982), pp. 134–44.

HATJE, GERD, *Design For Modern Living: A Practical Guide to Home Furnishing and Interior Design*, (translated from the German), London, 1975.

HEDQUIST, H., 'The Show Must Go On', *Form* (Sweden), vol. LXXVIII, no. 616 (1982), pp. 7–10. (1982 Milan Furniture Fair reviewed)

HESKETT, JOHN, *Industrial Design*, London, 1980.

HIESINGER, KATHRYN B., *Design Since 1945*, London, 1983.

HILL, MIKE, AND WOUDHUYSEN, JAMES, 'Thorn's New Light', *Design*, no. 388 (April 1981), pp. 34–5.

HILL, P., 'Breaks Rules, Feels Good', *Design*, no. 318 (June 1975), pp. 42–5.

HILLIER, BEVIS, *The Style of the Century: 1900–1980*, London, 1983.

HOFFMAN, P., 'Interview with Vico Magistretti', *Interior Design*, vol. XLVII (April 1976), pp. 176–7.

HOLLERITH, R., 'Global Ingenuity', *Industrial Design*, vol. XXVIII (Sept./Oct. 1981), pp. 28–9. (Hannover, West Germany, Industrial design exhibition)

HOLT, S., 'Irony, Novelty, Quality', *Industrial Design*, vol. XXXI (Jan./Feb. 1984), pp. 24–9. (Gallery 91, New York; Industrial design exhibition)

HOLT, S., 'Sony/Wega: Japanese Technology and German Design', *Industrial Design*, vol. XXXI (Jan./Feb. 1984), pp. 44–5.

HURLBURT, ALLEN, *The Design Concept*, New York, 1981.

INDUSTRIAL DESIGN, 'Design Japan', *Industrial Design*, vol. XXXI (Jan./Feb. 1984), pp. 2, 11–53, 58–61.

INTERIOR DESIGN, 'Readers' Choice: The 25 Most Popular Products of the Past Year', *Interior Design*, vol. LIV, no. 12 (Dec. 1983), pp. 182–7.

INTERIOR DESIGN, 'Roscoe Winners', *Interior Design*, vol. LIV (Mar. 1983), pp. 226–9. (1982 Product Design Awards sponsored by the Resources Council)

JONES, J. CHRISTOPHER, *Design Methods: Seeds of Human Futures*, New York, Chichester, 1981.

JONSON, L., 'Vad är mässa Paris värd? Jo, det här' (What is a Fair in Paris Worth?), *Form* (Sweden), vol. LXXVII, no. 603 (1981), pp. 12–13. (French Furniture Fair, Paris, 1981 with special reference to VIA)

BIBLIOGRAPHY

KAPLAN, A., 'Experiencing the Product', *Industrial Design,* vol. XXXI (Mar./April 1984), pp. 32–7.

KIMMELMAN, M., 'Sitting Pretty', *Horizon* (USA), vol. XXV, pt. 6 (Sept. 1982), pp. 16–24.

KUNST UND HANDWERK,, 'USA: neue handgefertigte Möbel', *Kunst und Handwerk* (GFR), vol. XXXIII, pt. 9 (Sept. 1979), pp. 259–63.
(American Furniture Makers' exhibition, summer 1979, at the American Craft Museum, New York)

LA TROBE-BATEMAN, R., 'Current Furniture', *Crafts* (UK), no. 41 (Nov./Dec. 1979), pp. 38–44.
(Neville Neal, Fred Baier, Floris Van Den Broecke, David Colwell)

LAURAEUS, R., 'Newsfront Finland', *Mobilia,* no. 301 (1981), pp. 5–18.

LINDKVIST, L., (ed.), *Design in Sweden,* Stockholm, 1977.

LOEWY, RAYMOND, *Industrial Design,* London, 1979.

LOTT, J., 'Are the British Going Gallic?', *Design,* no. 400 (April 1982), pp. 32–3.

LOTT, J., 'Big Brawny Bosch', *Design,* no. 391 (July 1981), pp. 36–7.

LUCIE-SMITH, E., *A History of Industrial Design,* Oxford, 1983.

LUCIE-MEYER, J., 'Conran Associates: 100% Design', *Novum Gebrauchsgraphik,* vol. XLVI (Nov. 1975), pp. 28–38.

LUCIE-MEYER, J.J. DE, 'Pentagrams' *Novum Gebrauchsgraphik,* (Feb. 1977), pp. 43–8.

LUNDAHL, G., 'Befria rummet!', *Form* (Sweden), vol. LXXVIII, no. 616 (1982), pp. 4–5.
(Modular Furniture)

LUNDAHL, G., 'Formgivarnas möbelmäss' (The Designers Furniture Fair), *Form* (Sweden), vol. LXXVIII, no. 614 (1982), pp. 38–40.
(Review of a Scandinavian Furniture Fair held in Copenhagen)

MacCARTHY, FIONA, *A History of British Design: 1830–1970,* London, 1979.
(First published as *All Things Bright and Beautiful,* 1972)

McFADDEN, D.R., 'With Loving Detail: The Scandinavian Marriage of Craft and Industry', *Industrial Design,* vol. XXX (May/June 1983), pp. 24–9.

MAGISTRETTI, VICO, *Twenty-one Years, Twenty-one Chairs: Liberty and designer-architect Vico Magistretti presents an exhibition to celebrate the first Designers Saturday in London,* London, 1981.

MAKEPEACE, J., 'Modern Living in Stately Circumstances', *Antique Collector,* vol. 51, pt. II (Nov. 1980), pp. 58–60.
(John Makepeace's commission to design a table for Longleat, Wiltshire)

MAYALL, W.H., *Principles in Design,* London, 1979.

MENDINI, ALESSANDRO, *Paesaggio Casalingo: La produzione Alessi nell'industria dei casalinghi dal 1921 al 1980,* Milan, 1979.

MOLINARI, T., 'Culture of Industry', *Abitare,* no. 26 (July/Aug. 1984), pp. 108–17.
(German Industrial Design)

MØLLER, S.E., 'Danes Design', *Architectural Review,* vol. CLXXIII (Jan. 1983), pp. 68–70+.

MORGAN, ANN LEE, (ed.), *Contemporary Designers,* London, 1984.

MURRAY, J., 'Joinings: Furniture and Other Useful Objects', *American Craft,* vol. XLI, pt. 2 (April/May 1981), pp. 36–9.
(Donald Lloyd McKinley)

MYERSON, J., 'Danish New Wave', *Design*, no. 399 (Mar. 1982), pp. 22–3.
(Industrial Design)

MYERSON, J., 'Spectacles: Finding a Fresh Focus', *Design*, no. 404 (Aug. 1982), pp. 26–9.

NELSON, G., 'The Design Process', *Interior Design*, vol. LIV, no. 9 (Sept. 1983), pp. 214–19.
(The Philadelphia Museum of Art presents an exhibition of post-war industrial design by leading designers and manufacturers, 16 Oct. 1983–8 Jan. 1984)

NEMECZEK, A., 'Keine Angst vor Kitsch', *Art: Das Kunstmagazin*, (G.F.R.), pt. 5, (May 1982), pp. 46–57.
(Memphis, Michael Graves, Michele de Lucchi, Alessandro Mendini, Ettore Sottsass, Paola Novone)

PAWLEY, M., 'Better by Design: Design and the Economy', *Architectural Journal*, vol. CLXXVIII (Oct. 1983), pp. 58–60.

PENTAGRAM DESIGN PARTNERSHIP, *Living by Design*, London, 1978.

PHILLIPS, B., 'John Tops the Bill; The Work of John Makepeace at the National Theatre', *Building Design*, no. 499 (6 June 1980), pp. 28–9.

PINKWAS, STAN, 'King and Queen of Cups', *Metropolis*, (Jan./Feb. 1983), pp. 12–17.
(Vignelli Associates)

POPHAM, P., 'Empty Vessels', *Design*, no. 404 (Aug. 1982), pp. 30–1.
(Japan's Tableware Industry)

POPHAM, P., 'Industrial Design Puts Osaka on World Map', *Design*, no. 421 (Jan. 1984), p. 4.
(First International Design Festival, Japan)

POPHAM, P., 'Sony: And Now, the Modular T.V.', *Design*, no. 394 (Oct. 1981), pp. 42–7.

RAMS, DIETER, (François Burkhardt and Inez Franksen ed.), *Design*, Berlin, 1981.

ROMANI, G., Olivetti Lexikon 82/83 DL: 'Analisi di un prodotto', *Casabella*, vol. 41 (Jul./Aug. 1977), pp. 20–31.

ROYAL COLLEGE OF ART, *Design Policy, 2. Design and Industry*, Richard Langdon (ed.), London, 1984.
(Proceedings of an International conference on design policy held at the RCA, London, 20–23 July, 1982.)

ROYAL COLLEGE OF ART, *Design Policy, 6. Design and Information Technology*, Richard Langdon (ed.), London, 1984.
(Proceedings of an international conference on design policy held at the RCA, London, 20–23 July, 1982)

SARTOGO, P., 'Italian Re-evolution: Design in the Italian Society of the '80s', *Domus*, no. 636 (Feb. 1983), pp. 54–7.

SCHMITTEL, WOLFGANG, *Design Concept Realisation*, Zurich, 1975.

SCHORY, K.C., 'Functional Aesthetics Can Help US Designs Compete Globally', *Industrial Design*, vol. XXVIII (July/Aug. 1981), pp. 37–41.

SIMPSON J., 'In the Showrooms: Saporiti Italia – Fine Craftsmanship – Classic Lines', *Architectural Digest*, vol. XL (July 1983), pp. 162, 164, 166.

SOTTSASS, ETTORE, 'Because of the late arrival of the aircraft', *Casabella*, no. 408 (1975), pp. 15–21.

SPARKE, PENNY, *Consultant Design: The History and Practice of the Designer in Industry*, London, 1983.

SPARKE, PENNY, *Ettore Sottsass Jnr.*, London, 1982.

SPARKE, PENNY, 'Ettore Sottsass Jnr., Anti-designer', *Mobilia*, no. 306 (1982), pp. 43–9.

STONE, M., 'Skill at Play: Edward Zucca', *American Craft*, vol. XLI, pt. 3 (June/July 1981), pp. 2–5.

SUDJIK, DEYAN, 'Comment: Backwards or Forwards', *Crafts*, vol. 56 (May/June 1982), pp. 16–18.
(John Makepeace)

SUDJIK, DEYAN, 'Sottsass and Co.', *Crafts*, vol. 59 (Nov./Dec. 1982), pp. 38–42.

TROTMAN, BOB, *American Craft*, vol. XL, pt. 4 (Aug./Sept. 1980), p. 38.

VERBAND DEUTSCHER INDUSTRIE DESIGNER E.V., *Krise des funktionalistischen Design? Dokumentation einer Veranstaltung des VDID*, Stuttgart, 1981.

VICTORIA AND ALBERT MUSEUM, *The Way We Live Now: Designs for Interiors 1950 to the Present Day*, London, 1979.

VOLLICHARD, D., 'Les créateurs italiens à Milan, *Oeil* (Switzerland), no. 340 (Nov. 1983), pp. 58–65.

VYAS, H. KUMAR, *Design and Environment: An Introductory Manual*, Ahmedabad, India, 1981.

WALKER, C., 'Magistretti rides a broomstick', *Design*, no. 369 (Sept. 1979), pp. 70–1.

WALKLING, G., 'Reproduction to Revolution', *Connoisseur*, vol. CCVI, no. 830 (April 1981), pp. 297–9.
(History of Hille Company)

WEBB, M., 'Robots are Here: The Robots are Here', *Design Quarterly*, no. 121 (1983), pp. 5–22.

WICHMANN, HANS, *Kultur ist unteilbar*, Starnberg, 1973.

WICHMANN, HANS, *Made in Germany*, Munich, 1970.